PUERTO RICAN AND CUBAN CATHOLICS IN THE U.S., 1900–1965

THE NOTRE DAME HISTORY
OF HISPANIC CATHOLICS IN THE U.S.
General Editor: Jay P. Dolan

Volume One
Mexican Americans and the Catholic Church, 1900–1965

Volume Two
Puerto Rican and Cuban Catholics in the U.S., 1900–1965

Volume Three
Hispanic Catholic Culture in the U.S.: Issues and Concerns

Puerto Rican and Cuban Catholics in the U.S., 1900–1965

Edited by

Jay P. Dolan

and

Jaime R. Vidal

UNIVERSITY OF NOTRE DAME PRESS

Notre Dame   London

Library of Congress Cataloging-in-Publication Data

Puerto Rican and Cuban Catholics in the U.S.,
    1900–1965 / edited by Jay P. Dolan and Jaime R.
Vidal.
        p.   cm. — (The Notre Dame history of
Hispanic Catholics in the U.S. : v. 2)
    Includes bibliographical references and index.
    ISBN 0-268-03805-8
    1. Puerto Rican Catholics—History—20th
century.   2. Cuban American Catholics—History—
20th century.   3. Catholic Church—United
States—Membership.   4. United States—Church
history—20th century.   I. Dolan, Jay P., 1936–   .
II. Vidal, Jaime R.   III. Series.
BX1407.P83P84   1994
282'.73'089687291—dc20   94-15463
                                                                          CIP

∞ *The paper used in this publication meets the minimum requirements*
of the American National Standard for Information Sciences—Permanence of Paper
for Printed Library Materials, ANSI Z39.48-1984.

CONTENTS

Acknowledgments   vii
Introduction   1

I. Citizens Yet Strangers: The Puerto Rican Experience
   Jaime R. Vidal

1. Church and People in Puerto Rico   11
2. The Attempt to Americanize Puerto Rico
   and the Problem of Identity   26
3. The Establishment of a North American
   Church Structure in Puerto Rico   38
4. The Great Migration   54
5. The Rejection of the Ethnic Parish Model   70
6. Implementing the Vision   88
7. Beyond New York   112
Conclusion   135

II. Cuban Catholics in the United States
    Lisandro Pérez

1. The Catholic Church in Cuba: A Weak Institution   147
2. The Nineteenth-Century Cuban Experience in the U.S.   158
3. The Cuban Communities in the U.S., 1900-1958   174
4. The Exodus from Revolutionary Cuba
   and the Catholic Church in South Florida, 1959–1965   189

Conclusion   208
Notes   209
Contributors   248
Index   249

Acknowledgments

The Notre Dame History of Hispanic Catholics in the U.S. began in 1989 when the Cushwa Center for the Study of American Catholicism at the University of Notre Dame and its director, Jay P. Dolan, together with Mary Ewens, O.P., at that time the associate director of the Cushwa Center, began to design a plan for the study. An essential component of this phase of the project was an advisory committee made up of individuals who were engaged in various aspects of Hispanic studies. Allan Figueroa Deck, S.J., Gilberto M. Hinojosa, Michael J. McNally, Moisés Sandoval, Anthony M. Stevens-Arroyo, and Olga R. Villa Parra comprised this committee and have guided the study throughout the four years that it took to complete it. We are truly grateful for their assistance. Also making an important contribution to the study was Jaime R. Vidal who replaced Mary Ewens at the Cushwa Center in 1990. He served as an important liaison between the Cushwa Center and the numerous scholars involved in the study. Another key person was the secretary of the Cushwa Center, Delores Dant Fain. She took care of a myriad of details and was mainly responsible for administering what proved to be a very complex project. We are very grateful for all her work on behalf of the study.

A special word of thanks must go to Jeanne Knoerle, S.P., and Fred L. Hofheinz of the Lilly Endowment. They continually encouraged us throughout the four years of the study; without their support the study would not have been possible.

Puerto Rican and Cuban Catholics in the U.S., 1900–1965 is only one part of the study. Another volume in this history is *Mexican-Americans and the Catholic Church, 1900–1965*. The third and final part of the study is *Hispanic Catholic Culture in the U.S.: Issues and Concerns*. All of these books are available from the University of Notre Dame Press. Together they comprise the Notre Dame History of Hispanic Catholics in the U.S., a landmark study of a people too long neglected by historians of American Catholicism.

INTRODUCTION

The essays in this volume of the Notre Dame History of Hispanic Catholics in the U.S. cover the two Caribbean groups which had established an important presence in the United States before 1965: the Puerto Ricans and the Cubans. Together with the Dominicans (whose presence in the U.S. does not become significant until after 1965) these two groups constitute a distinct entity within the U.S. Hispanic community, just as their lands of origin constitute a distinct subculture within the larger Hispanic world.

Puerto Rico and Cuba share the same tropical climate. At the time of the conquest, both islands had relatively small native populations, which were at a primitive stage of cultural development by comparison with the complex societies of the Aztec and Inca empires. Both islands, on the other hand, received a demographically and culturally important influx of African slaves, so that rather than a racial or cultural *mestizaje*, one must in this case speak of a *mulataje*. The Caribbean culture is much more a mixture of Spanish and African attitudes to life than of Spanish and Native American. Both islands remained Spanish colonies until 1898, and both have been subjected to American political and cultural influence—although in different ways—to a much greater degree than the rest of Latin America.

These shared cultural ingredients are not mixed in the same proportions in both islands. American influence in Puerto Rico, for example, has been much more direct than in Cuba. Cuba's history in the nineteenth century was marked by a much stronger desire for independence from Spain than was the case with Puerto Rico; this led to an important experience of exile even in the nineteenth century, and to a certain amount of residual resentment against Spain. Since one of the reasons for the Spanish American War was the United States' sympathy with the Cuban independence movement, it became politically imperative to give Cuba its independence as soon as possible, so that the rhetoric used during the war would not boomerang against the Americans. American interests and influence were safeguarded in the independence settlement,

1

but the idea of holding on to Cuba as an American possession could not be seriously entertained.

Puerto Rico, too, had its independentist exiles, but they were much fewer. The movement for independence had a good amount of popular sympathy, but unlike Cuba, this sympathy never translated itself into a viable rebellion. Eventually Puerto Rico chose the political struggle for a Home Rule solution—an arrangement which the Cubans rejected when Spain finally offered it to both islands. This made it politically possible for the United States to hold on to Puerto Rico as a possession, and to launch a cultural campaign to Americanize the island. This campaign was passively but adamantly resisted by the Puerto Rican people, and in the process Spain became the symbol of all that made Puerto Rico different from the United States. Thus *Hispanidad* became a conscious and important ingredient of the Puerto Rican sense of self-identity.

Finally, the African element has been much more significant, both demographically and culturally (contrary to the general American belief) in Cuba than in Puerto Rico. This has led to the emergence of a conscious Afro-Cuban subculture and to the preservation of African religion in the phenomenon popularly known as *Santería*. In Puerto Rico the African elements were much more successfully integrated into a Hispanic culture.

But while the ingredients may not be mixed in the same proportions, they are to a great degree the same ingredients, and the difference in their proportions pales into insignificance when the Puerto Rican and the Cuban compare themselves to a Mexican, a Peruvian, or an Argentinean, whose cultural ingredients are almost totally different from theirs except for the Spanish components. In the light of those comparisons, the Cuban and the Puerto Rican realize that their two islands truly are, in the words of the poet Lola Rodríguez de Tió, *de un pájaro las dos alas*—the two wings of a single bird.

In their history as Hispanics in the United States, and in their relations with the American Church, the Cubans and Puerto Ricans exhibit a similar pattern of visible differences belied by underlying similarities, a pattern which emerges as we compare the two essays in this volume. The kind of Catholic ethos which both groups brought with them to this country was formed by similar circumstances and shows many parallels.

In both islands the institutional Church was very weak. Because of scarcity of clergy and rural dispersion, it had lost touch with the peasantry except on special occasions of the Church year, so that the peasants were loyal to a Catholic symbol-system rather than to the hierarchy and its priorities.

In the nineteenth century the institutional Church also lost the loyalty of the elites in both islands. The Liberal elite came to perceive the Church as an instrument of Spanish colonialism and sought spiritual alternatives in Spiritism, Freemasonry, or the pantheistic German philosophies which they learned when they went to Europe for their education. The Conservatives, on the other hand, tended to use the institutional Church cynically as a prop of the colonial regime, while subordinating it to their own political, social, and economic agendas. This was most tragically demonstrated in the resistance of the plantation owners to the catechizing, baptizing, and marriage of their slaves; a resistance which was illegal under Spanish law, but which was generally successful because the colonial governments would not back the all too often weak efforts which the Church made in this direction. In this case the loss of the institutional Church's influence with the elite led to its losing touch also with the slaves and their descendants.

Thus, when they came to the United States, both the Puerto Ricans and the Cubans presented to American Catholics the paradox of a culture pervaded by Catholic symbols, attitudes, and traditions, but shockingly out of touch with the values and priorities of the institutional Church. In the case of the Puerto Ricans this perception led to a massive effort to integrate the newcomers into the American Church, but in such a way as to assimilate them into its structure and style. All concessions to their traditional way of expressing the Catholic faith were avowedly temporary and provisional, until they could be integrated completely into the American Catholic ethos. This goal led to the deliberate policy of not using the national parish model in the Puerto Rican community, a policy which was later extended to other Hispanic groups.

This policy of the U.S. Church was at cross purposes with the strong urge of the Puerto Ricans to preserve their identity and build their own community. At the secular level the Puerto Ricans have succeeded in this endeavor, but the policies of the institutional Church have made it difficult within the Catholic structure. This has led to a certain amount of marginalization of the Church within the Puerto Rican community.

The massive migration of Cubans in the early 1960s, which is the origin of the present day Cuban-American community, had a number of characteristics which produced a very different initial perception and reception on the part of the American Church and people. It was a flight from a communist regime, at a time when American public opinion was dominated by the Cold War mentality. The Cuban exiles, therefore, came with the aura of being victims of communism. Because the American Church perceived communism as the prime enemy of Christianity in our age, the exiles' rejection of it made them come across as people who had given up their homeland in order to practice their faith in freedom.

The fact that the majority of the exiles in the first waves of migration were from the upper and middle strata of Cuban society also meant that they were more familiar with English and more at home with American middle-class mores. Many of them were professionals and, although they had to revalidate their degrees before they could exercise them here, they had the social and business skills, and the general education, which could make them respected in American society. Many of them were the products of Catholic education, and some even active in organizations such as Catholic Action, and so their practice of Catholicism came much closer to institutional standards. Finally, since class and color are connected in the Caribbean, the class composition of the majority of the first exiles also meant that they were perceived as white, rather than "people of color."

These first impressions have lasted in the American people's general perception of Cubans as a group, even though later waves of migration have been more representative of the complete spectrum of Cuban society. The impressions have gained for them a much warmer welcome than the Puerto Ricans ever got, but they have also created certain expectations, especially that the Cubans would quickly mix into the white, middle-class American community, at both the religious and the social levels.

But here, as it turns out, the Cubans share an important issue with the Puerto Ricans—although its circumstances and expression may hide its similarity. The issue is *identity*. Both Cubans and Puerto Ricans, whether rightly or wrongly, tend to perceive themselves as being here "provisionally"—until the economy allows them to return home to Puerto Rico; until Castro's fall allows them to return home to Cuba—and therefore insist on holding on to their language and culture, and strive to build communities of their own, where these values will be preserved. Even as many individuals strike roots in America, the "exile" mentality is held on to for psychological reasons.

In this struggle the Cubans and Puerto Ricans have opposite assets and difficulties. The Cubans have the advantage of a strong and educated elite which can provide financial, educational, cultural, and political leadership, as well as a significant number of Cuban priests. But they have the disadvantage of not being able to visit their homeland (until recently). The Puerto Ricans, on the other hand, have suffered from the lack of an elite; their leadership (especially in the Catholic context) has often come from persons who care very much for them, but who do not always share their vision of the importance of preserving identity and building a distinct community. But they have had the advantage of easy access to their homeland, so that frequent visits and the pattern of travel which has been called "revolving door immigration" constantly reinforce identity.

Aside from these shared themes which are important in both of the essays in this volume, certain factors are unique to each island. In his essay on the Puerto Ricans, Jaime Vidal stresses the importance of the effort at Americanizing the people in the island itself, beginning immediately after the change of sovereignty in 1898. This was met by an unorganized and passive but very stubborn and ultimately successful resistance on the part of the people of the island. This was not an anti-American movement; its slogan was not "Yankee, go home," but "I am not an American." Its ultimate incarnation was the commonwealth status by which the Puerto Rican people chose to keep at once the political and economic connection to the United States and their own cultural identity.

This resistance to cultural Americanization in the island meant in turn that at the time of the Great Migration the Puerto Ricans who came to the U.S. were already used to the idea that they were American citizens, but not *Americanos*, and that they had no wish to become assimilated to American culture. The fact that they were already American citizens actually made it easier for them to resist assimilation, since it precluded the imposition of quotas or other restrictions on the growth of the Puerto Rican community and made possible the "revolving door immigration" which reinforced the values of Puerto Rican culture. The struggle to create a community of their own is central to the Puerto Rican experience in the U.S. In this struggle the Church has been, often with the best of intentions, an obstacle rather than a helper, because of its commitment to the role of Americanizer of the immigrants.

At the same time, the American Church expended a tremendous amount of energy on behalf of the Puerto Ricans within the parameters of the policies it had chosen. Vidal dedicates a chapter to the efforts of the New York Archdiocese, under the leadership of Joseph Fitzpatrick, S.J., and Iván Illich, to make the integrated parish serve the Puerto Ricans in fact and not just in theory. The most important result of this effort was the massive training of New York clergy in the Spanish language and Puerto Rican culture which enabled the archdiocese to place a Spanish-speaking priest on the staff of most if not all integrated parishes. This, however, tended to create the very situation of a "parish within the parish" which the integrated parish model was supposed to avoid. Lay movements such as the *Cursillos de Cristiandad*, where the Hispanic laity had a position of effective leadership, also served as instruments for the preservation of a distinctively Hispanic way of living one's Catholicism, and for the creation of a Puerto Rican community within the Church.

In a final chapter, Vidal surveys the relations of the American Church and the Puerto Ricans outside the city of New York, with special emphasis on Chicago, the second largest Puerto Rican community in the U.S., and on the very successful community of Lorain, Ohio.

In his essay on the Cuban-American community, Lisandro Pérez stresses the importance of the experience of political exile in the making of the Cuban ethos; much of Cuba's history in the nineteenth century was made in New York, and much of its nineteenth-century literature was written or published there. Connected to this was an economic immigration which was centered in southern Florida; political turmoil in Cuba led to economic instability which in turn led much of the island's tobacco industry to move its operations to nearby Florida. Since Havana is only seven hours away from Key West by steamship, this was a "revolving door immigration" similar to that of the Puerto Ricans in the 1940s and 1950s. In fact, when conditions stabilized, large numbers of cigar makers returned permanently to Cuba. Pérez studies the religious attitudes of these exile and worker communities and notes that they were on the whole secular and even anticlerical. The institutional Church's influence was negligible.

After the decline of the Florida cigar industry in the early years of the twentieth century, Cuban immigration was very small. The large Cuban community now in the United States is overwhelmingly composed of post-1960 exiles and their children. Pérez therefore gives special attention to the events which led to the massive self-exile of Cubans following the victory of the Revolution, and to the developments which gave this migration a religious dimension. The response of the diocese of Miami is closely analyzed; its extraordinary efforts in support of the exiles are described, but also the underlying assumption that the Cubans were to assimilate into American Catholicism.

The large number of educated persons among the exiles, however, enabled the Cubans to create a viable community, with its own professional class offering it medical, legal, commercial, cultural, and educational services on its own terms. At the religious level the presence of a relatively large number of priests and religious in the exile community, as well as alumni of elite Catholic institutions and members of Catholic Action groups meant that the Cuban community was able to re-found schools such as the Jesuit *Colegio de Belén*, and to keep alive the religious aspects of Cuban culture, as an integral part of the community's cultural life.

This volume takes the history of the Caribbean Hispanics in the U.S. as far as 1965. After that date developments occur in both American culture and the Catholic Church which make a significant difference to what it means to be a Hispanic in the U.S., and a Catholic Hispanic in the U.S. A large Dominican immigration also adds another strand to the Caribbean Hispanic community. The repercussions of the cultural and political phenomenon we call "the sixties" and of the Second Vatican Council on the history of Hispanic Catholics in the United States are covered in another volume of this study, *Hispanic Catholic Culture: Issues and Concerns.*

Jaime R. Vidal
Jay P. Dolan

PART I

Citizens Yet Strangers:
The Puerto Rican Experience

Jaime R. Vidal

1

Church and People in Puerto Rico

The island of Puerto Rico, settled by the Spaniards under Juan Ponce de León in 1508, became an American possession in 1898 as a result of the Spanish-American War. Its inhabitants were granted American citizenship by unilateral act of Congress in 1917, and in the mid-1940s Puerto Rican migration to the mainland—which up to that point had been barely significant—suddenly increased to enormous proportions, becoming a challenge first to the archdiocese of New York and eventually to the rest of the American Church, especially in the Northeast and in Chicago: a challenge which still stands after forty-five years, in spite of enormous efforts on the part of these local churches.

This essay will chronicle and analyze the interaction of the American Church and its Puerto Rican communicants, especially from the period of the Great Migration until the middle of the 1960s, when a number of social, political, and ecclesial factors—most especially the changed self-image of Americans as a result of the Vietnam War and the counterculture, and the new ecclesiology ushered in by the Second Vatican Council—changed the "rules of the game" as to what it meant to be a Puerto Rican in the U.S. (and a Puerto Rican Catholic in the U.S. Church).

It is a commonplace of American social history that the arrival of an immigrant at Ellis Island was the equivalent of a new birth, a "bath in a purifying Jordan"[1] in whose waters were drowned (supposedly) the immigrant's past allegiances or attitudes to life. The Pole, German, Norwegian, or Italian was, by the act of crossing the Atlantic, reborn as an American. Similarly it was an archetypal American, Henry Ford, who gave us the phrase "History is bunk." America is a practical land, interested in the present and the future, not in the "dead past," especially when—as in the case of the immigrants—it has been left behind in the "old country." To come to America was to turn your back on your old identity and to face the future as a "new person."

This, of course, is mythology, but rarely has a myth been farther from reality than this one is when applied to the Puerto Rican migration. The Puerto Ricans arrived at what was then Idlewild

Airport in New York with strong ties to the Puerto Rican community in the homeland—most emphatically not "the old country,"
but "homeland"—and remained "absent members" of that community, to which most if not all expected to return eventually, and
with which they stayed in touch, especially by frequent visits in
holiday seasons. Thus it is impossible to understand the U.S. Puerto
Rican community without understanding the social, political, and
religious ethos of the homeland, including even the developments
which this ethos may have undergone after the immigrant arrived
in this country. And it is impossible to understand the religious
ethos of the Puerto Rican community on both sides of the sea
without examining the historical forces which shaped it and the
roots which still nourish it.

From the religious point of view, the primary component of
the Puerto Rican ethos is Iberian Catholicism.[2] While in areas like
Mexico and Peru the Native American peoples had a relatively
large population and high levels of civilization which ensured
racial and cultural survival to a greater or lesser degree in the
post-Conquest society,[3] the Taínos of the Caribbean were still at
a neolithic stage of development and could offer little resistance
to European ways. They were also relatively few in number and
were decimated by epidemics and by the heavy work of the mines.
Many others died in the fierce rebellion of 1511 or fled to the
Lesser Antilles when it failed.[4] When in the 1540s the Council
of the Indies decreed the emancipation of the natives, the bishop
reported (possibly with some exaggeration) that only sixty were
left to receive their freedom.[5] By 1582 Governor Juan Melgarejo
reported to Philip II that the Indians in Puerto Rico were very few,
and some of them not native to the island, but imported from the
mainland. At that time they had no separate villages, had forgotten
their language and religion, and were integrated into the island's
society; some of them were even soldiers in the garrison.[6] Eventually some congregated in a mountainous region near Maricao (la
Indiera), and in the eighteenth century numbered some 2,000 souls.
At present, however, there are no pure-blooded Indians in the
island, although a high proportion of Puerto Ricans show Indian
characteristics (facial or genetic) transmitted by intermarriage.[7]

In contrast to Mexico, Central America, and the Andean nations, the religion of the Puerto Ricans is therefore not so much
the result of the evangelization of native populations as of the
immigration of a Spanish population which was already traditionally Catholic and which, like the other peasantries of Europe, had

already formed its own version of popular Catholicism. While it was to be developed and modified in important ways by its new environment, it was this Mediterranean popular Catholicism that would form the basis of Puerto Rican folk Catholicism; indeed many practices and devotions which are commonly believed to be autochthonous are in fact familiar to anyone versed in Mediterranean folklore.

Much more important in the creation of Puerto Rican culture than the survival of the Indian strain as a component in the blood of a racially mixed people was the importation of African slaves to work in the sugar plantations. Since the slave population was concentrated in the areas suited for such plantations, certain sections of the island, especially the coastal plain, have a much higher proportion of blacks than the mountain areas, where coffee plantations (worked by white peasants in various degrees of dependence on the great landowners) were prevalent.[8] For a number of reasons this black population became culturally assimilated in Puerto Rico to a much greater degree than in the rest of the Spanish Caribbean. While the high bourgeoisie carefully avoided intermarriage, the lower and lower middle classes did not share such prejudices, and the offspring of such unions were socially considered white if their proportion of white blood was sufficiently large—even if it was clear that there was some non-white ancestry. Except for the most exclusive clubs and neighborhoods there has never been any segregation in the island, and this constant interaction has led to a certain amount of cultural *"mulataje,"*[9] a presence of important African elements in the Puerto Rican ethos at the levels of art, music, religious sentiment, ethics, and attitudes to life. On the whole these elements have been integrated into a basic Hispanic culture; only in areas of unusually high concentration, such as the municipalities of Guayama and Loíza Aldea, did they produce a distinct Afro-Puerto Rican ethos. The African attitudes which succeeded in entering the general culture are present in all Puerto Ricans—those families which avoided intermarriage had black nannies, who could be as influential as mothers—and most descendants of slaves have integrated a great amount of Spanish attitudes into their worldview. Puerto Rican blacks did not preserve their African religion—as happened in Cuba—in a syncretized form with Catholicism.[10]

Up to the late eighteenth century most Puerto Rican *criollos*[11] were of Castilian ancestry; in the nineteenth and twentieth centuries there was significant immigration from the Canary Islands,

Catalonia, and Mallorca. French refugees from the Haitian slave rebellions and Corsicans imported as middle management for the coffee plantations came in the nineteenth century and their influence was notable in some parts of the island, while individual Irishmen, Englishmen, Germans, and Americans came as businessmen and intermarried with leading local families. Even more than the Africans, these European strains quickly assimilated into the local ethos, while making their own contributions to it. The children of the Catalan entrepreneurs grew up speaking Castilian and those of the Protestant planters grew up Catholic like the local heiresses their fathers married; the leaders in the struggle for independence or autonomy from Spain were often enough the sons of Spaniards.

Racially, therefore, the people of Puerto Rico are a combination of white Europeans (primarily Spaniards) with Africans brought in as slaves and Indians, both native to the island and imported from the other Spanish colonies. While the presence of these groups is unevenly distributed, there are probably few Puerto Ricans who do not have at least a little of each of these strains in their genetic composition. Culturally, the Puerto Rican ethos is a combination of Spanish/Mediterranean attitudes to life, death, love, work, etc., modified by a different natural and historical environment and by the contributions of other strains, particularly those of the Africans, which are especially significant but unevenly spread across the geography and society of the island.

The natural environment and historical vicissitudes of the island have also affected the development of both its institutional and its popular Catholicism. Technically the institutional Church came to Puerto Rico in its full late-medieval development, not as a small seed which would later grow into a full-fledged local church, but as a fully established diocese, just like the ones in Spain—with bishop, chapter, inquisition, prebends, and benefices, as well as friaries.[12] All of this was endowed by the Crown, following the established practice of the *Reconquista* (and of the recent conquest of the Canary Islands) where as soon as a city was taken or founded by the Christians a diocese was erected and endowed, not as a "missionary church" but as a normally functioning local church, a new province of Christendom.[13] The circumstances of the New World soon forced modification of this vision, so that in Mexico, for example, the Church was begun as a missionary endeavor and centered in its first decades not on the bishops but on the mendicant orders. Even there, however, the now current notions of starting with a vicariate apostolic and then erecting a missionary diocese with minimal staffing were not even dreamed of.

At the request of King Ferdinand, Pope Julius II erected in 1511 the diocese of Puerto Rico, together with those of Santo Domingo and Concepción de la Vega in Hispaniola as the first three dioceses of the newly settled territories, making all three suffragan to the metropolitan church of Seville.[14] Santo Domingo was shortly after given metropolitan rank, and therefore ranks as the premier see of the Americas, but as a diocese it is no older than San Juan; it is worth noting that both were close to 300 years old when John Carroll became the first bishop of Baltimore.

The first bishop of Puerto Rico was don Alonso Manso (1511–1539), a canon of Salamanca and former rector of that city's university; he took possession of his see in 1513 and was the first bishop to arrive in the New World. On his arrival he had to use a hut made of dried palm fronds (yaguas) as his cathedral, but already before leaving Spain he had set up the cathedral as a corporate body or chapter (cabildo), with a dean, archdeacon, precentor, master of the schools, treasurer, archpriest and a number of canons and prebendaries.[15]

Since everyone expected Puerto Rico to live up to its name as an emporium for gold, a stone cathedral was begun in 1525 on a scale comparable to that of Seville. In a few years, however, the gold ran out in the island's rivers just as the rich empires of the Aztecs and the Incas were being discovered. The attention of the Spanish authorities was drawn away from the Antilles to the mainland viceroyalties, and Puerto Rico became a backwater of the Spanish empire. The cathedral begun on such an ambitious scale—until the building of the new St. Peter's at Rome, Seville was the largest church in Christendom—had to be finished as a much smaller building and except for the sanctuary and crossing, which were already covered with late Gothic star-vaulting in stone, the rest of the church was roofed in beams and tiles. The chapter, too, never reached the glory intended by Manso; by 1589 there was no master of the schools, and by 1647 there was only a dean, an archdeacon, a precentor, three canons, and two prebendaries who, in the words of one of their number, received "the most limited stipend in all these Indies."[16]

The bishops of Puerto Rico in the colonial period tended to be men of a high cultural and moral level, especially in comparison to their secular counterparts, the governors of the island, whose training was military rather than legal or political. Almost all of the bishops had master's or even doctor's degrees, and the friars among them had usually been "lectors" in the *studia* of their orders.[17] One bishop, don Bernardo de Balbuena, was a well-regarded poet in the *Siglio de Oro*, highly praised by Lope de Vega. Unfortunately the see of Puerto Rico, not being well endowed, was often refused by the candidates to whom it was offered, and bishops who proved to be outstanding were rewarded after a few years by promotion to a better see on the mainland. This, together with the slowness of communications and the snail's pace of Spanish bureaucracy,[18] made for exceedingly long vacancies in which the island's clergy were left without leadership or any stimulus to self-improvement.[19]

Indeed the number, training, and morale of the clergy were an ongoing problem. In the sixteenth century Governor Melgarejo reported that no priest could stay on the island unless he held a benefice because the people were too poor to support unbeneficed clergy. Starting with Manso, the bishops began ordaining the sons of settlers[20] and even an occasional *mestizo* such as Diego Polo, prebendary and succentor of the cathedral whom Bishop Mercado and his chapter recommended to the king for a canon's stall, "for fear that he might otherwise want to leave the island, where he is much needed"[21] since he was also the teacher of grammar and pastor of the cathedral parish. In the periodic reports of the bishops to the Council of the Indies, the phrase "born in this island" occurs as often as "Spaniard" among the names recommended for promotion, and the Puerto Rican canon Diego de Torres Vargas (who died as dean of the cathedral) goes so far as to say in 1647 that "normally all the dignities and prebends of this cathedral are given to natives of this island by the Royal Patronage, which prefers them to outsiders."[22] While no Puerto Rican was promoted to the episcopate until 1803 (don Juan Alejo de Arizmendi), the post was by no means reserved for Spaniards; as early as 1599 the Peruvian-born fray Martín Vázquez de Arce, O.P., became seventh bishop of Puerto Rico and as late as 1814 Arizmendi was succeeded by the royalist Peruvian don Mariano Rodríguez de Olmedo.[23]

While the two friaries of St. Thomas Aquinas (1511) and St. Francis (1645) managed to keep up some minimum standards of ecclesiastical culture until they were suppressed in 1838 by the Liberal government, the intellectual quality of the diocesan clergy was, with honorable exceptions, appallingly low. As a result, the bishops' reports to the Crown constantly harp on the incompetence of the local clergy, begging for better qualified men, recommending the qualified for rewards and prebends lest they be tempted to seek greener pastures, or sometimes in despair admitting a subject's incompetence but recommending him for a post because no one better can be had.

This situation improved slowly until the nineteenth century when a conciliar seminary—the cherished dream of more than one bishop—was finally able to operate. In the early part of the century at least half of the priests on the island were Puerto Rican, but, in spite of the foundation of the seminary, by the second half of the century the proportion of natives to Spaniards in holy orders had significantly decreased. One reason for this was the gradual impoverishment of the old Castilian-descended Puerto Rican families, whose properties were pulverized by being divided among all the children in each generation. As the descendants of these families lost access to such schooling as could be had and became an underclass of landless or virtually landless peasants, their place as the island's elite was taken by a new breed of bourgeois Spanish immigrants, mostly from Catalonia and the Balearic Islands—areas of Spain where secularization and anticlericalism were already rising. The Puerto Rican–born sons of such immigrants rarely sought the priesthood, and so the parishes had to be filled more and more with imported clergy.[24] In the mid–twentieth century a myth arose to account for the scarcity of Puerto Rican vocations: the cause was a—wholly imaginary—Spanish law which forbade ordained Puerto Ricans to serve in the island. The prospect of lifelong exile as the price of ordination supposedly discouraged vocations over the centuries and created the expectation that priests would always be from the outside.[25] The material presented in the previous pages should be sufficient to lay this myth to rest.

The scarcity of priests in Puerto Rico, whether native or Spanish, was aggravated by the fact that a high percentage of them were concentrated within the walls of the capital, in the cathedral and the two friaries, although the population was scattered all over the island. Thus in 1765 Field Marshal Alejandro O'Reilly reports forty-two priests in San Juan (seventeen in the cathedral plus fifteen Dominicans and ten Franciscans) while the rest of the island had only twenty-six.[26] Even if these priests had been evenly spread out this would have averaged, according to O'Reilly, 660 souls per priest, but since, aside from the concentration in San Juan, a number of them were doing indispensable non-pastoral work and others were sick or otherwise impeded, "it may be seen that there is an urgent need to increase the number of priests in those areas which are more populated."[27]

One reason for this imbalance was the Mediterranean culture's emphasis on the centrality of the city. While many Americans merely put up with city life and dream of moving to small towns (or at least to the suburbs), the Spaniard—and the Latin American—can think of no life to compare with city life. Thus to many of the leaders in Church and State the city of San Juan for all practical purpose was Puerto Rico.

Not unconnected with this is the Spanish penchant for solemn and rich religious spectacles, which could only happen in the city. Their priorities led them to concentrate as many priests as possible in one place where the ceremonies could then be celebrated in their full splendor, rather than to spread them out so that everyone in the island could see a priest with some regularity.[28]

Besides this, the Church had to deal with the problem that the country people, having a great amount of unclaimed land at their disposal, tended to scatter widely, frustrating the constant efforts of the bishops to gather them in villages and towns where at least they could have a church and a resident priest. These efforts began in the sixteenth century when Bishop Mercado came across some thirty households living scattered on the southern coast "very far from any town, without a church or cleric or hearing Mass in a year or receiving the Church's sacraments; in fine, living like savages although almost all are Spaniards by birth."[29] Mercado and his successor fray Diego de Salamanca struggled to gather these families into a village (now known as Coamo) and to set up a parish for them.

In the seventeenth century three more towns were founded (Arecibo, Aguada, and Ponce) in places which up to that time had been mission stations, visited every so often by a priest from the city; they in turn became foci from which a resident priest could travel to new mission stations. The eighteenth century was a time of great progress in setting up towns; by 1765 some sixteen new towns had been founded (compared to three each for the two preceding centuries) including Mayagüez, Yauco, Santurce, Río Piedras, and Bayamón. Some of these had stone churches with three naves, roofed in tiles; others had wooden churches.

These centripetal forces were countered, however, by the centrifugal force of hunger for land and its easy availability at a time when the island was still underpopulated. In the sixteenth and seventeenth centuries the Crown would grant large areas called *hatos* in the coastal plain; these were inherited collectively by all the descendants of the grantee, who would split the profits among themselves. These profits would of course be spread a bit thinner in each generation, so by the eighteenth century the governors promoted an agrarian reform which resulted in the granting of Crown lands in the mountainous interior to families who were willing to leave the coastal plain and settle there.[30] These families, too, founded towns, but tended to settle in scattered farms within the municipal jurisdiction, so that according to O'Reilly's report "except for the city of Puerto Rico the towns have no permanent resident except for the Parish Priest; the rest of the 'inhabitants' live permanently in the countryside except for Sundays, when those who live near the Church come to Mass, and for the Easter Triduum, when all the parishioners generally come together."[31]

This scattering of the population had already forced Bishop fray Damián López de Haro, in the Synod of 1645, to establish a correlation between the distance from people's dwellings to the parish church and the frequency of their expected Mass attendance. Persons who lived one or two leagues from church had to hear Mass every other Sunday, those who lived three leagues away, once a month; four to six leagues, every other month, while those who lived more than six leagues from the parish church had to attend only on Christmas, Easter, Pentecost, and one of the Sundays of Lent.[32] This legislation remained in force until the Synod of 1917 and should be kept in mind as a caveat against using Mass attendance as an "indicator of religiosity" in the case of Puerto Ricans. While roads and transportation had improved notably by the late nineteenth century, Picó gives a vivid picture of the difficulties encountered by peasants who wanted to hear Mass in the mountain town of Utuado in the 1880s and 1890s:

> People had to travel long distances on foot and fasting to be able to receive communion at the 9 AM Sunday Mass, which was the second and last Mass of the day. From barrio Paso de Palma people would leave around 4:00 in the morning; in the rainy season those who had shoes or Sunday clothes didn't put them on until they could wash themselves in the river Viví in the outskirts of the town. They confessed during the 7 AM Mass and went to communion at the 9 AM Mass.[33]

Not only did these distances, and the difficult roads, keep the people from Mass, but they also kept the priests from having effective contact with the people, since it took all their time and energy to keep the minimum services going. Fray Iñigo Abbad y Lasierra, who wrote the first history of Puerto Rico in the late eighteenth century, says that a country priest would get a sick call, ride two, four, or six leagues, hear the man's confession, anoint him, give him Viaticum, and then ride back to town, where already someone would be waiting to call him to another deathbed, and so he spent most of his life on horseback, making sure that people had Christian deaths, but with no time to teach them the Christian life.[34] He agreed with O'Reilly that the rural dispersion was the cause of these problems.

At first the scattered Spanish settlers of Puerto Rico were aware that this situation was anomalous. In 1597, for example, Blessed Carlo Spínola, S.J., forced to spend some time in Puerto Rico while the ship that was taking him to Japan was being repaired, decided to make a tour of the island to preach to the settlers. He visited Coamo (whose priest had been sick in San Juan for a year), Bucaná (a barrio between Coamo and the present site of Ponce), San Germán, and the settlement that would later become Arecibo. Everywhere the scattered settlers had been without sacraments for years, but when the news spread that a Jesuit was in the area they flocked from miles around to confess and receive communion. Already, however, he found a serious lack of instruction in matters of the faith, as well as a number of superstitions beginning to grow like weeds in the untended field of their religiosity. These, however, do not seem to have resulted from contact with native or African religion, but could as easily have arisen in any isolated valley of Spain—e.g., the belief that the Pope had sent out a bull with certain words of power which, if copied and worn on one's person, would render one immune from contagious diseases.[35]

The people to whom Spínola preached were still only one or two generations removed from a situation in which Mass, sacraments, and preaching were still normal and normative, even if their quality might have been considered less than ideal by Tridentine standards. But after a number of generations of removal from this situation, the religion of the scattered peasants underwent an inevitable number of transformations which would make its notion of what was essential in religious practice significantly different from that of the institutional clerics.

By the nineteenth century habits of behavior which had been normal and normative to their European ancestors had slowly become unusual, and thus passed from the center to the periphery of the people's religious consciousness. Basically, whatever could not be celebrated without an educated and ordained leader had to be done without except on extraordinary occasions. After centuries of this, people did not see the importance of attending such events regularly, even if they had come to live in a situation where they were readily available. This does not mean that these things have no importance for the people, but that they are perceived as unusual, for special occasions only. A prime example is Holy Week; a person who thinks nothing of staying home every Sunday of the year will often go to great lengths in order to attend the services of the Triduum, especially the processions.

Since nature abhors a vacuum, the place left empty by the loss of formal liturgy as a normal event was filled by a number of folk devotions that the people could celebrate on their own, led by a *rezador* or *rezadora* who had memorized the texts:[36] the rosary, the setting up of home shrines or altars, the celebration of major feasts in the Church calendar with folk customs such as the Candlemas bonfires or the Fiesta de Cruz.[37] Some of these are very beautiful, bearing comparison with the best in Christian spirituality, and most if not all are basically orthodox, so that it should now be possible to integrate or combine them with the liturgy if pastoral authorities are willing to go to the trouble of doing so with some care. In this sense the people, by making the best of an unhealthy ecclesial situation, have produced customs and songs of lasting value which can be used to enrich the life of the Church even after the ecclesial situation has become healthier.

But other, less healthy results also derived from this situation. Generations without religious instruction resulted in a dangerously widespread religious ignorance, which made the people's cultural Catholicism vulnerable to Protestant challenges after 1898 and to syncretisms such as Spiritualism and Afro-Cuban *santería*.

Moreover, the religion of the people tended to become individualistic, or at the most family oriented, rather than ecclesial. This has not been an unmitigated drawback, since it can protect the individual's relationship with God from the pettiness of a narrow-minded community or from the demands of an overbearing institution. Puerto Ricans can feel they are *muy católicos* while totally ignoring the wishes and pressures of the institutional Church when it cannot convince their conscience, because the institution does not control the things that mediate the individual's religious experience. At the same time this attitude can also neutralize more valuable hierarchical efforts, not to mention that a non-ecclesial Catholicism is always an anomaly.

This non-ecclesial character of Puerto Rican folk Catholicism has been a scandal to American priests and bishops from the first encounter between the American Church and the Puerto Rican people and the American Church has never really been able to accept its reality. This incapacity has led American bishops and clergy both on the island and on the mainland to continually act as if they could expect Puerto Ricans to give up their wishes and follow those of the institution's leaders out of mere institutional loyalty, only to be disappointed again and again.

The nineteenth century, in which the Puerto Ricans became a people conscious of their own identity, brought about some major changes in the relationship between the Church and the people of the island. After a false dawn during the episcopate of the first native bishop, don Juan Alejo de Arizmendi y de la Torre (1803–1814), when it looked as if the Church would play a leading role in the creation of this consciousness,[38] the Puerto Rican institutional Church became afraid of the wave of revolutions sweeping Europe and America and, following the lead of Pope Gregory XVI, became a firm and unconditional prop of Spanish colonial rule. This was particularly ironic because during most of the century the Spanish governors were Liberals who on arrival at the colonies lost every aspect of Liberalism except the anticlericalism which was a hallmark of Liberalism in Latin countries.

Because of this unconditional support of the colonial government and opposition to any political or social innovation, the Church lost the support of the emerging intelligentsia, despite the fact that many of them began their intellectual life in the classrooms of the conciliar seminary, which for much of the century was the only secondary institution in Puerto Rico. Perceiving popular Catholicism as a primitive religiosity fit only for women or uneducated peasants, they also rejected elite or institutional Catholicism as a tool of the government and sought to fulfill their spiritual aspirations in Freemasonry or the newly fashionable "scientific spirituality" of Spiritism; others dabbled in pantheistic German philosophies or made a religion out of patriotism. As a result in 1898 the local church discovered that the Puerto Rican élite—politicians, professionals, and thinkers—was at best indifferent to it and at worst overtly hostile.

At the same time the Church's lack of touch with many sections of the masses had reached alarming proportions. While baptism remained an important sacrament without which a child was in a sense not yet a member of the community,[39] delays in baptizing children became more common, as did emergency lay baptism by the midwife or a *rezador*. Still, most children were baptized sooner or later, and baptism remains the most important sacrament in the Puerto Rican popular mind. The spiritual relationship contracted between godparents and godchild—as well as between godparents and blood parents, who become co-parents (*compadres*)—is taken by the people with extreme seriousness; it creates bonds comparable to kinship by blood or marriage.

Marriage, on the other hand, became in the nineteenth century the most traumatic sacrament for the common people of Puerto Rico. Spanish law demanded Christian marriage for slaves and forbade the separation of spouses and children at the time of sale or inheritance. But in the nineteenth century the closing of the slave trade with Africa made the sale of home-grown slaves an almost irresistible financial investment and, since by law married couples had to be sold as a unit, slave owners began to discourage matrimony with the connivance of the civil authorities.[40] In the eighteenth century the bishops would have insisted on enforcement of the laws, and the planters would have been heavily fined or even had the slaves confiscated as a result of such conduct.[41] But in the nineteenth the Church was not up to taking on the slave-owning class which was now politically powerful, often anticlerical, and—because of their wealth and political position—had the Church by the purse-strings. This situation led to a sharp rise in concubinage and illegitimacy among the slaves and this became normal by the time slavery was abolished in 1873. This attitude also spread among the free poor in those areas where a large proportion of the population had been slaves, i.e., the cane-growing coastal plain.[42] This part of the island still has the highest proportion of consensual unions, and of unions which are perceived by the partners themselves as being impermanent.

The free white peasants in the mountains, meanwhile, were having their own problems with the sacrament. Both the isolation of the mountain barrios and the advisability of avoiding divisions in their small holdings by inheritance led to a great amount of marriages between kinfolk, even first cousins. But to marry in church these persons needed a dispensation from the impediment of consanguinity, and these dispensations were prohibitively expensive: 25 pesos for relatives in the fourth degree, 50 for those in the third, and 200 for first cousins. (This at a time when a *cuerda* of land—roughly an acre—in that area sold for one peso.) Even the regular stole fees for a non-consanguineous wedding (5 pesos) would equal a day laborer's wages for a month. In this situation the simplest solution was to elope, have a couple of children, and then go to the parish priest with a sad story about wanting to live in holy wedlock like good Christians, but being unable to afford it; could the priest get the chancery to waive the dispensation fees? Sometimes when a bishop arrived for the pastoral visitation he would see the situation and grant a general dispensation; in such years the number of church weddings would rise 500 percent over the previous average.[43]

The nineteenth century marks a massive descent in the percentage of church weddings, and this was not helped by the fact that for some thirty years (1847–1876) the government set up a committee in each town with power to force the unemployed to accept employment at whatever wage was offered and to compel couples living in concubinage to marry or separate. Because of the Church's jurisdiction over matrimony, the parish priest was an ex officio member of this board, and his presence was required at its meetings. It goes without saying that this board was perceived as a group of "haves" trying to rule the lives of the "have nots" for the benefit of their own class, and the priest's participation did nothing to endear the institutional Church to the poor.[44]

As a result of these developments the matrimonial attitudes of Puerto Ricans by the time of the Great Migration were divided along lines of class and region. The upper classes, for whom inheritance and dignity were important, were married almost without exception and, since their women at least remained strongly religious, these marriages were practically always church weddings. The emerging middle class tended to imitate these attitudes, and it was not uncommon for couples to "fix their matrimonial situation" (*arreglar su matrimonio*) as their social situation improved. Among the peasants elopements were common, but over 85 percent of these couples eventually got married in church; marriages were viewed as permanent and divorce was therefore rare. In the coastal plain the communities which arose from the sugar-cane culture have a much higher rate of consensual unions and these are not necessarily seen as permanent; indeed even the persons married in church will not let that stand in their way if the marriage fails. Finally the urban proletariat which arose in the twentieth century has the most casual attitudes towards marriage, although even there we find a good number of religious marriages.[45] By the standards of the U.S. Catholic community in the 1940s and 1950s this situation was shocking, especially since the upper and middle classes rarely emigrated, so that the attitudes and mores of the peasants, coastal laborers, and urban slum dwellers were perceived as typical. The pastoral documents at the time of the Great Migration were close to obsessive about this issue.

Thus from the sixteenth to the nineteenth century historical and economic developments led the settlers of Puerto Rico to develop a popular Catholicism which was basically orthodox and Iberian, but which came to be out of touch with the institutional Church and with many of its priorities. It was not "pagan" or syncretistic or schismatic; it was based on the traditional Catholic symbol system, and while it gave priority to individual experience and to those aspects of Catholicism which the people could produce on their own, it did not deny the role of the institutional Church.

The Spanish official Church served this popular Catholicism by celebrating the liturgies of the great feasts, by baptizing the children, by blessing the *santos* and candles that would be used in the home altars. It also sometimes used it, or tried to use it, for its own institutional purposes, although the Spanish and native clerics had a pretty good idea of how far they could push the peasants and still expect to get results. Nevertheless, people and clergy shared certain basic assumptions of Mediterranean Catholicism and could live with each other.

The events of 1898 would create a situation that in many ways exposed the weaknesses of this cultural Catholicism, and this challenge was answered by importing an American institutional Church that in many ways was stronger and more effective than its predecessor, but was unable to understand and appreciate the religiosity which the Puerto Rican people had created out of their Iberian Catholic heritage.

With the Great Migration some fifty years later, a confrontation took place between the Puerto Rican people's passive but stubborn attachment to its own way of being Catholic, and the very institutional—and Northern European—Catholicism of the American Church. This Church would try to rise to the challenge but, in spite of the love and good will of many of its members, it would be limited in what it could do because it was imprisoned in its own ecclesiological presuppositions, which had no room for the Puerto Rican Catholic ethos. And it was *to that ethos*, and not to the institution, that the Puerto Ricans were loyal, because that ethos, and not the institution, had sustained them in their times of trial.

2

The Attempt to Americanize Puerto Rico
and the Problem of Identity

In the year 1898, just months after Spain had granted Home Rule (*Autonomía*) to Puerto Rico, the United States declared war on Spain, ostensibly because of American sympathy for the cause of Cuban independence. A number of Puerto Ricans who would not accept the Home Rule solution had been living as exiles in the United States and formed a Puerto Rican branch of the Committee for the Independence of Cuba.[1] These exiles approached the American government and convinced it to invade not only Cuba but also Puerto Rico. As a result of this American troops landed in Guánica Bay on July 25, 1898 (ironically, the feast of the patron saint of Spain) and later also in the port of Ponce—the second largest and the most commercially and politically progressive city in the island—which surrendered without a shot. The Spanish army made a desperate stand on the mountain road leading from Ponce to San Juan and had at least for a moment checked the American advance towards the capital, but at that point the Spanish government, realizing that its position was militarily untenable on all fronts, sued for peace.

By the Treaty of Paris Spain was forced to hand over Cuba to the United States in preparation for its independence; Puerto Rico and the Philippines were ceded absolutely as American possessions. In their case, however, Spain stipulated a number of safeguards for Spanish subjects who chose to continue residing in the lost colonies, for the free entrance of Spanish literary and cultural material, and for the protection of the interests of the Catholic Church insofar as this was compatible with the American Constitution. These safeguards were written into the treaty, and thus bound the United States in international law.[2]

In spite of the granting of Home Rule, most Puerto Ricans welcomed the invading forces as liberators, and the new order became the object of great hopes, which ranged from the democratization of Puerto Rican society to the granting of full independence, as had been formally promised to Cuba. It soon became obvious,

26

however, that the United States had no desire to relinquish Puerto Rico, which in an age of naval power could be the key to the defense of the Panama Canal. Indeed the very independentist exiles who had found Home Rule inadequate became divided when the occupying power was the democratic United States rather than monarchical Spain. While some still felt that independence was the only acceptable solution and accused the Americans of betraying their own ideals by holding on to Puerto Rico as a possession, others had become such admirers of the American system that they felt Puerto Rican aspirations for liberty would best be served by permanent annexation and eventual statehood.

The American government quickly took steps which showed that it intended to maintain permanent control of the island. In 1900, while the Puerto Rican politicians were still in disarray and lacked experience in dealing with American politics, Congress passed the Foraker Law, which put an end to U.S. military rule in Puerto Rico and set up a civil government. This relied primarily on a governor appointed by the president of the United States with the consent of the Senate and on an appointed Executive Council; the decisions of the elected House of Delegates could be vetoed by the governor and were subject to congressional review.

The Puerto Rican legislators found this situation unacceptable and struggled for seventeen years to widen the participation of their constituents in the decisions affecting the running of their country. This was at last achieved in 1917 by the passage of the Jones Law in the U.S. Congress. This replaced the appointed Executive Council with an elected Senate, but the governor was still appointed by the president, and his cabinet was to be confirmed by the U.S. Senate. Some of its clauses also reinforced the economic dependence of Puerto Rico on the United States.[3] Except for the fact that the governorship became elective in 1944, the Jones Law was the equivalent of a state constitution for Puerto Rico until 1950, and some of its provisions are still in effect.

The most important provision of the Jones Law was the granting of American citizenship to all Puerto Ricans. The annexationist Partido Republicano had advocated the corporate granting of American citizenship to all Puerto Ricans, but the Partido Unión de Puerto Rico (which had won every election since 1904) was formally opposed to the collective and unilateral imposition of United States citizenship on Puerto Ricans. In 1914 the House of Delegates, with a Unionist majority, passed a resolution to that effect. By 1917 the Unionists had come to realize that the bicameral legislature—

which was the principal plank on their platform—would not be granted unless American citizenship was also accepted, and so gave in on the issue.[4]

The immediate result of the granting of U.S. citizenship was to raise an almost insurmountable obstacle to any Puerto Rican aspirations to independence, since it would be constitutionally impossible for Congress to grant independence to the island, thus depriving millions of legal Americans of their citizenship at the stroke of a pen. Only a practically unanimous pro-independence plebiscite would make such a decision possible; a mere majority, even over a repeated number of elections, would not be sufficient. Thus the granting of citizenship, over the formal objection of the elected representatives of the Puerto Rican people, signified clearly the American government's intention to hold on permanently to the island, whether as a possession or an eventual state.

Two other results would surface over the years. The first was that, although the citizenship as granted by the Jones Law did not make residents of Puerto Rico eligible to vote for the president of the United States,[5] it did make them eligible for the draft in times of war. Due to the short duration of U.S. participation in World War I, only a few Puerto Ricans saw action, but in World War II, Korea, and Vietnam a large proportion of the draft-age male population of the island saw action on foreign soil. In World War II and the Korean conflict most Puerto Ricans fought in the ranks of the 65th Infantry Regiment, which was recruited in Puerto Rico and staffed by Puerto Rican officers. Since these wars were perceived as noble and altruistic struggles for freedom, and since the regiment distinguished itself on the field, Puerto Ricans tended to be very proud of it, with a pride which was at once pro-American and Puerto Rican. Still, a number of soldiers came across American prejudice and returned soured on the American dream. In Vietnam, where a great number of Puerto Ricans fought in an unpopular war under American officers and as part of American units, the army experience often created bitterness towards the United States.

The other consequence was that as American citizens Puerto Ricans could enter the United States by right, and the government could make no law restricting migration from Puerto Rico to the mainland. In 1917 this migration was minimal, but by 1945 it would acquire massive proportions. A nation which had xenophobically closed its doors to all but a few immigrants by the immigration laws of 1924 saw itself invaded once again by an overwhelming flow of immigrants of just the type these laws had been designed to keep out, but whose entrance or movements could not be restricted or controlled in any constitutional way.

The years from 1898 to 1919 were a honeymoon period between Puerto Ricans and the United States. Especially in the coastal area—where the important cities were located, and therefore the important newspapers and other organs of opinion—union with the nation which had been for decades the principal consumer of Puerto Rican sugar was economically most advantageous. Everything American, from sports and fashions to political institutions, was seen as better than its Spanish equivalent, while politicians of every stripe hoped that the Americans would fulfill their disparate agendas for the future of Puerto Rico. Even on the issue of religion, Protestants had as one of their strongest cards the claim that Protestantism was "the American religion," associated with the values of progress and democracy embodied in the American ethos, while Catholicism was the religion of the defeated and authoritarian Spanish ethos. Catholics, meanwhile, pointed to the devout behavior of Irish soldiers in the American occupying forces, who came to the communion rail every Sunday while the gentlemen of the local elites would only accompany their wives and children as far as the church door.[6]

Meanwhile the American authorities were pursuing a policy of cultural Americanization of the island. The Spanish educational establishment before 1898 had been rather skimpy, and so a new public school system—with such school names as Washington, Lincoln, Hamilton, and McKinley—was created. Like its counterpart in the mainland, one of its main values was its capacity to socialize the children out of their parents' culture and into the American Way. A key element in the system was that English was the compulsory medium of teaching for all subjects except Spanish—which had to be kept as a compulsory subject in all grades as a concession to public opinion. The scarcity of native teachers—especially with sufficient English fluency to teach in that language—brought into the island scores of American teachers intent on "civilizing, Christianizing and Anglo-Saxonizing" the Puerto Ricans.[7] Indeed, it is still the custom in Puerto Rico to refer to teachers by the English titles of "Mr.," "Miss," or "Mrs." even if they are natives and the speakers are using Spanish.

Even in the era of American-born teachers, the effort to turn the children into English speakers did not succeed, in spite of such draconian measures as the prohibition of Spanish in the halls and schoolyard; that generation became, at least in the cities, admirably

fluent in English, but English remained in all cases a second language which Puerto Ricans never used among themselves.[8] As
more natives of the island acquired teacher certification the rule
of teaching in English, although still on the books, came to be
less observed in practice, although for a long time the textbooks
remained in English. It was only in 1950 that teaching in Spanish
became legal and Spanish textbooks for history, science, and other
subjects could be used.[9]

Around the year 1920 the Puerto Ricans' honeymoon with the
United States came to an end. At the end of World War I the
American government put quotas on Puerto Rican sugar which
occasioned a serious setback to the economy of the coastal areas,
and dampened the coast's enthusiasm for the American connection. At the same time it was becoming clearer that the United
States had no intention of granting independence to the island,
so that pro-independence elements became disillusioned with the
"liberator nation." The 1920s and 1930s were marked by the effort
to define a "Puerto Rican identity" and to defend it from erosion by
outside values. This led to a rediscovery and reevaluation—even an
idealization—of Puerto Rico's Spanish past and to an insistence on
the preservation of Spanish culture and traditions. The Nationalist
Party, which arose at this time under the leadership of the charismatic don Pedro Albizu Campos, spoke with frank nostalgia about
the good old days before 1898. Albizu himself was strongly influenced by the nineteenth-century Spanish philosopher Jaime Balmes
who presented a vision of Latin Catholic civilization as superior
to the Nordic Protestant culture in terms of human values,[10] and
therefore presented the island's Spanish heritage as essential to its
spiritual identity, which was threatened by American imperialism
not only at the political and economic but also at the cultural
level. This message appealed to the small landowners and to certain educated but not wealthy sectors of the city and small-town
electorates, although it alienated the cane laborers and blue-collar
workers, as well as the emerging number of women in the labor
force, for whom there was no place in the good old traditions of
the Spanish family.[11] In despair of achieving independence by non-
violent means, the Nationalists resorted to force and were brutally
repressed by the Americans, and Puerto Rican policemen who were
"more American than the Americans."[12] While most Puerto Ricans
rejected the violent approach of the Nationalists, the government's
overreaction gained them a grudging amount of public sympathy;
many Puerto Ricans came to feel a certain admiration for their

ideals, even if they deplored their methods. In the early 1950s the Nationalists attempted to proclaim the independence of Puerto Rico by a coup, which failed for lack of popular support but cost a number of lives. They also attempted to assassinate President Truman and on one occasion a few of them smuggled guns into the visitors' gallery of the U.S. House of Representatives and sprayed the floor with gunfire. These incidents were condemned by the vast majority of Puerto Ricans and added fuel to the prejudice against Puerto Rican migrants in the U.S., yet today in the Puerto Rican neighborhood of New York City there is a large public school named after don Pedro Albizu Campos.

Although most Puerto Ricans did not react to the situation of the 1920s and 1930s with the dogmatism and violence of the Nationalists, this period brought to the fore two interlocked issues which haunt Puerto Ricans both in the island and in the mainland to this day: the issues of *identity* and of the *status* of the island. As early as the first decade of the nineteenth century Puerto Ricans had begun to develop a sense that the island on which they were born was "their country." While their ancestors in the sixteenth to the eighteenth centuries might have seen themselves as Spaniards who happened to come from Puerto Rico, these later generations began to see themselves as Puerto Ricans. By the middle of the century this led a number of persons to work actively for the independence of the island, but their efforts proved premature. While they may have had the sympathy of many or even most of the population, people were not ready to resort to violence. In the later part of the century politicians came to see Home Rule as more feasible than independence, and in 1898 Home Rule was granted, only to disappear practically untried as a result of the war. So in 1898 the Americans took over an island whose inhabitants considered themselves a people, who were attracted to American values of progress and democracy, but also firmly attached to their own language and traditions.

By the 1920s it was clear that while most Puerto Ricans were not willing to revolt against American rule, they also had no wish to trade this Puerto Rican identity for an American one. They might be very pro-American, but *Americano* was something they were not and had no wish to become. Even in the honeymoon days of 1898–1919 there were certain signs of resistance, and it is interesting that even then these tended to cluster around the Spanish language as a symbol of Spanish tradition. The blood, language, and cultural heritage of Spain were already seen by some as the bulwark which would keep the Puerto Rican people's sense of identity from being absorbed into the American ethos. Thus as early as 1900 the poet José Mercado published a poem on the Castilian language which culminates in the wish that Puerto Rico should never give up that tongue, and that the bonds of union with Spain and the Hispanic world which force had snapped asunder would be retied by the common language. The final couplet cries out (with double exclamation points) that "one can easily change flags, but feelings do not change!!"[13] The great Puerto Rican statesman don Luis Muñoz Rivera, who as a leader of the Home Rule Party before 1898 had written scathing attacks in prose and verse against the Spanish colonial establishment, also expressed a new appreciation of the Spanish heritage in a poem written on the back of a postcard which showed the Spanish flag and coat of arms:

> Ayer, amenazante, esa bandera
> flotó de mi país en los castillos
> y habría dado yo mi vida entera
> por mirarla salir, mares afuera,
> con sus matices rojos y amarillos.
>   Hoy que en sus reales se plegó sombría
> se va con ella un ideal fecundo:
> un símbolo de honor y de hidalguía.
> Y, creedlo: no sé lo que daría,
> ¡ay! para verla dominar el mundo.[14]

José de Diego, the leader of those who held on to the ideal of independence after 1898, also expresses the sense of Spanish heritage, dignity, and *hidalguía* in his poetry and prose. He was instrumental in the restoration to the seal of the island of the coat of arms granted by King Ferdinand in 1511—full of castles, lions, and other Spanish insignia—which had been replaced by the Americans with a heraldic monstrosity symbolic of the dawn of a new day for Puerto Rico under American auspices.[15]

    This Spanish symbolism and attachment to Spanish values did not signify (in spite of Muñoz Rivera's obviously hyperbolic closing line) a desire to return to Spanish colonial rule nor a desire to deny the Indian and African blood which runs in the veins of almost every Puerto Rican in varying proportions. They signified rather an instinctive affirmation that Puerto Ricans see their identity as rooted not in race but in *culture* and in *language*, and that it is this which unites Puerto Ricans of all races into one people, a people which at the same time feels bonds of brotherhood with the other nationalities that share this language and heritage, as well as with Spain, the source of both.[16] In the United States, this sense of culture and language as the sources of identity has kept white Puerto Ricans from blending into white middle-class America even when they are in a position to do so, and has also kept darker or distinctly black Puerto Ricans from joining the American black community. The Puerto Rican, whether black or white, tends to think of those who speak Spanish as "our people"—no matter what their color—while those whose first language is English (be they black or white) are "the others."

This is particularly confusing in that American culture tends to divide people along color lines. White Americans are surprised when a white Puerto Rican refuses to "pass" or "blend," especially if he at once insists on his whiteness and his Puerto Ricanness. Black Americans are offended when darker Puerto Ricans remain aloof from the black community and its interests, and interpret this as a desire to "pass for" or be accepted as white. Both sides find it hard to understand that in the eyes of Puerto Ricans, American blacks and whites have more in common with each other than with them.

Some American liberals have a particular problem in this regard, since their sympathy tends to go to the oppressed *as oppressed*, and thus tend to use oppression as the common denominator. However, the Puerto Ricans will not accept "poor" as a primary identification. They know too many well-off Puerto Ricans back home who, whatever their class differences, are undoubtedly Puerto Rican, and they know too many people in the U.S. who share their economic and social conditions, but not their language or culture. For the same reasons, neither will they identify primarily as "people of color." What Puerto Ricans are aware of—and socially conscious Americans are blinded to by their culture's obsession with color and economic status—is that other groups which share with them the classifications of "poor" or "non-white" may have very different agendas and interests, which need not coincide with theirs and may even on occasion be opposed to theirs. If such a coalition is ever successfully formed, it will have to begin by accepting and respecting the differences among its components, and safeguarding the interests of each. Otherwise Puerto Ricans will feel that their identity is being swallowed, and their interests shortchanged, in the name of a spurious "unity."

Inextricably united to the issue of identity is the issue of the political status of the island. We have seen that by the mid-nineteenth
century Puerto Ricans had formed a clear sense of peoplehood
and of *patria*, but efforts to acquire independence by violent means
were few, and failed for lack of broad support. This kind of ambivalence was reinforced under American rule by a number of
factors. From their earliest years in school Puerto Ricans were led
to feel that their island was too small to be economically viable
as an independent nation, and at a more practical level American
legislation has tended to make the island economically dependent
on the mainland. The sight of dictators like Trujillo and Batista in
the neighboring islands led many to believe that American tutelage
was necessary to keep Puerto Rican politics from deteriorating in
the same direction, precisely because Puerto Ricans felt that they
were not all that different from Dominicans and Cubans. These
feelings and attitudes were widespread in all classes and led to
the conclusion that independence was, of course, a beautiful and
noble ideal, but in the Puerto Rican reality it was utterly impractical. Young independentists were seen as being infected with the
idealism of youth and were expected to get practical as they grew
older (as most of them did); those who remained independentist
into middle and old age were regarded as new Don Quixotes,
admirably noble, but dangerously mad. This attitude was reinforced in the 1960s when Castro brought the threat of Communism
to the Caribbean, with the aggravating factor that he explicitly
advocated the independence of Puerto Rico. The independentists
openly embraced Marxism and thus alienated the mainstream of
Puerto Rican society, which tended to feel about Communism as
sixteenth-century Spaniards felt about heresy.

All of these circumstances produced a mentality which we
might describe as "passive aggressive," in which it was considered
taboo to express or even have anti-American feelings, and in which
those who expressed the desire for political independence were
marginalized into a fringe movement.[17] At the same time, however,
Puerto Ricans instinctively and stubbornly clung to their identity,
resisting the use of English as anything but a second language and,
while superficially accepting many aspects of American culture,
subtly "misunderstanding" them or "translating" them into something very different. They continued to feel that Puerto Rico was
their country and the United States a foreign land; that the Puerto
Rican flag was their flag, and the Stars and Stripes the flag of the
Americans; and that they were Puerto Ricans, not *Americanos*.[18]

If the feeling that the island could not manage without American protection made independence unacceptable to most Puerto Ricans, the feeling that they are not *Americanos* makes the idea of statehood equally unacceptable to a less overwhelming but still large majority. Even members and leaders of the Statehood Party, when caught off guard, forget their professions of Americanism and identify themselves as *Puertorriqueños*, and their pro-statehood speeches are of course made in Spanish, not in English.[19] During the years that Fidel Castro was perceived as a threat those Puerto Ricans who had something to lose if the island became a Socialist Republic—and by that time they were many—were attracted to the idea of statehood because this was perceived as the only infallible guarantee that the United States would never relinquish the island. But even now the Statehood leadership has to insist that their concept of statehood would include guarantees for the preservation of the island's language and identity.

Thus ever since the American occupation, Puerto Ricans have been obsessed by the problem of the island's status; all political parties define themselves not by their social agendas, but by their position on this issue. Even second and third generation U.S. Puerto Ricans can get emotional over this—and are just as much divided about it as their cousins in the island. When a project for a plebiscite on the status was recently canvassed, the "absent Puerto Ricans" of the United States loudly clamored for the right to vote in it; they considered themselves Puerto Ricans, and it was the future of their country that was being decided.

In the late 1930s don Luis Muñoz Marín, in many ways a New Deal pragmatist, founded the Popular Democratic Party whose agenda was centered not on the status of the island but on correcting its abysmal socioeconomic situation. His goal was to give the island a viable economy and a just social structure but in a capitalist pattern, by raising the poor to a middle-class standard of living. In order to build a winning coalition of peasants, laborers, and white-collar liberals he had to avoid the divisive problem of the island's status and, in a piece of Spanglish that became celebrated, proclaimed "el *status* no está en *issue*." This allowed a large number of people whose ideas on the status were incompatible with each other to lay aside this divisive and insoluble issue and work for immediately soluble and desperately needed goals. This position led to resounding victories in 1940 and especially in 1944. In this year an amendment to the Jones Law allowed Muñoz to become Puerto Rico's first elected governor—an office he would hold until his retirement in 1964. But ultimately the question of the island's status could not be kept "not in issue," and Muñoz and his party were forced to pronounce themselves on it.

Here Muñoz showed his political genius. He realized that the Puerto Ricans' phobia of independence, coupled with their stubborn reluctance to relinquish their identity, meant *de facto* a choice for colonial status, but that this, when put bluntly, was emotionally unacceptable to the people's sense of dignity. Nobody could admit to wanting to be a colony, but the two other alternatives were even more abhorrent to the majority of Puerto Ricans. He therefore devised a sort of "colony with dignity" which was presented to the U.S. Congress under the name of "Commonwealth," but to the Puerto Rican voters under that of *Estado Libre Asociado*: a free state which freely associated itself to the United States while keeping its own identity as a distinct people.[20] As a potent symbol of this the Puerto Rican flag—up to then banned by law as a Nationalist symbol—would now fly next to the American flag in all public buildings, so also the Puerto Rican anthem *La Borinqueña* was to be played immediately after the *Star-Spangled Banner* at all public events. Spanish was proclaimed to have parity with English as the official language of the Commonwealth. The new status and its constitution were overwhelmingly approved in a plebiscite in 1952 and entered into effect on July 25 of that year,[21] which meant that celebrations of the landing of the American troops in Puerto Rico (July 25, 1898) would now be superseded by the anniversary of the Commonwealth constitution.

The great weakness of the Commonwealth solution is that, in spite of its proponents' claim that it is an ideal and thus permanent synthesis of statehood and independence, with the advantages of each and the drawbacks of neither, most Puerto Ricans soon came to perceive it as a compromise which sooner or later would have to evolve in one direction or the other. Forty years later, however, it is still the official status of the island, and looks to remain so for the foreseeable future, having survived the collapse of Popular Democratic hegemony in 1968 and further plebiscites in 1967 and 1993. This it owes to its great strong point: it is the only dignified face that can be put on the situation which not too many Puerto Ricans want as the ultimate destiny for their country, but which almost all Puerto Ricans hope will last their time.

The problem of identity is one that all U.S. Hispanics have to deal with, and indeed all immigrant peoples who have come to this country. In the case of Puerto Ricans, however, the peculiar status of the island and its peculiar relationship to the United States have added unique twists. Puerto Ricans have already had to deal with it at home, and have managed to hold on to their identity through more than ninety years of American domination and more than seventy years of American citizenship. There is therefore in the Puerto Rican psyche a firm determination not to become American or identify as such. But this determination is expressed in the form of passive resistance rather than open defiance. When Puerto Ricans came to the mainland, therefore, they were well versed in the art of cheering the American flag, but with the unconscious reservation that this was the flag of a wonderful nation, the protector of their own . . . but not *their* flag.

Indeed the very granting of American citizenship ironically contributed to the preservation of identity: other immigrants had to *decide* to become Americans, aspire to it, demonstrate proficiency in English, attend lectures on civics. After the granting of citizenship they were no longer Italians, Germans, or Poles but Americans, even if hyphenated by first-generation loyalties. Italy, Germany, or Poland was now "the old country." But the Puerto Ricans, without asking for it, had been born American citizens, and entered the country as American as they needed or wanted to be for their own purposes, i.e., *legally* American but emotionally Puerto Rican. They were here by right and did not have to prove loyalty, undergo indoctrination, or even learn English, unless they wanted to. The ambivalence which had been developed in Puerto Rico was simply continued in the mainland.

It is important to understand this deep-seated and stubborn ambivalence—which is partly the result of decisions made by the United States without consulting the people of Puerto Rico. Otherwise apparent signs of Americanization and open expressions of love and loyalty to the United States may mislead Americans into thinking that all that is needed is a slight push and Puerto Ricans will gladly become fully integrated into American culture, whether at the secular or the religious level.[22] Both in the island and in the mainland the American Church has succeeded with Puerto Ricans to the degree that it has understood, accepted, and identified with their strongly held sense of identity and with that identity's religious aspects. To the degree that it has not understood it or accepted it, and has clung to its traditional agenda of Americanizing the immigrant, it has failed.

3

The Establishment of a North American Church Structure in Puerto Rico

The previous chapter has examined the effects of the American invasion on the political and cultural life of the Puerto Rican people. It is now time to look at its effects on the religious life of the island and especially at the momentous changes it occasioned in the Catholic Church.

The events of 1898 were traumatic for the institutional Church in Puerto Rico on more than one level, and the reaction to this experience produced important changes which were to affect its relationship to the people—sometimes positively, sometimes negatively—for the rest of the century. At the core of the trauma stood the union of Church and State—and the deeper and more significant *unity of society and religion* which this union sought at once to express and to effect. Such a union had been central to the Spanish Church's self-image and pastoral strategies. From the first days of the settlement and conquest, and even before in the Spanish *Reconquista*, the aim had been to create a Christian society in which assent to the teachings of the Church, the celebration of its feasts, the observance of its moral code, and the internalization of its devotion would not be the responsibility of the individual, but would be acquired almost by osmosis, by being part of a society where these were the shared and lived values. To achieve this the Spanish Church had counted, from the dawn of the Middle Ages, on the cooperation of the State, because both State and Church shared a common ideal of what constituted the good society. Thus both in the Spain of the *Reconquista* and in the New World of the *Conquista* the Crown had endowed cathedrals, built monasteries, paid clerical salaries, enforced Christian ideals, and protected the people from anything perceived as heretical propaganda.

In the nineteenth century the Spanish Church both at home and in the colonies had to deal with the fact that the Spanish government had fallen into the hands of anticlericals who closed the monasteries and restricted the Church's freedom. Still, even the anticlericals were not ready to totally repudiate the ancient connection between Church and State, and the Church put up with their harassment because the alternative of disestablishment was unthinkable.

In 1898, with hardly any warning, the unthinkable happened in Puerto Rico. The new colonial power not only had a constitutionally guaranteed "wall of separation" between Church and State, but had a strong tradition of Protestantism which informed the American ethos. All of a sudden, the clergy had no visible means of support and neither they nor the people had any idea of how the Church was to be financed in the new situation. Both clergy and people would now have to deal with the challenge of Protestantism and had no idea how this could be done in a pluralist society. It was therefore understandable that Rome should decide to appoint for the island's see a series of bishops who would be familiar with the American constitutional ethos and experienced in the preservation of Catholicism in a pluralist environment. This, of course, meant American bishops. It should be noted, however, that Rome hedged its bets on the eventual Americanization of the island, so that while the bishops of Puerto Rico throughout the first half of the twentieth century would be American, the diocese—which up to then had been suffragan to Santiago de Cuba—was not incorporated into an American ecclesiastical province, but made immediately subject to the Holy See. Neither was the apostolic delegate at Washington given authority over the island's Church, which received an apostolic delegate of its own (usually the same prelate who concurrently served as nuncio to the Dominican Republic). So, while the island got an American hierarchy, it was not made a part of the American Church.[1]

Unfortunately, the American bishops appointed to Puerto Rico tended to see their mission as helping to Americanize the people of the island on the ecclesiastical level, as the public schools and other institutions supposedly were doing at the secular level. A number of them became vocal advocates of statehood in the mainland press; they saw this advocacy as a defense of the Puerto Ricans as being "good enough to become full Americans." But when their statements were reported in the island they were perceived as unduly meddling in an issue that should be determined by Puerto Ricans, and on which an American bishop should remain publicly impartial both as an ecclesiastic and as a foreigner. Being convinced of the superiority of American Catholicism over European and especially Mediterranean religiosity, they set out to transform the Puerto Rican institutional Church in the image of its American counterpart, and the popular religion of the Puerto Rican people into the hierarchically controlled devotionalism of Irish Americans.

In 1897 the last Spanish bishop of the island, fray Toribio Minguella de la Merced, O.S.A., had been promoted to the see of Sigüenza in Spain. His successor don Francisco Valdés y Noriega (nominated by the Queen Regent in March 1898) had not yet received papal confirmation when it became clear that Spain would lose the island to the United States. He then resigned his rights to the see, having no wish to serve in the new situation. This freed the Vatican to nominate, for the first time in the history of the diocese, a bishop on its own initiative. The chosen candidate was James Humbert Blenk, born in Germany of Protestant parents, but brought to America as a child and converted to Catholicism in his early teens. He had joined the Marist Congregation where he became a professor and later president of the congregation's college in Louisiana and had fulfilled delicate missions in Europe and North Africa. When Archbishop Placid Chapelle of New Orleans was named apostolic delegate to Cuba and Puerto Rico he asked Blenk to take a post in his entourage, and it seems that he recommended him to the Vatican for the see of Puerto Rico.[2]

An urgent priority in Blenk's episcopate was the financial grounding of the island's Church. As we have seen, an anticlerical Spanish ministry had confiscated the Church's landed endowments in the 1830s. But in 1851 a concordat was signed by which the Spanish Crown, in exchange for the Church's acceptance of the confiscations, engaged itself to pay the salaries of the cathedral and parochial clergy and other ecclesiastical expenses. This meant that the change of rule in Puerto Rico from Spain to a nation which by its Constitution could not subsidize the clergy or worship of any denomination left the island's Church—both the diocese and the individual clergymen—without any visible means of support. Neither the Spanish clergy nor the native priests understood the American ethos on this issue, and their requests for aid from the American military government were argued in such a way as to be self-defeating. It was therefore imperative that a talented man with diplomatic gifts and a clear understanding of what an American government could and could not do be put in charge of the matter. Blenk, who to a great extent had been selected precisely because of these talents, was therefore instructed to remain on the mainland until he could resolve these issues in Washington, and only then to take possession of his diocese.

Blenk's mission was complicated by the fact that the municipalities of a number of island towns, composed of anticlerical members of the elite, were claiming that the parish churches, rectories, and other ecclesiastical buildings of their towns had been built with public monies or on land donated by the government, and that separation of Church and State meant that these buildings became the property of the people of Puerto Rico to be put to secular use. If these claims were accepted, the already impoverished Church would have to start all over again, by buying land and building new churches and rectories. Moreover, the church would lose its symbolic place in the plaza at the heart of each town. Luckily for Blenk, these anticlerical councilmen did not understand the American religious ethos any more than the Spanish-trained clergy of the island. In the Latin mentality separation of Church and State always meant State hostility towards the Church and when the Church was disestablished in Latin countries this tended to be done in a vindictive way designed to curtail the Church's effectiveness in society. They did not realize that in the American ethos separation of Church and State means that the State is fair to all denominations and is sympathetic to their ethical and charitable aims while avoiding direct aid. Thus lawsuits which were clearly anticlerical and vindictive would only damage their cause in American eyes.

Blenk's trump card was the clauses in the Treaty of Paris by which the United States was bound to honor Spain's outstanding commitments in its new possessions and to guarantee the freedom of the Catholic Church in them. Measures that were vexations to the Church, such as the confiscation of churches which had been built wholly or in part with State money at a time when the Church was established, were thus presented as a violation of the treaty. The American Constitution did not invalidate gifts made before it came into effect in a given territory, and the Treaty of Paris obliged the U.S. Government to protect this property as it would protect any other property legally acquired under Spanish law.

The salaries of the clergy had been paid by the Spanish Crown as a compensation for its confiscations of Church property in the 1830s, to which compensation Spain had engaged itself by the Concordat of 1851—a treaty which created valid obligations in international law. By the Treaty of Paris the United States had become committed to honoring such Spanish engagements in its new possessions, and since the method by which Spain had fulfilled them was unconstitutional in the United States, another method had to be devised. This was for the government to pay the Church

a lump sum based on the value of the confiscated properties—some
of which the Spanish government had kept and transferred in 1898
to Federal hands, while others, which the Spanish government had
sold, were now producing tax revenue for the island's government.
These buildings and lands were eventually evaluated at $300,000—
a very important sum in those days—which was given to the
diocese of Puerto Rico. The diocese invested this and used the
capital as an endowment.[3]

Even before the final adjudication of this case Bishop Blenk
had been transferred to succeed Chapelle as archbishop of New
Orleans; it was his successor, William Ambrose Jones, O.S.A. (1907–
1921) who became the real builder of the American institutional
church in Puerto Rico, although in many cases he was only implementing with skill and enthusiasm policies which had been
initiated by Blenk.

A native of New York state, Jones joined the Augustinians at
eighteen and after a brief parochial experience was assigned to
Villanova as master of novices and clerics for his province. Three
years later, upon the American occupation of Cuba, he was sent to
Havana to take charge of the old Augustinian church in that city.
In his seven years there, he expanded the Augustinian presence
to a second parish and founded a respected secondary school,
the Colegio San Agustin. He was still at this post when he was
appointed to the see of Puerto Rico.[4]

Jones's principal achievement was the celebration of a diocesan
synod in 1917. This synod's legislation replaced that of the last
previous synod, celebrated by fray Damián Lopez de Haro in 1645.
The new diocesan statutes embodied and gave permanent form to
the new policies initiated by Blenk and Jones in order to rebuild
the Puerto Rican Church in the pattern of a successful American diocese. Two of these policies were designed to end institutions of the Spanish Church which were incompatible with the
American-style diocesan government, the cathedral chapter and
the lay mayordomos de fábrica.

The cathedral chapter was a normal part of a European diocesan structure; its *raison d'être* was twofold: to chant the Liturgy
of the Hours corporately and daily in the cathedral and to serve
as the "senate" of the bishop. According to canon law the bishop
is obliged to consult his chapter on certain issues of the administration of his diocese, especially in the sale or lease of diocesan
property, and if the value of the property is sufficiently high, may
not act without the chapter's consent.[5] The chapter thus provides

some form of "checks and balances" to the power of the bishop. Blenk and Jones found themselves in Puerto Rico with an almost 400-year-old chapter, but almost all of its canons were Spaniards, who felt out of place in the new regime and kept begging the Queen Regent of Spain for appointments to Spanish cathedrals. As they one by one received their transfer or died, the American bishops simply did not replace them, and the chapter erected by Manso in 1512 was allowed to wither away into nonexistence, thus freeing the new bishops to administer the diocese as they saw fit.

At the parish level the Church's temporalities were administered in Spanish times by an elected lay official called mayordomo de fábrica, the rough equivalent of an English churchwarden. The mayordomo, in consultation with the rector or vicar, ran the day-to-day administration of the parish funds and made the disbursements for items such as wax, incense, linen, vestments, and church plate, and for common repairs to the building. The mayordomo also collected and administered the rents owed to the parish by the tenants of any land belonging to it and the *censos* or perpetual annuities which landowners often set up in their wills for the benefit of the parish fabric or the greater splendor of its worship.[6]

Under Jones's new legislation the parish priests, under the effective control of the bishop, became the administrators of parochial finances and lay involvement was kept to a minimum.[7] The demise of the cathedral chapter and the abolition of the mayordomos de fábrica meant that two important checks to episcopal authority had disappeared, and the bishop was in a position to govern the diocese as he saw fit, according to the more "efficient" American model.

Having removed the two principal institutional obstacles for the remaking of Puerto Rico into an American-style diocese, Bishop Jones was free to pursue this goal by means of four policies already begun by his predecessor: the Americanization of future native clergy, the introduction of American religious orders, the erection of a parochial school system, and the popularization of American-style lay organizations.

The efforts to Americanize the island's future native clergy were begun by Bishop Blenk's decision to close the conciliar seminary which had been founded in the 1830s and to send its students to American seminaries. Given the nature of a seminary as a "total institution" whose purpose is to "form" its students into its pattern of the "ideal priest," the expected result was that the Puerto Rican seminarians would be socialized into the clerical style of the American Church. Instead the result was the loss of a great many

Puerto Rican vocations; young men sent to the U.S. seminaries would suffer culture shock and leave, or resist certain aspects of the "formation" process and be therefore dismissed as unsuitable. Those who persevered spent as many as twelve years away from their country.[8] The result of this was that by 1925 the number of Puerto Rican priests reached a record low of twelve,[9] probably the lowest number since the end of the sixteenth century. This would later have important repercussions on the ministry to Puerto Ricans in the mainland. Because of this low number of priests, Puerto Ricans became the first major immigrant group which did not have members of its own clergy ministering to it.[10] In the 1940s and 1950s American Catholic sources tended to blame this situation on Spain or on the Puerto Rican character, but surely the negative results of Blenk's policy of sending Puerto Rico's seminarians to be trained in the mainland—a policy which was still in force at the time—seems to have been a contributing factor. At the same time, it should be realized that Blenk and Jones were not out to strangle the Puerto Rican clergy and replace it with Americans, but to produce a new generation of Americanized Puerto Rican priests to serve the new generation of Puerto Ricans, whom everyone at the time expected to be Americanized. This policy, like its secular counterpart, failed because the policymakers did not understand the quiet but stubborn attachment of the Puerto Ricans to their own culture and ways.

Meanwhile the Spanish diocesan priests were leaving the island. To supply this need Blenk invited religious orders—mostly American, but some Spanish and one Dutch—to send priests to Puerto Rico where they would be given charge of parishes. Once again this policy was initiated by Blenk but implemented by his successor. This was a tempting solution since, while American or Spanish diocesan priests might be reluctant to leave their homelands, members of religious orders could be assigned to Puerto Rico under obedience by their superiors. It was therefore not very difficult to convince a Provincial to send a small band of his men to staff a parish or two in Puerto Rico and, if the venture was successful, to send more men to spread out over a whole district of the island. While in 1900 there were only 8 religious priests in the island, as compared to 105 diocesans (38 native and 67 foreign), by 1960 there were 394 religious (of whom only 4 were Puerto Rican) as compared to 86 diocesans (44 native and 42 foreign).[11] From this it can be seen that the policies initiated by Blenk and Jones changed the configuration of the Puerto Rican clergy from two-thirds foreign (mostly Spanish) and one-third native to nine-tenths foreign (mostly American) and one-tenth native, as well as from overwhelmingly diocesan—the normal European arrangement—to overwhelmingly religious—the typical missionary arrangement.

Most of these orders were American communities, and this contributed to the Americanization of parish structures; the American religious also attempted to remold the parishioners according to American patterns of practice and devotion. Most prominent among them were the Redemptorists of the Baltimore Province who by 1952 had parishes in the four principal cities of San Juan, Ponce, Mayagüez, and Caguas as well as in nine other lesser towns. In that year they had eighty-one priests active in the island[12]— almost as many as the diocesan priests in the whole island, almost twice as many as the native priests, and close to a quarter of the island's regular clergy. The Baltimore Redemptorists would later have an important role in Cardinal Spellman's response to the "Great Migration."

While the orders of priests were primarily brought in to staff the island's parishes, congregations of teaching sisters were invited to staff another pillar of the new system: the network of parochial schools which spread across the whole island, reaching its apogee in the 1950s. In the United States the purpose of the Catholic school system was to protect the youth of the Catholic ghetto from alien intellectual influences; at first from the overt, although non-denominational, Protestant atmosphere of the nineteenth-century public schools, and later from the secular attitudes of twentieth-century public education. In Puerto Rico this purpose was somewhat modified. In the first place, the American clergy was appalled at the low level of catechetical instruction in the island, and attributed to this the inroads of Protestantism among people who were not equipped to answer the evangelists' arguments against traditional beliefs or practices. Where the Spanish Church had been able to rely on the basically Catholic atmosphere of Puerto Rican society, the new situation demanded from every Catholic the capacity to understand and defend the tenets of the Faith. The bishops counted on the Catholic schools to produce graduates with such a capacity.

The bishops were also concerned about the cavalier attitude of the average Puerto Rican toward the sacramental laws of the Church (Mass attendance, Easter duty, marriage in church, etc.)

which had resulted from centuries of rural isolation, and which continued even when a family moved to town or when a chapel was built in their rural barrio. A system of Catholic schools would train the new generation in regular habits of churchgoing, not only by stressing the importance of this obligation, but by making continued attendance at the school contingent on it. Not only the school children but also their parents were expected to attend Mass every Sunday at the parish church if they wanted their child to be readmitted to the school the following year, and no child was admitted whose parents were not married in a Catholic ceremony. The bishops hoped that exposure to a Catholic education after the American pattern would produce a new generation whose Catholicism would be closer to the American ideal. The Catholic schools were also expected to produce native vocations, both to the diocesan priesthood and to the male and female American orders.

These expectations were only fulfilled to a certain degree. In the first place, it was never feasible to have "every Catholic child in a Catholic school"—even less in Puerto Rico than in the United States. Even with the nominal salaries nuns received in those days and with the consequently low tuition, the cost was prohibitive for families below the lower middle class. Since only the elite *colegios privados* took boarders and the Church could not afford to build and staff schools in the country barrios, Catholic schooling for all intents and purposes was not available to the children of the peasantry. Thus the Catholic schools, in spite of the enormous energy expended on them, rarely reached beyond the urban upper and middle classes.

The efforts to socialize the students into a more institutional and sacramental religiosity were again only partially successful. By indicators such as fidelity in Mass attendance and fulfillment of Easter duty the upper and middle classes were definitely "more Catholic" in 1960 than they had been in 1900. But things like compulsory Mass attendance can be double-edged; they can create resentments or become part of what one leaves behind when one graduates into the adult world. It must also be kept in mind that the solidarity, parish centeredness, and strong sacramental practice of the pre-1965 American Church were not in fact based primarily on Catholic education; factors such as a sense of anti-Catholic discrimination had an important role to play in creating and preserving the U.S. Catholic ghetto. When that sense of being a beleaguered minority collapsed with the election of John F. Kennedy and the new spirit of Vatican II, much of the American Catholic ethos which

Blenk, Jones, and their successors tried to re-create in Puerto Rico collapsed with them. In Puerto Rico that crucial ingredient was lacking. Indeed it was the Protestant minority which felt discriminated against in a society whose whole culture was dominated by a Catholic symbol-system, and so in Puerto Rico it was the Protestants who closed ranks, voted as a bloc on certain issues, made it a point to attend church faithfully, and used their religion as their primary self-identification. The type of Catholicism which the American bishops tried to create in the island depended to a great degree on this sense of being a "people set apart," who were willing to pay a price for their beliefs. It therefore could not be developed in a society where being a Catholic remained, when all was said and done, the line of least resistance.

In the field of vocations too, the Catholic school system achieved some success, but not very much; by 1960 there were forty-four Puerto Rican secular priests. The religious orders, however, had only managed to recruit and ordain four Puerto Ricans, in spite of having a greater number of parishes and a reputation for being more active than the diocesan clergy.[13] The orders of teaching sisters had also reaped a very meager harvest of vocations, and American sisters occasionally expressed their disappointment about this fact. It is particularly ironic that while the American sisters, who by the standards of the time were refreshingly commonsensical and human, hardly attracted any vocations, the *Madres del Sagrado Corazón* (mostly Spanish and Latin American) whose attitudes were close to medieval, had a few Puerto Rican sisters teaching at each of their schools in the island. The Spanish Carmelites of Charity and the two recently founded Puerto Rican congregations (*Dominicas de Fátima* and *Hermanas del Buen Pastor*) also did much better than the American congregations. It seems that at least in the case of women, language and culture were definitely a barrier to entering the American congregation. It should be kept in mind that while a diocesan priest is often on his own, nuns and religious priests must live in community, so that joining an American order meant living the rest of one's life in an American, English-speaking environment even if one was assigned to Puerto Rico.

Part of the Church's trauma in 1898 had been the discovery that it had to a great degree lost the Puerto Rican elite, which over the nineteenth century had turned to Masonry, Spiritism, Theosophy, or various forms of German philosophy picked up in their university years in Europe.[14] While the women of the upper class remained attached to traditional religious practices, the men were often anticlerical or contemptuous of the Church. The independentist members of the elite considered the clergy a tool of the colonial Spanish government; the assimilationists after the American takeover, while not going so far as to become Protestant, tended to admire the Protestant ethos.[15] The lawsuits by which the municipal councils of many towns tried to despoil the Church of her land and buildings at the time of the change of sovereignty were particularly alarming, since they showed that the most influential members of society had become anticlerical.

The Catholic school system implanted by the American bishops was therefore an important move in a campaign to regain the Puerto Rican elite for the Church. By offering a first-rate education in the *colegios privados* of the Jesuits, Marianists, and *Madres del Sagrado Corazón* the Church hoped to attract the next generation of the influential families, while the parochial schools would train middle-class children, some of whom would rise by their talents into political, literary, or commercial leadership. Like the other policies started by Blenk and Jones, this too was partially successful. By the 1960s the Church was much more respected by the island's elite, but with few exceptions the elite was not committed to the Church, nor did it allow the Church to channel its thought or mold its policies.

Connected with this issue was the distrust felt by the hierarchy for the University of Puerto Rico and for the secular intelligentsia. Even when in the 1920s the intellectual leaders began to place a positive value on the island's Catholic heritage, this reevaluation was a result of the general disillusionment with Americanization and took place in the context of the intellectuals' efforts to define and defend the Puerto Rican identity. What they wanted was a revival of the old Spanish–Puerto Rican tradition of Catholicism, and their great Catholic hero was Arizmendi, the first Puerto Rican bishop and herald of the island's identity as a *patria*. While a politician like Albizu Campos made it a point to be seen attending Mass—which would have been unthinkable in the previous two or three decades—he openly expressed his dream of a Puerto Rican Church ruled by Puerto Rican bishops in the style of an idealized Spanish tradition. He had no use for a hierarchy which tried to impose on an island with a centuries-old Mediterranean Catholic culture the religious style of a minority church in an Anglo-Saxon Protestant society. Clerically oriented Catholics resented such statements as veiled attacks on the Church itself, under the pretext of trying to reform it. They preferred leaders like don Luis Ferré in the 1950s: a rich philanthropist who gave generously to the Church without overtly trying to influence its policies.

One important issue on which the "Hispano-Catholic" intelligentsia disagreed bitterly with the hierarchy was that, when the public schools finally began to teach in Spanish, the Catholic schools—staffed mostly by American religious—remained strongly committed to English as the vehicle of teaching. Indeed, some American sisters were even discouraged from learning Spanish by their superiors, so that students who wanted to converse with them, even informally, would be forced to "practice their English." Rumors circulated about Catholic schools where the students were encouraged to go to confession in English, or which sponsored English language spiritual retreats for Puerto Ricans.[16] To those who saw the Catholic tradition as an essential component of the historical Puerto Rican identity, this effort on the Church's part at Americanizing the very religion of the people constituted a supreme betrayal. To the bishops, on the other hand, the intellectuals' efforts to impose a change of policy on the hierarchy appeared insolent and uncalled for.

Worse yet in the bishops' eyes were those elements of the intelligentsia which, especially in Muñoz Marín's time, would endeavor to solve Puerto Rico's problems along purely secular lines, not hesitating to use methods condemned by the Church such as a massive campaign of sterilization and birth control. This would eventually lead the Church into a head-on collision with the Popular Democratic Party at a time when this party commanded the loyalty of the overwhelming majority of Puerto Ricans.

In order to attract the laity which was already past school age, Blenk and Jones fostered the introduction of American-style lay Catholic associations such as the Holy Name Society and the Knights of Columbus.[17] The former was instituted in every parish and tended to attract lower middle and upper lower class men; the latter was non-parochial and attracted upper middle and lower upper class men. Because of its appeal to men of the popular class, the Holy Name Society in particular became quickly Puerto Ricanized. Many of the Society's characteristics in the U.S. quietly disappeared, while it took on many aspects of a traditional Spanish-style *cofradía*, such as the members referring to each other as *hermano*. The ostensible purpose of the Society—combatting casual and irreverent use of the Holy Name as an expletive—was close to meaningless in Puerto Rico, where this habit has always been considered devout rather than irreverent. But the purpose for which it had been primarily introduced—creating a group of men who frequented the sacraments and became involved with the parish—did succeed to a great degree during this period, although the membership transformed the spirit of the Society into their own style of religiosity at least as much as the Society influenced them.

By the 1950s the policies set up by Blenk and Jones had met with an apparently marvelous success, to the point that the island had been divided into two dioceses (San Juan and Ponce) in 1924 and would later (1960) be erected into an ecclesiastical province with San Juan as its metropolitan see and Ponce and Arecibo—to which Caguas was soon added—as its suffragans. While the proportion of priests to people was still alarmingly low, native vocations had quadrupled from 12 in 1925 to 48 in 1960, and the total number of priests in the island was 480, as compared to 113 in 1900.[18] It should be noted, however, that the percentage of natives in the island's clergy had sunk from 33 percent (38 out of 113) in 1900 to 10 percent in 1960, which gives away the artificial quality in the increase in the clerical force.

The Catholic school system was flourishing. Since it was staffed by native English speakers who taught in English (while the public schools were more and more staffed by Puerto Ricans who spoke English as a second language, and taught in Spanish), it was very attractive to middle and upper class parents who, even if they didn't speak English at home, wanted their children to be perfectly fluent for business reasons. While the Sisters were often aware that this, rather than religion, was the motivation of most parents, they trusted that the religion classes were creating a more religiously knowledgeable and committed elite in the island.

In 1947 the newly consecrated third bishop of Ponce, James Edward McManus, C.Ss.R., founded an interdiocesan Catholic university in his cathedral city, known at first as Universidad Católica Santa María and later as Universidad Católica de Puerto Rico.[19] This was supposed to present Puerto Rican youth with an alternative to the secular education provided by the University of Puerto Rico, so that ideally a child could now have a Catholic education from kindergarten through college without having to leave the island. However the quality of the Catholic University never allowed it to compete with the University of Puerto Rico. Therefore, although the children of the elite usually attended Catholic grammar and high schools, they tended to go for higher studies to UPR, or else to universities in the United States. It was the poorer students—more poorly educated in the public schools—who filled the classrooms of the Universidad Católica, where the theology professors often complained of their religious illiteracy which turned theology courses into catechism classes.

The Holy Name Society, Knights of Columbus, and other lay societies were flourishing and the Legion of Mary, introduced in the mid-1950s, was growing by leaps and bounds and presenting to the people a vision of the Christian life which was apostolic, rather than merely devotional. While many people had not been yet reached by the new currents, Mass attendance and reception of the Eucharist were at record highs, partly because the increase in priests—as well as the increase in parishes and in rural chapels where Mass was said every other week or once a month—made the sacraments more available and partly because a significant percentage of the population had internalized the notion that weekly Mass was imperative, or at least rather important. All in all the American bishops and priests had reason to feel that, while much yet remained to be done, their vision and methods had met with reasonable success and that it could be hoped that some day, with more clergy and more of the same methods, Puerto Rico would become a flourishing local church by American standards.

The 1950s were therefore a "decade of self-confidence" for the institutional Church in Puerto Rico, but the decade's end would put all these achievements to the test and show that to a great degree they were a house of cards. The years 1959 and 1960 brought to a head a crisis which had been building up for some years between the hierarchy and the majority Popular Democratic Party, and the eventual rejection of the hierarchy's position by the overwhelming majority of the Puerto Rican electorate produced in the institutional Church a trauma almost comparable to that of 1898; it also was a catalyst for the replacement of the American hierarchy with a native one.

The issues of government encouragement for birth control and of religious instruction for public school children combined in the late 1950s to produce a head-on clash between the secularizing forces of Popular Democratic liberalism and the hierarchy's efforts to build a U.S.-style institution-centered Catholicism in the island. Caught in the middle was the average Puerto Rican who valued the island's Catholic ethos but—precisely because the island's ethos was Catholic—did not see the necessity of closing ranks and making the hierarchy's priorities into a *casus belli*, especially against political leaders who had earned the people's loyalty on economic and social grounds to a far greater degree than the bishops had earned it on religious grounds.

After efforts to influence legislation on birth control and "released time" by non-partisan pressure tactics proved unsuccessful, the island's bishops reached the conclusion that only a Catholic or "Christian Democrat" political party would produce the desired results. The apparently flourishing state of institutional Catholicism in the previous decade led them to believe that such a party stood a fair chance of winning the elections in 1960, or at least of winning a sufficient number of seats in the legislature to achieve its goals. They therefore encouraged the founding of the Partido Acción Cristiana (PAC) and publicly identified themselves with it. The injection of religion into the 1960 electoral campaign made it unusually bitter, and the opposition between the Popular Democratic Party and the hierarchy escalated to the point that in a collective pastoral letter the bishops declared that party's platform to be irreconcilable with Catholic principles, so that to vote Popular Democratic would constitute a mortal sin.

Finally Election Day arrived, and the resulting landslide in favor of the Popular Democratic Party demonstrated that when a choice was forced on them the people of Puerto Rico would choose political loyalties over loyalty to the institutional Church.[20] The vote was not, however, a rejection of Catholicism; the churches were just as full on the Sunday after Election Day as on the Sunday before. It was rather a rejection of the institutional Church's efforts at influencing the secular life of the island on issues where it had not been able to convince the people. The people showed that they would only follow leaders whom they trusted implicitly, and that the clergy had not achieved this position. The election also demonstrated that ultimately the religion of the vast majority of Puerto Ricans was still a personal matter between themselves and God and was not mediated by the institution, which was there to serve this relationship, not to control it.[21]

The results did demonstrate, however, that the success of the American-style Church in the 1950s, and of the tactics adopted by Blenk and Jones at the beginning of the century, had been more apparent than real. Increased attendance at Mass, Catholic education, and membership in the Holy Name Society or the Knights of Columbus could not be translated into unconditional following of hierarchical directives. Indeed many Catholic societies became divided between those who had finally chosen loyalty to Muñoz and those who had obeyed the hierarchy and now wanted to expel the "traitors" or exclude them from office. It took years to heal these rifts. Before the next election Rome had promoted Archbishop Davis from San Juan to Santa Fé and had asked Bishop McManus to resign the see of Ponce.[22] Both were succeeded by Puerto Rican bishops, one of whom—the present Cardinal Aponte—many years later gave the last rites to the dying Muñoz and celebrated his funeral in San Juan Cathedral as a final gesture of reconciliation.

4

The Great Migration

When Puerto Rico became an American possession in 1898 there was already a small but long-standing Puerto Rican presence in the cities of the Eastern United States. Throughout the nineteenth century the sugar industry of Puerto Rico had been directed primarily to the American market, and strong economic and business links had been forged between the sugar-producing coastal areas of the island and cities such as New York, Boston, and Philadelphia.[1] This situation naturally resulted in the temporary or permanent residence of Puerto Rican businessmen in these cities, and a number of the business elite coming to the United States rather than to Europe for their higher education. In the second half of the century the growth of the independence and home-rule movements led to the exile of a number of politically active Puerto Ricans, many of whom settled in New York where they conspired in union with their Cuban counterparts for the independence of both islands. These exiles were an important factor in the American decision to invade Puerto Rico in 1898, and many of them returned to be leaders under the new regime, some as independentists, but others as converts to the cause of annexation. Others, however, had sunk roots in the mainland and remained there as a small Puerto Rican community, which also served as a link with the homeland for the now growing number of young members of the elite who came to American universities. This Puerto Rican colony increased gradually in the first third of the century: in 1910 there were 500 persons of Puerto Rican birth living in New York City; by 1920 they had increased to 7,000 and by 1930 to 45,000.[2] In the earlier part of this period they shared with Spaniards and other Latin Americans the neighborhood between West 14th and West 25th Streets (Chelsea); in Brooklyn other communities were clustering around the Navy Yard—a major source of employment during World War I—and in the Borough Hall area.[3] By the early 1930s the neighborhood around 116th Street (up to then primarily Italian) began to have the highest concentration of Puerto Ricans in the city; it came to be known by Americans as "Spanish Harlem" and by Puerto Ricans as El Barrio—*the* Puerto Rican neighborhood par excellence. This is significant, since Harlem was the neighborhood "where most colored people in Manhattan lived before World War II"[4] and so is an early indicator of an emerging perception of Puerto Ricans as "non-white" by the average New Yorker. Probably involved in this incipient perception was the changed nature of the Puerto Rican community over those decades. Around 1900 the small Puerto Rican colony had been composed primarily of businessmen, political exiles who had chosen to stay after 1898, and students from the elite families—all of whom could easily blend with the Spaniards and Latin Americans in Chelsea. But by 1930 most New York Puerto Ricans were from the poorer classes, which had never had a taboo against miscegenation and therefore came in many shades of pigmentation. By their types of employment they were considered socially inferior, and by the color of their skin they came to be considered "not white," although many of them were lighter than a good number of Italians.

In 1934 Fiorello La Guardia, who had represented East Harlem in Congress, was elected Mayor of New York, and was succeeded in Congress by Vito Marcantonio, an Italian-American politician whose power base was the labor movement and who had definite socialist sympathies. While Marcantonio was not a Puerto Rican, most Puerto Ricans in the area empathized with him as a fellow *Latino*[5] because of his Italian roots and were very open to his social justice platform.[6] In return Marcantonio vocally advocated self-determination for Puerto Rico and defended the Puerto Rican Nationalist party.[7] It should be noted that Marcantonio represents the secularizing and even anticlerical wing of the *Latino* tradition— as Muñoz Marín did in the island, although Muñoz did so in a much milder form until the bishops forced him into stronger opposition. But, as in the case of Muñoz, the Puerto Rican people saw in Marcantonio a champion of their interests while the institutional Church was perceived as pursuing its own agenda and as relatively indifferent to their social welfare.[8] The Puerto Ricans did not turn against the Church, but neither were they about to turn against a benefactor because the Church disapproved of some of his positions.

The 1930s did not present a great increase in New York's Puerto Rican population. While the Depression was even more crushing in the island than in the mainland, and had been anticipated by the devastating hurricane of San Felipe (September 1928) which totally ruined the island's agriculture, conditions in the United States were not such as to attract economic refugees. But after World War II the expansion of the mainland economy and the improvements in air travel led to a massive migration—encouraged by Muñoz Marín's Popular Democratic government for the same reason that it encouraged birth control: the density of the island's population had reached such proportions that any effort to alleviate its economic and social situation required a drastic thinning of the population.[9] By 1950 there were 301,375 Puerto Ricans in the mainland, of whom 81.6 percent were in New York City; by 1960 they had increased to 887,662, with 69 percent in New York, and by 1970 to 1,429,396, with 56.8 percent in New York.[10]

From these figures it can be seen that the city of New York felt the initial shock of this massive migration, and that while the percentage of Puerto Ricans on the mainland who lived in New York had steadily decreased, in 1970 more than half the Puerto Ricans in the mainland still lived in that city. It should also be noted that while, of the total number of Puerto Ricans in the U.S., the *percentage* of those living in New York kept decreasing, this does not indicate a decrease in *real* numbers; while losing 12 percentage points between 1960 and 1970 in relation to the total U.S. Puerto Rican population, New York's Puerto Ricans actually increased by close to 200,000. Hence the response of New York to the Great Migration—both at the secular and the ecclesiastical levels—became a paradigm that was followed by many municipalities and dioceses as the Puerto Ricans began to spread out into other cities and regions.

To understand the reaction of New Yorkers and other Americans to this great wave of migration it is necessary to realize that this country, after having been in the nineteenth century a "nation of immigrants," had in the early 1920s closed its doors to immigration except for small quotas favoring Northern European over Mediterranean and Slavic nations. By this time, a generation was growing up for whom the immigrant experience was history. By the 1950s many descendants of the nineteenth-century immigrants were turning their backs on their ethnic roots and embracing middle class values and conformism with a vengeance. The willingness to be monolingual and monocultural was seen as a test of true loyalty to the American way.

The Puerto Rican newcomers were poor, "different," often dark-skinned, and (in spite of their citizenship) foreign in language, behavior, and cultural presuppositions. They settled in the deteriorating inner-city neighborhoods which other ethnic groups were abandoning for the suburbs and took low paying and menial jobs. Indeed, as Clara Rodríguez points out, "not only were jobs few, low paying and often insecure, but once a job was obtained, mobility was also poor. Where could you go from being a sewing machine operator? Perhaps to the post of supervisor, earning $10 more a week. Similarly, in the food trades, the ladder to success started with dishwasher and ended with waiter. . . . Most jobs were dead-end jobs."[11]

If they could not get a job, the welfare system provided a resource which had not been open to previous immigrants. But this also backfired at the collective level because it created the image of the Puerto Rican as a parasite on an American society built on the work ethic. In fact a large number of Puerto Ricans whose economic situation definitely qualified them for welfare preferred not to take advantage of this resource, which they perceived as humiliating,[12] and instead tightened their belts and had recourse to friends or relatives, whose help could be accepted without loss of *dignidad* on the principle of "today it's my turn, tomorrow it may be yours." But all too many New Yorkers accepted the myth of the Puerto Rican as a shiftless welfare addict as uncontestable truth.

The younger generation, caught between two often incompatible systems of socialization, often struck out on its own and produced its own codes of behavior and survival, of which the most notorious were the street gangs—another negative image which, under the guise of liberal concern, was patronizingly stereotyped in the musical *West Side Story*.[13]

To a great degree this history of pain, confusion, and humiliation is not much different from the story of most immigrant groups. There are, however, certain significant peculiarities which render the situation of the Puerto Rican immigrant unique in American history.

A major cause for these differences was the changing economy of New York, the preferred port of entry and city of first settlement for Puerto Ricans. "Automation, and the movement of surviving blue-collar jobs to the suburbs, the South, or to other countries . . . caused a sectoral decline in the number of manufacturing jobs available in New York City. Since these trends occurred more rapidly than out-migration or the retraining of blue-collar workers to fill white-collar jobs, a severe problem of blue-collar structural unemployment arose."[14] Because of this, the jobs which helped earlier immigrant groups climb the socioeconomic ladder were not available to the Puerto Ricans. Yet the members of these older ethnic groups were not always aware of this diminishment of opportunity and assumed that if the Puerto Ricans were not

working, or were stuck in undesirable jobs, it was *their* fault, and
not the economy's. The blue-collar members of the older ethnic
groups were desperately holding on to the few desirable blue-
collar jobs that remained in the New York area, and since they
controlled the unions, they used this as a means of keeping the
new immigrants out of these jobs.[15]

Other factors which made the Puerto Rican migration significantly different from that of earlier ethnic groups were the consequence of the political and religious history of the island—and
these are all connected with the issue of identity.[16] As we have seen,
language and culture are the primary factors in Puerto Rican self-
identification, while race is secondary, due to the fact that in the
island the races have on the whole successfully integrated. While
prejudice is not entirely absent, "dark or black Puerto Ricans are
not an ethnically distinct, lower class minority [in the island] as
Black Americans are in the US."[17] This integration, as Rodríguez
points out, is not a "one way integration," as in American society
(i.e., blacks integrating into white society) but rather, a "two way
integration," with whites too assimilating many African traits and
attitudes into their worldview.[18] Except for the most aristocratic
families, there is no taboo on intermarriage between the races—a
situation which has produced over the centuries a wide spectrum
of shades which make it impossible to divide the population into
"black" and "white." Puerto Rican society is thus an integrated,
multiracial society where the unitive factors of language and culture are much stronger than the potentially divisive factor of race.
But precisely these unitive factors make Puerto Ricans, both in the
island and in the U.S., very conscious of their difference from the
Americanos. Those who speak Spanish are "us," those whose first
language is English are "them."

This self-image based on language and culture caused a clash
when Puerto Ricans came to live in a society which strictly divided people into "black" and "white" and which expected them
to assimilate into the language and cultural standards of the culturally dominant ethnic group: the white Anglo-Saxon Protestants.[19]
Puerto Ricans found that Americans had a psychological need to
fit them on one side or the other of the "black-white" dichotomy,
and that their standing in American society would depend on
which side they fell. This was particularly traumatic for individuals
who by Puerto Rican standards were considered white, but who
discovered that by U.S. standards they were classified as black—
and were then discriminated against to a degree unimagined by

blacks in Puerto Rico. Americans expected that white Puerto Ricans, once they had achieved the required education and financial status, would blend into the white American middle class, while the darker Puerto Ricans would blend into the black American community. Puerto Ricans, however, clung to their cultural and national identity, and resisted being divided from other Puerto Ricans and "melted" into American communities on the basis of color; this would have amounted to the giving up of a powerfully meaningful self-identification for an alien identification which they found meaningless. A white and a dark Puerto Rican had things in common with each other which they valued intensely, and while these created solidarity between them, they also divided the black Puerto Rican from black Americans, and the white Puerto Rican from white Americans.

This solidarity causes resentment in the black community, which often feels that Puerto Ricans "deny their blackness" or want to "pass for white"—since American blacks, being American by culture, accept the "black-white" dichotomy, and so perceive a refusal to identify with them as equivalent to an identification with white America. Living as they do in a society which rewards whiteness and punishes blackness, it is understandable that racially white Puerto Ricans insist on the fact that their race is "white."[20] But contrary to the expectations of sociologists, they still insist on identifying themselves by language and culture (Hispanic) or by nationality (Puerto Rican), in the sense that their primary group is still determined by these factors rather than by race. They are Puerto Ricans who *happen to be white*, but when they see a darker Puerto Rican being discriminated against their reaction is one of solidarity with their fellow Puerto Rican, rather than disassociation from him and solidarity with fellow whites.

This stubborn clinging to language and culture as primary self-identifiers causes a further problem because American society, while strongly divided by color, has an equally strong expectation that newcomers should abandon their ancestral languages and cultures and wholeheartedly adopt the English language and the American ethos, which are seen as the bonds of union of the society. The insistence of Puerto Ricans on speaking Spanish among themselves and on speaking Spanish at home in order to pass on the language (as a *first* language!) to the next generation was therefore deeply disturbing and even offensive to Americans, who instinctively perceived it as a rejection of the "melting pot," a symbolic way of clinging to an alien identity.

Two other factors facilitated this resistance to assimilation or Americanization. Both of these factors were totally new in the history of immigration to the United States and both were important to such a degree that their presence made analogies between this and previous waves of immigration misleading. These were the ease with which Puerto Ricans could travel between their homeland and New York, and the fact that they arrived in the United States already American citizens.

While earlier immigrants had to undergo a long, dangerous, and often traumatic ocean crossing, one of the contributing factors of the Great Puerto Rican Migration was the establishment of frequent, cheap, and relatively short flights between San Juan and New York City. This also meant that Puerto Ricans who settled in New York were able to fly home with very little physical or financial inconvenience. It soon became common to fly to Puerto Rico for the Christmas holidays at least every two or three years or to send the children to spend their summer vacations with their grandparents in the island. Such frequent visits meant that the Puerto Rican worldview and cultural attitudes were constantly reinforced, making up for the attrition of daily life in a different culture, and thus significantly counteracting the natural processes of assimilation.

Furthermore, the ease of traveling between New York and Puerto Rico meant that many Puerto Ricans came to New York with no commitment to their new environment. Indeed many of them came with the clear intention of returning home as soon as they had made enough money to buy a small farm or start a small business there. A good number of these migrants were in fact able to return home in better circumstances after a number of years in the mainland.[21] And even in the case of those for whom such a return remained an unfulfilled dream, it was a dream which was not perceived as unrealistic, and it kept many Puerto Ricans from emotionally settling down in New York.

Indeed, many of them practiced what could be called "commuter immigration" or "revolving door immigration." They would come to New York every so often for relatively short periods and return home after having made enough money to avert a family financial crisis or when a job became available in the hometown. But they returned to New York if they lost their job in the island, or if friends in New York got them an even better job. Ivan Illich tells the story of a country woman whose husband did not return from the cane fields one evening; she was naturally distraught until, two weeks later, a money order from him arrived in the mail, postmarked in Chicago. It seems that on the way to work he met a labor-recruiting crew, and on the spur of the moment decided to spend a couple of months there, making some extra money, and then return to his wife and children. "In a case like this," Illich comments, "in which a man 'drops in' on New York with no intentions of staying but of eventually commuting 'home,' how can the transient have the same effect on his neighborhood in New York as the old immigrant who came to stay? Yet the statistical curve of emigration from the island is in exact correlation with the curve of employment on the mainland. If employment is scarce, the reflux increases correspondingly. Many, even after years in New York, feel that they got stuck there because of money."[22]

There was yet another very important difference between the Puerto Ricans and earlier immigrant groups. Puerto Ricans arrived at New York's Idlewild Airport already American citizens —usually by birth, but, even in the case of those born before 1917 (who would be in their fifties by the time of the Great Migration) by Congressional *fiat* rather than by an individual decision. This had a number of practical and psychological consequences.

First of all, it made possible the Great Migration at a time when the immigration laws of the 1920s sought to prevent just such a phenomenon. At the legal level the Puerto Ricans were not actually immigrants and their movement constituted an *internal migration* comparable to the migration of Southern blacks to the industrial North, or to the Westward move of pioneers or Forty-niners. While at the *existential* level the Puerto Rican experience is truly one of emigration, at the legal level it is not, and this means that there was and is no constitutional means of controlling it. "*La Migra*," that nightmare of illegally entered Hispanics, has never been a Puerto Rican issue, and indeed it is not now uncommon for illegally entered Dominicans to try to pass for Puerto Ricans, so as to remain unmolested by the immigration service.

Secondly, citizenship combined with the ease of air travel to make possible the "revolving door" or "commuter" character which the Great Migration had for a significant number of Puerto Ricans, as well as the frequent short visits to the island of an even larger number. Even if the transatlantic crossing had been easier and cheaper than it was, most nineteenth and early twentieth-century European immigrants would have been deterred from temporary return to their homelands by the fact that if they then came back to America they would have had to undergo the entry process once again. But for Puerto Ricans, moving back to the island for a couple of years and then returning to New York if the job market got tight at home, was as easy as moving to Chicago for a couple of years and then returning to New York. In each case they would be American citizens moving between two points under the American flag. As Ivan Illich put it, "this was a new type of immigrant: not a European who had left home for good and strove to become an American but an American citizen, who could come here for one harvest and return home for vacation with a week's salary spent on a coach ticket."[23]

The most important aspect of the Puerto Ricans' citizenship, however, was that it had been imposed on them by *fiat* in 1917 rather than being the product of a collective aspiration of the Puerto Rican people, or of personal decisions on the part of each individual immigrant. For the earlier immigrants the act of requesting citizenship, even more than the act of coming to America, was a decision which affected one's identity. One had decided that one was here to stay; that this was now one's country, while Germany or Italy, Ireland or Poland was "the old country." Loyalty, memories, and customs could continue to be cherished, but one had decided no longer to be "an Italian in America," but an "Italian-American," i.e., an American who happened to come from Italy.

Since Puerto Ricans arrived in New York as citizens, but without having chosen this in a personal decision, none of the emotional concomitants of citizenship applied to them. By the 1940s Puerto Ricans with very few exceptions had come to appreciate the advantages of being American citizens—and besides, since there was no such thing as Puerto Rican citizenship, even the minority that was avowedly anti-American did not have any viable alternative to choose. But citizenship was a purely legal identity. At the emotional level the Puerto Ricans thought of "Puerto Rican" and "American" as two distinct nationalities, each with its own homeland, language, culture, and flag. To leave the island for the mainland was to leave one's country and emigrate to a foreign country—of which, by an anomaly of fate, one happened to be a citizen.

These sentiments are clearly expressed in the song which has become the classic expression of the Great Migration, *En Mi Viejo San Juan*, written by Noel Estrada in 1943. After describing his youthful dreams and early loves in his old San Juan, the immigrant sings:

... one day I set forth
for an alien nation (*extraña nación*)
because fate so decreed,
but my heart remained behind, by the sea,
in my Old San Juan.
Farewell, my dear Borinquen
... I am leaving, but some day I'll return
to seek out my old love
to dream once again in my old San Juan.
But time passed
and fate made a mockery
of my terrible homesickness
and I never could return
to the San Juan I loved,
to that piece of my country (*patria*);
my hair has turned white,
my life is ebbing away; I hear death calling me,
and I can't bear the thought of dying
far away from you,
Puerto Rico of my heart![24]

Much of this may be put down as mere sentimentality, but its enduring popularity shows that it expresses widely shared and deeply held sentiments.

In terms of the "passive-aggressive" ambivalence of Puerto Ricans towards the United States which was discussed earlier, we might say that while the Puerto Rican citizen-immigrants would be horrified at the suggestion that they are anti-American, they have no intention of changing their identity and becoming *Americanos*. They are already as American as they need or want to be—i.e., *legally* American—and they intend to exercise all the rights which this legal status entails. But they have no intention of becoming *emotionally American*; they reject American culture and insist on holding on to Spanish as their primary medium of communication with their fellow Puerto Ricans. Any efforts to change these attitudes will be resisted passively, but very stubbornly.

This clinging to an identity based on culture, language, and nationality is all the more potentially problematic in that religion, which in older societies had a crucial role as a source of legitimation and social cohesion, cannot fulfill such a role in the United States with its plurality of denominations. Since denominational religion came to be perceived as a potentially divisive force, American

society—which needed agents of emotional legitimation and cohesion as much as any other—was forced to create a *civil
religion*, in which American values, the "American Way," and
America itself have acquired religious connotations. Americans
of all denominations are free to pursue their various dogmatic
and ritual preferences *as long as these don't threaten, but rather le-
gitimize and strengthen those commonly held values.* The rejection or
questioning of these values, whether for denominational religious
reasons or for reasons of loyalty to a different culture, thus becomes
in America a threat comparable to that presented by heresy to
medieval Christendom.[25]

In the nineteenth century the Catholic Church had been perceived as alien and un-American precisely because it had ties of
loyalty and obedience to a European pontiff, and because its ethos
and traditions were perceived as linked to undemocratic philosophies of life. Throughout that century the leaders of the American
Church counteracted these accusations by proclaiming the compatibility between Catholicism and the American ethos, and by turning the Church into the great Americanizer of the immigrants. By
the 1940s this had resulted in a conscious and belligerent identification of Catholicism and American patriotism, all the more emphatic
in that American Catholics, while never doubting the compatibility
between their faith and the American ethos, realized that many
other Americans did doubt it.[26] The incompatibility between this
important agenda of the U.S. Church and the determination of the
Puerto Ricans to hold on to their own identity is central to the
story of the relations between the Puerto Ricans and the Church in
the period we are studying.

It should be noted that the problem was not limited to the issue
of language and culture, central as these may be. There was also a
whole issue of class difference involved. Over the previous century
the earlier Catholic ethnic groups had engaged in a successful
struggle for economic improvement and had gradually risen from
the lower to the middle class. As long as immigration continued
unchecked, however, new arrivals kept ethnic Catholics, and their
ecclesiastical leaders, in touch with their original roots among the
poor. The immigration laws of 1924, however, by placing quotas
on the very nationalities that provided the influx of poor Catholic
immigrants, allowed for the growth of a generation of Catholics
which identified with the middle class and its values and mores.
The encounter of this generation of clergy and parishioners with
a new wave of poor immigrants, whose values and mores were

not those of the middle class, created a shock for the American Church which was not commensurate with the effect of earlier immigrants on their more established American confreres.[27] Catholics whose experience of their own ethnic groups was by now almost exclusively middle class were encountering another Catholic ethnic group as represented by its lower class, and this tended to get in the way of their appreciation of the Catholic values embodied in the total spectrum of Puerto Rican culture. For that reason the American priests in the island, who met Puerto Ricans of all social classes and all levels of education, were in a much better position— although not all of them took advantage of it—to appreciate the Catholic values of even the poor Puerto Ricans, perceiving them as part of a continuum.

The difficulty in communication and mutual understanding was—and is—aggravated by the fact that at the unconscious and involuntary levels of nonverbal communication and "body language," the U.S. and Puerto Rican cultures "are cultures almost in total reversal of one another: what is acceptable and permissible in one is practically always not so in the other."[28] Even more than in consciously held values, it is in areas like "kinesics, proxemics, haptics, polychromism vs. monochromism, tone of voice" etc.[29] that Puerto Ricans and Americans "get on each other's nerves" without either of them realizing that they are doing so, or how they are doing so.[30] Because of these factors, communication between people of these two cultures is full of hidden traps, and each side can produce very negative reactions in the other just by doing what comes naturally, and without the least realization that one has given offense. Indeed, while the offended parties may sometimes be conscious of their dislike for certain specific forms of behavior ("Puerto Ricans are so loud," "Americans are so cold and unfriendly") very often all that is perceived is a vague, but cumulatively powerful, feeling of discomfort or unease in the presence of the other—which each side can later justify in terms that make sense to it, but which actually have nothing to do with the real cause. Many reactions which are simplistically ascribed to "prejudice" actually have their roots in these unconscious discomforts and are all the harder to correct because neither side understands the dynamics involved in the interaction.

When this clash of historically engendered presuppositions and agendas, of class-engendered values and mores, and of unspoken expectations at the level of everyday behavior is applied to the encounter between the American Church and the Puerto Rican people, we come in touch with the religious aspect of the "Puerto Rican problem" caused by the Great Migration, as perceived by the American Church. American and Puerto Rican Catholics might believe the same dogmas, but at the existential level their experience of Catholicism was quite different. It must be kept in mind that, outside of theological manuals, there is no such thing as a "chemically pure Catholicism." In real life the Catholic faith is always incarnated in local communities which must live out their faith in a certain historical and sociological context, which in turn affects the way in which that local community lives and experiences the commonly held faith. As a result of these contextual forces different aspects of the Catholic ethos are emphasized or deemphasized by Catholic communities in different times, places, and cultures.

For example, the Irish-Catholic community, after centuries of penal laws at home and of cultural and economic oppression in America, managed to retain the sense of obligation about attending Mass on Sundays and holy days but was not able to retain a sense of the importance of *celebration* in this respect. A clandestine and persecuted eucharistic community could not afford to ring bells, hold processions, or take holy days off from work—even in America, absence from work on a Catholic holy day could mean loss of employment. As a result the obligation of attending Mass became central to Irish-American clergy and laity—but most of the time their masses could hardly be called "celebrations," and on holy days they simply got up an hour earlier so as to hear Mass before going to work. For this reason holy days became a burden to the laity rather than the festivals which they were intended to be, with the result that the American Church has always felt a certain amount of pressure to reduce the number of holy days. In the Hispanic world, on the other hand, where the union of Church and State was the official expression of a union between religion and society, holy days were also legal holidays, and liturgical celebrations combined with civic ones to produce a major fiesta in honor of the saint or mystery of the day. Even in remote mountain regions, where a trip to the church was not feasible, the peasants would take the day off on such feasts and spend the time in such religious celebrations as they could produce without a priest (processions, singing of folk hymns, etc.) and in dances or other festivities, which were also perceived as honoring God and the saints.

Both of these situations are valid but partial expressions of the Catholic tradition and ethos, and both are the result of historical circumstances in which a Catholic people who could not have it all made the best of their historical predicament. But in the long run each of them created very different forms of *lived* Catholicism, making it very difficult for Irish-American and Puerto Rican Catholics, when history brought them in contact with each other, to recognize their own faith in the faith as lived by the other group. Each side was shocked at the other's lack of attention to aspects of Catholicism which it had come to regard as central, while thinking it was totally unreasonable on the part of the others to expect that they should now give more importance to what was so "obviously" optional and peripheral. Of course the side that had all the power—in this case the Americans—was in a position to impose, or at least to try to impose, its own vision as normative. The Puerto Ricans, who for reasons we shall see below were the most ecclesially powerless immigrant group to have arrived in America, could only comply—or offer passive resistance. Such resistance, however, only reinforced the dominant culture's negative view of their religious ethos.

The Puerto Ricans, then, came to New York with a culture pervaded by the Catholic ethos—but it was a different kind of Catholic ethos. Jay P. Dolan has pointed out four central traits of pre–Vatican II American Catholicism: "authority, sin, ritual and the miraculous."[31] Of these four, their historical development had left Puerto Ricans—especially those of the poorer classes—notably unimpressed with the first two, and very much in touch with the latter two. Throughout their stay in the United States, the Puerto Ricans have held on to this configuration of attitudes. Before the Council they were considered "bad Catholics" for lacking a strong sense of authority (institutional loyalty) and of sin ("Catholic guilt"). After the Council many of the "renewed" clergy and laity have difficulties with the Puerto Ricans' continued attachment to ritual and their persistent belief in the possibility of the supernatural world's intersecting with and intervening in the everyday, secular realm. Thus both before and after the Second Vatican Council the Puerto Rican Catholic ethos has been out of tune with the prevailing ethos of American Catholicism.

In the 1940s and 1950s, this clash of cultural emphases and presuppositions at the religious level led American Catholics to complain about the religious "bad habits" of the Puerto Ricans, precisely at the level of authority and sexual morality. Accustomed to measure Catholic loyalty by a strict fidelity to institutionally mandated practices such as regular attendance at Mass, compliance with one's "Easter duty," and obedience to the laws of fasting and abstinence, American Catholics were shocked at the Puerto Ricans' cavalier attitude towards these rules. Most American Catholics lacked the historical perspective that would have enabled them to understand the causes which had led Puerto Ricans to this attitude—and to realize that their own religious ethos, too, contained historically conditioned practices. Similarly, the moralism which came to characterize the post-famine Irish-Catholic ethos had combined with American Puritanism and middle class values to produce a very strict code of sexual morality, which had been profoundly internalized by most U.S. Catholics. On the other hand historical conditions had led the poorer strata of Puerto Rican society—from which came practically all of the immigrants—to accept consensual unions either as a preliminary to marriage or as a substitute for it.

In fact the differences between the Puerto Rican and American practice of the faith were not as drastic as Americans perceived them to be. Faithful attendance at Sunday Mass, for example, was commonly perceived as a basic indicator of whether an individual or collectivity could be identified as "practicing" as opposed to "nominal" Catholic. In 1953 the figure for Mass attendance for all Catholics in New York was "slightly more than one third," while the Puerto Ricans who attended were "not much more than one in ten."[32] This would imply that while Puerto Rican attendance was at about 10 to 12 percent, general attendance was about 33 to 35 percent—certainly much better than the Puerto Rican figures, but still significantly less than half.[33] American priests tended to be very aware of the low index of sacramental practice in the case of Puerto Ricans[34] but they did not seem equally aware that the archdiocese as a whole had a problem of "rather low Mass attendance."[35] On the issue of consensual unions—"probably the most serious block to the understanding of Puerto Ricans by people on the mainland"[36]—Americans tended to ignore the qualities of fidelity and stability which were often enough present in such unions; since they were not blessed by the Church, nothing good could be present in them. Such unions were simply "living in sin," and made those involved in them—and the society which tolerated them—socially contemptible, and only nominally Catholic.

As a result of these culturally conditioned differences, many American Catholics went so far as to deny the Catholic character of the Puerto Rican ethos and culture.[37] Whenever Catholic reviews published articles which defended this Catholic character or described in laudatory terms the popular religion of the island,[38] letters to the editor would promptly appear in which the religion of the Puerto Ricans would be judged by U.S. Catholic standards and found wanting. Some of these were even by American priests serving in Puerto Rico.

Hence many American Catholics came to see the role of the American Church towards the Puerto Ricans—even in the island, but especially in New York—as primarily a *missionary* enterprise, in which a people who had been superficially evangelized would now be brought to the full understanding and practice of true Catholicism by their providential encounter with a vital and committed local church: the American Church in the archdiocese of New York. Thus Cardinal Spellman would speak lyrically of the sidewalks of New York having become "a mission field 'white for the harvest'" and of every New York priest becoming "by Divine Providence . . . a missionary to these people of Puerto Rico,"[39] while George Kelly spoke bluntly of "the conversion of the Puerto Ricans to Christianity in America,"questioning whether this could be done "quickly enough and effectively enough within the framework of our traditional parochial organization, which assumes some kind of Christian community,"[40]—something which, it seems, one could not assume in the case of the Puerto Ricans.

Such attitudes and presuppositions led the archdiocese of New York—and the American Church as it came to follow New York's lead—to see its ministry to Puerto Ricans in terms of converting them from a defective form of Hispano-Caribbean Catholicism to an American form of Catholicism, and to hope that this could be done in one generation. This vision and this hope were behind Cardinal Spellman's response to the Great Migration.

5

The Rejection of the Ethnic Parish Model

The initial response of the archdiocese of New York to the presence of Spanish-speaking Catholics within its territory had been a variation on the classic pattern of the *national parish*: a parish whose membership was not determined by place of residence but by country of origin. By means of such a parish immigrants from a particular ethnic group would receive spiritual care in their own language, usually at the hands of priests from their own country, and in the style of lived Catholicism to which they were accustomed, with stress on the feasts, devotions and liturgical customs which had been important in their homeland.

By the early years of this century a number of small Spanish and Latin American *colonias* had begun to form in New York City, and since none of them was particularly large and all shared the Spanish language and the traditions of Hispanic Catholicism, a small national parish, Our Lady of Guadalupe in Fourteenth Street, was founded for them in 1902. Although the Spanish-speaking inhabitants of the immediate neighborhood tended to be Spaniards, the name given to the parish was a clear indication that it was intended as a common home for members of the *raza hispana* from both sides of the Atlantic—including therefore the small Puerto Rican *colonia*. Guadalupe was therefore technically a "language parish" rather than a "national" one. Curiously, the parish was put in the care of the Augustinians of the Assumption, a French congregation which had many members fluent in Spanish. This foreshadowed an important feature of the future Hispanic apostolate in New York: Hispanics would be cared for primarily by priests for whom Spanish was a second language and whose primary cultural milieu was not Hispanic.

In 1912 a second Hispanic parish was founded, Nuestra Señora de la Esperanza in Washington Heights. This was built on land given by Archer Huntington, founder of the Hispanic Society of America, at the suggestion of the widow and daughter of the Spanish consul in New York and was meant to complement the buildings of the Society's museum and research library. As a result it attracted a good amount of Spanish patronage; King Alfonso XIII donated a bronze copy of the hanging sanctuary lamp in a famous Madrid church; ladies of the royal family donated chalices and vestments; and the famous artist Joaquín Sorolla y Bastida painted a canvas of St. Joseph for a side altar as his personal contribution. But, like Guadalupe, this was from the beginning a church for all Spanish-speaking nationalities. Although the royal arms of Spain are conspicuously displayed in stained glass and in bronze plaques, it is the patroness of Cuba, Our Lady of Charity, who presides over the main altar in an exact replica of the miraculous image of El Cobre, donated by popular subscription of the people of Cuba.[1] La Esperanza was also placed under the Assumptionists and remained in their charge until 1982, when it was transferred to the archdiocesan clergy.

Both Guadalupe and La Esperanza were intended to be shared by all the Hispanic national groups in New York City since at the time of their foundation no one of these groups had a numerical preponderance over the others. In neither parish was the Puerto Rican *colonia* particularly noticeable, especially since it lacked the prestige of diplomatic representatives from the home country. By the late 1920s, however, the number of Puerto Ricans in the city had increased to the point that they were ceasing to be a part of the "Hispanic community" and were becoming a large community with its own identity. They also were settling in East Harlem, which was not convenient to either of the Hispanic parishes.

The increased Puerto Rican presence led Cardinal Hayes to establish two specifically Puerto Rican national parishes in East Harlem: La Milagrosa (Our Lady of the Miraculous Medal) in 1926 and Santa Agonía (Holy Agony) in 1930. Since Puerto Rico could not spare any of its native priests, both parishes were entrusted to the Madrid province of the Vincentians, which already staffed a good number of parishes and rural chapels in Puerto Rico. This meant that the New York Puerto Ricans were at least being served by priests who often had firsthand knowledge of the island, and who were already known to those parishioners who came from Vincentian parishes in Puerto Rico.

In the 1940s and 1950s, and even into the early 1960s, La Milagrosa was *the* center of Puerto Rican Catholic life in New York, with parishioners coming not only from all over el Barrio but from other neighborhoods and even from the Bronx, in spite of the fact that their territorial parishes were by then also offering services in Spanish. Eventually, however, the nature of the neighborhood changed; it became a "dangerous neighborhood" where one was likely to be mugged on the way to church, and this began to discourage Puerto Ricans from other neighborhoods. By the 1970s the area was noticeably changing from Puerto Rican to black American. La Milagrosa began to decline swiftly and was closed in 1978. Santa Agonía, which had never been as important to the New York Puerto Rican community, was more fortunate since its neighborhood has remained very Hispanic.

Pre–World War II work with Hispanics in New York City was not limited to parishes. In 1927 Father Adrien, an Assumptionist from Guadalupe parish, founded Casa María (later renamed Centro María) as a residence for single young working girls from Spain; this later became open to girls from other Spanish-speaking countries. A few years later Casita María was founded as a settlement house in el Barrio by the Sullivan sisters, two Irish-American laywomen who were concerned that Puerto Ricans were not being served by the territorial parishes in the area. They had been sending Puerto Rican children to parish catechism classes, but when they were ignored there, the two women set up CCD classes with the Spanish Vincentians at the recently founded La Milagrosa; later they extended this work to programs such as day camps. In the early 1960s the center moved to the Bronx.[2]

The lack of response shown by the territorial and diocesan parishes of el Barrio to the Puerto Ricans was not as reprehensible as it may seem. Up to that time the archdiocese had been following the classic arrangement of the national parish, which meant that in point of fact the Puerto Rican children of the neighborhood were not the responsibility of the territorial parishes but of La Milagrosa and Santa Agonía, and of the Spanish religious to whom these parishes had been entrusted. While the lack of interest on the part of the diocesan clergy may have been caused, in part at least, by racism or prejudice, it also corresponded to a policy which was by no means disadvantageous to the Puerto Rican community.

This policy changed, however, when Francis J. Spellman became archbishop of New York in 1939. Shortly after coming to his new see, the archbishop removed the diocesan priests from St. Cecilia's Church, in the same general area as La Milagrosa and Santa Agonía, and entrusted it to the Baltimore province of the Redemptorists, a province which also served a great number of parishes in Puerto Rico. Although the Redemptorists "made it a matter of policy to assign only bilingual personnel to the parish"[3] and often assigned priests with previous experience in Puerto Rico, St. Cecilia's remained a territorial parish and continued to offer

English services to the English-speaking Catholics who remained in the area.

Subsequent events would show that Spellman did not subscribe to the national or ethnic parish as an ideal, but preferred the new model which came to be called the *"integrated parish."* This would be a territorial parish which would include on its staff at least one priest who could speak the language of whatever ethnic group was present in its territory, and which would offer services in that language in addition to its regular English services. The English language services remained the principal services of the parish, and it was expressly intended that, as the immigrants became comfortable with English, the special second-language services would be dropped, thus producing a unified parish community as soon as possible.[4]

Though the Mass at that time was always in Latin, the sermons and the hymns were in English or Spanish depending on the congregation. Other services, such as devotions or novenas, could be in the vernacular and therefore would also have to be held separately for each language group—although in practice many integrated parishes simply offered a Spanish Mass every Sunday, and held all other scheduled worship services only in English. Weddings and funerals would be held in a combination of Latin and the language of the family involved. Confessions, as well as any form of personal counseling, were in the language of the recipient, and even the most sanguine advocates of quick integration admitted that, long after the Puerto Ricans would come to attend the English Mass, they would still have to be provided with confessors who understood Spanish.[5]

The fact that public worship, especially the Mass, was conducted in Latin is of crucial importance to the model of the integrated parish and to the expectations that were placed on it. As long as the Mass itself was celebrated in a language which was not understood either by Americans or Puerto Ricans, American priests and bishops could hope that once Puerto Ricans came to learn English well enough to understand the sermon, the "Spanish Mass" could be dropped out of the parish schedule with minimal resistance. The introduction of a vernacular and inculturated liturgy in the late 1960s would widen the gap between those parishioners who attended the Spanish Mass—now completely in Spanish and in a strongly Hispanic style—and those who attended the "regular" liturgies of the parish, celebrated completely in English and in a style which, as it inculturated more and more into the middle class American ethos, became less compatible with the Hispanic ethos.

It is often said that the policy of the integrated parish was devised as a response to the overwhelming numbers of the Great Migration, and that it was, therefore, a decision based on practical necessity. In fact there is every reason to believe that Spellman had made up his mind on that policy from the time of his arrival in New York, five years before the influx of Puerto Ricans into the city began to take on massive proportions.[6] In this decision Spellman seems to have been influenced by the advice of John F. O'Hara, C.S.C., former president of Notre Dame and future cardinal archbishop of Philadelphia, who had just been appointed his auxiliary bishop for the military ordinariate. O'Hara had traveled extensively in Latin America and had been in residence at St. Cecilia for a few years, and the new archbishop found it natural to seek his advice.[7]

The spirit of the American community in the 1940s and 1950s was another important factor which contributed to Spellman's decision to integrate the Puerto Ricans as soon as possible into the American Church, and through it into the American ethos. At the popular level, the strong patriotism generated by World War II and intensified afterward by the Cold War promoted a stress on Americanism and a downplaying of ethnic differences and ethnic identities among the older immigrant groups. In the intellectual community the common vision at this time was that the history of American immigration was "a process of Americanization, the gradual blending of many diverse elements into one people."[8] It was granted that the descendants of the immigrant groups would keep certain superficial traits of their heritage (e.g., ethnic food or ethnic music) which might even pass into the general American mix, but they were expected to assimilate into the primary identity of Americans and to take on the "American character."

The new archbishop of New York was a sincere and enthusiastic believer in this ideology. He did not see such Americanization as a forced imposition of an alien worldview on the Puerto Ricans, but as the offering of an opportunity for a better way of life. He saw the national parishes as reinforcing ethnic identity and retarding assimilation, but he also saw them as akin to the segregated churches which had been imposed on black Americans—as a denial of the opportunities that came with integration into the greater American community. Just as the American bishops in Puerto Rico had insisted that Puerto Ricans were "good enough for statehood," so Spellman would see his policy as defending the Puerto Ricans' capacity for becoming good Americans, and their right to be welcomed into American parishes, without being "segregated" into separate churches.[9]

The arrangement introduced at St. Cecilia's thus represented Spellman's policy, chosen in the light of his personal ideals and later justified as being most suitable for the "state of emergency" created by the Great Migration. As the Puerto Rican migration spread to other major cities the policy of integrated parishes, with Cardinal Spellman's prestige behind it, was widely imitated and has become, with local variations and exceptions, the generally accepted policy of the American Church for the care of Puerto Ricans and later Hispanic immigrants.

There were a number of reasons behind the decision to discard the national parish model, which had undeniably served other ethnic groups with excellent results, and replace it with the integrated parish as a "normative" model.[10] Considering the importance of this decision for the subsequent ecclesial development of Puerto Ricans and other Hispanics in the United States it is important to examine these reasons, and to evaluate their validity. They are most coherently presented in Father Joseph Fitzpatrick's 1966 article "The Role of the Parish in the Spiritual Care of Puerto Ricans in the New York Archdiocese,"[11] and the pages that follow owe much to this presentation by an author who was closely involved in the archdiocese's ministry to Puerto Ricans at an early period. Some of these reasons are also discussed in Fitzpatrick's *Puerto Rican Americans*[12] and in the *Report on the First Conference on the Spiritual Care of Puerto Ricans* held in San Juan under the auspices of Cardinal Spellman in 1955,[13] as well as in Robert Stern's "Evolution of Hispanic Ministry in the New York Archdiocese," in the archdiocesan publication *Hispanics in New York: Religious, Cultural and Social Experiences*.[14] In the absence of official statements from the archdiocese or of personal statements from Cardinal Spellman, these authors, who were intimately involved in the implementation of the archdiocesan policy, seem to be the most trustworthy guides to the rationale behind that policy.[15]

In the first place, by the time the Puerto Rican migrants arrived in force, New York and other large cities of the Eastern seaboard had fully developed the land within their city limits. Not only would it be difficult to acquire land for a new church, but it seemed wasteful not to utilize the many churches already present in the city. Moreover, at that time no parish was considered complete without a parochial school and convent, so new national parishes would need land for those too. Obviously it made more sense to use the already existing schools of the territorial parishes. From this perspective, serving the Puerto Ricans from the territorial parishes was a very attractive solution.[16]

Secondly, a combination of factors made it harder for Puerto Ricans to create their own neighborhoods than it had been for other nationalities in earlier times; especially important is the fact that "the only housing within reasonable range of the income of the Puerto Ricans is the public housing projects. Selection for these is on a non discriminatory basis. . . . Therefore Puerto Ricans can not easily move in where brothers, cousins, relatives or friends are living, and find themselves within a conglomerate group. It is obviously much more difficult to maintain the cohesiveness of a stable Puerto Rican community similar to that of early immigrant groups."[17] Indeed to this day most Puerto Ricans, and Hispanics in general, tend to live dispersed among non-Hispanics, and to be a numerical minority in their territorial parishes.[18] They tend to rent rather than buy and therefore easily pull up stakes if they change jobs by choice or necessity; it is also easy for landlords to drive them out if a neighborhood begins to become desirable again. Urban redevelopment and slum clearance programs can also radically diminish or even destroy the Puerto Rican character of a neighborhood.[19] Thus diocesan officials had an understandable fear that a national parish, if founded, could be left "high and dry," since it would not be firmly anchored in a stable ethnic neighborhood. Indeed, as we have seen, this fate overtook La Milagrosa in the late 1970s.

It should be noted that the first two objections to the national parish imply the unspoken assumption that you can't have a Catholic parish without a great amount of brick and mortar, real estate, etc. The rented storefront model that was doing wonders for the Pentecostals was not seriously considered, though its success was noted and deplored.

Certain characteristics of the Puerto Rican ethos made it easier for the archdiocese to impose its policy without meeting any significant resistance. Throughout the nineteenth and twentieth centuries, the majority of Puerto Ricans seem to have had a marked preference for passive resistance over confrontation. On the issue of Americanization, especially, the population of the island has consistently shown a firm unwillingness to give up its own language and culture in the face of persistent government policies in that direction which lasted from 1898 until at least 1950. And yet at the same time any clear statement of opposition to American rule, or of dislike for the Americans, is socially taboo. Like many powerless people, Puerto Ricans of the poorer classes have perfected the art of letting persons in authority think that one is in agreement with them, and then quietly following one's own preference. As a result of this Puerto Ricans who were not satisfied with the integrated parish would naturally tend to "vote with their feet" rather than to forcefully express their desires to their priests or to the archdiocesan authorities whether individually or in an organized form. For historical reasons Puerto Ricans of the popular classes did not have a strong commitment to the *institutional* aspects of Catholicism, and so did not feel an urgent need to fight (as the Poles did, for example) for the kind of parish they might prefer. If they didn't feel at home in the parish church, they could just as easily stay at home and pray there, or join a storefront church led by a Puerto Rican Protestant minister.

Puerto Rican priests might have had the motivation and the capacity to organize pressure on the archdiocesan authorities, as other ethnic priests had done in the past, but there were no Puerto Rican priests in New York at the time, since the island's dioceses could not spare any of their few native clerics.[20] At the ecclesial level the Puerto Ricans were "a community without an elite of its own,"[21] and therefore had no leadership capable of dealing effectively with the hierarchy, or even of making the people conscious of their interests if these did not coincide with those of the hierarchy.

Thus by both temperament and circumstances, the Puerto Ricans were in no position to let it be known if they would have preferred to have their own parishes rather than integrating into the existent ones, and their silence was taken for consent.

If by chance a priest or lay person did question the wisdom of the new policy, they were often told that Rome discouraged, or even disapproved of national parishes. Thus Father Frederick O'Brien, who started the Puerto Rican ministry in the archdiocese of Boston, was given to understand at the time that the setting up of more national parishes had been ruled out by the Holy See, and he was therefore very surprised when many years later Cardinal Medeiros set up a Portuguese national parish in that city.[22]

The strongest argument for the integrated parish apparently arose from the fact that, as the children and grandchildren of the original immigrants assimilated into American society, they tended to lose their language and move out of the ethnic neighborhoods into the suburbs or other neighborhoods, where they would attend the local territorial parish. Just as the Puerto Ricans were arriving in force, Cardinal Spellman was having to deal with a great number of moribund German, Polish, and other ethnic parishes whose buildings were becoming or had already become white elephants in the hands of the archdiocese. If he erected new national parishes for the Puerto Ricans, he would only be bequeathing more white elephants to his successors. If he followed the integrated model, all that would have to be done when the Puerto Ricans came to assimilate and lose their language was to discontinue the Spanish services—they would already be members of the territorial or "American" parish.[23]

Finally, there was one other reason why many American priests and bishops considered the integrated parish intrinsically superior and preferable to the national parish. They regarded the latter as an element which undermined diocesan unity[24] and which retarded the Americanization of the immigrants. Even in the heyday of the national parishes, there seems to have been a certain ambivalence about them in the minds of a number of American bishops. The national parishes were sometimes perceived as standing aside from the concerns and policies of the diocese as defined by its episcopal leadership, and therefore as weakening the united front needed for the defense of Catholic interests in a Protestant society. This same society often used the "foreignness" of the Catholic community as a reason for anti-Catholic hostility; Catholics were presented as being imbued with the authoritarian and undemocratic values of their lands of origin and as owing allegiance to a "foreign power." To these accusations the American bishops responded by emphasizing the compatibility between Catholicism and American values, and by presenting the Church as the most effective transmitter of these values to the immigrants. While the ethnic parishes were in fact extremely effective in helping the newcomers make the difficult transition from one culture to another, by giving them the emotional security which is essential for such a transition, they could also be perceived as preserving foreign attitudes and loyalties, and therefore as retarding the goal of Americanization.

While in the 1940s and 1950s it was the "practical" arguments for the integrated parish that were most often voiced, and on which the decision to discontinue national parishes was consciously based, the ideal of Americanization and integration was also present in the minds of the decisionmakers. It was expressed in lyrical terms by Cardinal Spellman in the "Dedication" of the *Report on the*

First Conference on the Spiritual Care of Puerto Rican Migrants where integration was presented in terms of the right of Puerto Ricans, as baptized Christians and American citizens, to be welcomed as members of the same parishes as everyone else, without being excluded or relegated to separate parishes because of "superficial discrepancies or deficiencies of code, creed or cult."[25] This begged a number of questions by implicitly equating the national parish with the segregated parishes set up for blacks in the South. These, however, were a result of discrimination on the part of American Catholics who did not want to worship in union with other American Catholics because they were of a different race. The national parishes, on the contrary, had been set up at the desire of the immigrants, who wanted parishes where their own language, feasts, and customs would be preserved. In other words, while the integration of black and white parishioners in the same parish meant that the powerful white Catholics were being forced to accept the *persons* of black fellow Catholics who shared their language and culture, the integration of Puerto Ricans into American parishes was designed to make the powerless Puerto Ricans give up their language and culture and accept those of their powerful neighbors as soon as possible. This discrepancy between the two senses of the term "integration" was probably hidden from many Americans of good will because the U.S. culture's emphasis on race—and the racist opposition of many American parishioners and even priests to having Puerto Ricans in their parishes[26]—blinded them to the fact that the Puerto Ricans themselves, for reasons of language and culture, were anything but eager for this integration.

The goal of Americanization at the speediest rate possible as a rationale for the integrated parish was also expressed at the time by a number of pastoral agents, most clearly and even bluntly by Phillip Bardeck, C.Ss.R. pastor of St. Cecilia's, in his presentation at the 1953 Conference on Spiritual Care of Puerto Rican Migrants. Although he was aware that his suggestions contradicted the directives of the Council of Trent and the Third Council of Baltimore, he felt "that it would be better not to have Masses in Spanish, [i.e., with Spanish sermon and hymns] nor special Spanish Societies, nor a special place for their services, because in doing so we retard tremendously the unification and solidification of the family life of the parish."[27] He also felt that "in any parish that has less than twenty-five percent Puerto Ricans the thought of establishing a special Spanish Mass should be discouraged."[28] "Focal parishes, " such as St. Cecilia's, should be set up for recent arrivals but as soon as individual Puerto Ricans learned enough English they should be encouraged to go to the English Mass in their own territorial parishes, and to join the English-speaking parish societies, although even in parishes with no Spanish Mass a curate should be available to hear confessions in Spanish.

When he became pastor at St. Cecilia's Bardeck had found flourishing Puerto Rican chapters of such societies as the Holy Name and the Children of Mary. Indeed, he admitted that they were more active than their English-speaking counterparts. But while he felt he could not now suppress them without creating resentment, he was opposed on principle to the founding of independent Spanish-language societies where they did not already exist. Similarly when he tried to bring the Spanish Mass out of the basement into the main church he discovered to his dismay that the Puerto Ricans were attached to the basement because it was exclusively their own.[29] In fact, what he found was an incipient Puerto Rican community forming itself within the supposedly integrated parish—a situation which was to spontaneously arise in most if not all such parishes. While he could not deny its success in pastoral terms, he deplored and discouraged this development because it would retard the integration of the Puerto Ricans into a united parish of American Catholics.

Few American priests or pastoral agents have been that honest on the issue of Americanization. As a result the mystique of integration or parish unity has come to be the argument of choice among defenders of the integrated parish—especially after 1965, when the hitherto accepted ideals of assimilation began to be regarded as "cultural imperialism" in progressive Catholic circles. When assimilation ceased to be respectable, a stress on parish unity offered a post-conciliar rationale for pressing the Hispanic "sub-group" to integrate more and more with the greater parish "family." In practical terms this integration means the purposeful weakening and eventual dissolution of that "parish within the parish" which the Hispanics spontaneously create as a response to the integrated parish situation. The desire for a national parish, or even the desire to maintain a sense of identity and community among the Hispanic members of the integrated parish—of being "the Hispanic Community at St. Bridget's" rather than merely "those parishioners of St. Bridget's who go to the 11 o'clock Mass"[30]—are perceived and described by many American clerics and religious educators as divisive, uncharitable, and even incipiently schismatic. But lurking underneath the more theological arguments is the American resentment towards the immigrant who refuses to assimilate, who resists the Melting Pot and insists that on at least some issues "our culture's way" is preferable to the American Way.

It is especially for these ideological reasons that the desirability of the integrated parish over the language or ethnic parish has become almost an article of faith among the English-speaking decisionmakers in the American Church. It is clear to any close and impartial observer that this ideal of integration is seen in a rather different light by American pastoral agents than by the Puerto Ricans whom they serve. While most of them are by now not aware of the ethnic parish as an alternative model, they tend to work at cross-purposes with the American leadership (clerical and lay) of their parishes on the issue of integration. While the American leaders are constantly urging them towards ever greater "parish unity," the Hispanics hold on as much as they can to their identity as *la comunidad hispana*, as a distinct community within the parish. Often enough they are kept within the Church more by movements such as the Cursillos and the Charismatic Renewal, which by necessity have had to develop parallel structures divided by language, than by the parish itself.[31]

In the light of this we should take a closer look at the reasons given above for the adoption of the integrated parish as the normative model, and ask if they are in fact as compelling as they seem.

The difficulty of finding space for building new churches could have been bypassed by renting space such as halls or storefronts, or by buying the churches of those denominations whose constituencies were being replaced by the Puerto Ricans.[32] The Pentecostals did not think storefronts were beneath their dignity, and this certainly did not drive the Puerto Ricans from their doors. Indeed the storefront churches provided an intimacy, as well as a sense of being in one's own territory, which made them quite attractive.[33] Renting space would also have avoided the danger of an ethnic parish being left high and dry if the Puerto Rican population moved out of its neighborhood.

Another reason given was that most Puerto Ricans lived in neighborhoods that were not overwhelmingly Hispanic. On reflection, however, it would seem that this only made it all the more important for them to have "turf" of their own, since there seems to be a psychological need for some sort of spatial basis if a healthy and stable community is to be formed. Although Father Fitzpatrick was closely associated with the implementation of Spellman's plans for

Puerto Rican ministry, and in that capacity has presented some of the most coherent articulations of the case for the integrated parish,[34] he has also clearly expressed the problems inherent in the policy of integration. Puerto Ricans, he says, "have not had the confidence of knowing that this parish church, or school, is 'theirs' in the sense in which Italians, for example, knew the Italian parish was 'theirs'. As a result, the parish has not been able to serve as the basis of a strong, stable Puerto Rican community the way it had served for earlier immigrant groups."[35] This psychological need for a geographical focus for community—the community's need for a figurative "room of one's own"—has been filled at the religious level by Hispanic storefront churches, and at the secular level by social and civic clubs. But the Catholic Church as an institution has, by its own choice, been on the fringes of this community-building process, and as a result has often found itself left out of the Puerto Rican community, which has arisen mostly without its help. This building of ethnic community was, as Fitzpatrick points out, an important function of the old national parishes; it was there that local leaders could arise and later move into ward and city politics as representatives of their ethnic group. For such leaders the ethnic parish was both a benefactor with a claim on their gratitude and a power base whose wishes had to be seriously considered. The integrated parishes have not served this function, but the storefront churches and the secular organizations did. As a result a disproportionate number of the community's leaders have been Protestants, and those leaders who identify as Catholic do not have a strong identification with the Church. To the degree that Puerto Rican community is being built in a Pentecostal or a secular context, the Catholic Church may find that when Puerto Ricans come into power they will regard her with indifference or even in some cases with hostility.

The fact that Puerto Ricans display an indifferent attitude toward the parish by not getting involved and by supporting it with "nickels and dimes" is also a function of this feeling of detachment from an institution which they perceive as "not theirs." Experience shows that in those rare occasions when a diocese allows a Puerto Rican parish to be formed, financial support and lay involvement suddenly appear—as they always have for the Pentecostal storefronts.[36] Puerto Ricans, for historical and temperamental reasons, may not be willing to fight for a parish of their own, but the difference in their reaction when they can have one is an indication of how valid the model still is.[37]

In this context it is important to note that at the 1953 Conference on Spiritual Care of Puerto Rican Migrants, voices were raised repeatedly which questioned the validity of the integrated parish as the policy of choice for Puerto Rican ministry. The report does not specify who these persons were; they may have been some of the Puerto Rican priests who participated in the conference—which took place in San Juan[38]—or representatives of a few mainland dioceses which refused to give up the national parish model.[39] In the words of the conference's official report,

... the request was made a number of times that some effort be made to learn the sentiments of the Puerto Rican people themselves [with regard to the issue of national or integrated parishes]. This seems based on the fear that, perhaps, it is taken for granted too lightly that the Puerto Rican people are quite willing to be integrated with the territorial parishes. *No definitive steps were taken to determine what the Puerto Ricans felt about the matter.*[40]

Persons who questioned the advisability of giving up the national parish model were often told that Rome in some way "disapproved" of national parishes. This impression seems to originate from a peculiar reading of Canon 216, par. 4 in the 1917 Code of Canon Law, according to which national or personal parishes could not be set up without a special indult from the Holy See; such an indult being also necessary for any change in the status of existing ones.[41] A cursory reading of this canon may indeed lead to the conclusion that its intent was to discourage national parishes. But it is significant that the canon makes it as difficult to close national parishes, or to convert them into territorial ones, as to open new ones; when Rome really wants certain customs or institutions to die out it does not tend to be so even-handed. Judging from other situations, if Rome had in fact wanted national parishes to die out it would have made them difficult to open and easy to close.[42] From a careful and impartial reading of the canon one cannot conclude anything about Rome's attitude to national parishes except that it wanted to keep some control over them. The fact that dioceses like Trenton and Camden found no difficulty in obtaining indults to constitute new national parishes would seem to indicate that this is a more correct reading of the Vatican's attitude.

This understanding is reinforced by the apostolic constitution *Exsul Familia*, on the Spiritual Care of Migrants, promulgated by Pius XII in 1952.[43] This document praises the work of the national parishes, which were "most frequently requested by immigrants," singling out for mention those of the United States. Canon 216:4, the very rule which Americans interpreted as discouraging national parishes, is explicitly presented by *Exsul Familia* as an approval of such parishes, and the document supports this interpretation by citing ("to give just one example") the "very recent" decree of the Consistorial Congregation setting up Chinese national parishes in the Philippines.[44] The great experiment of integrating a whole wave of migrants into the territorial parishes receives no mention, positive or negative, in *Exsul Familia*—in spite of its being sponsored by Cardinal Spellman, who was on particularly close terms with the pope.

For dioceses where the bishop preferred not to set up formal national parishes, *Exsul Familia* created a new option, which was not, however, the integrated parish. Such bishops were advised to obtain priests of the immigrants' nation, or at least of their language, and give them faculties for the *cura animarum* with respect to the group in question. Such "ethnic missioners" would be the equivalent of the pastor of a parish (*aequiparatur parocho*), and therefore should have their own parochial record books, but their parochial powers only extend to the immigrants of their language or nation—although the word "immigrant" is defined most amply to include the direct descendants of immigrants, even if born in the new country or naturalized into it, as well as foreign students. Those who migrate from a colony to the metropolis—the very situation of the Puerto Ricans in the U.S.—are also specifically included among those for whom this model of ministry can be used. With regard to all such "immigrants" the ethnic missioner would have equal powers with the pastor if he was working out of a regular (non-ethnic) parish—an arrangement which, if applied in New York, would have turned every integrated parish into two parishes, each with its own pastor, but sharing the same facilities. In such a situation the local bishop should set up norms by which the ethnic missioner would be enabled to do his work freely and without hindrance; however, the pope suggested that whenever possible the missioner should be assigned some church or chapel for his headquarters.[45]

The *Exsul Familia* model was intended to have the advantages of the national parish, but in a more flexible and adaptable form. An ethnic mission along these lines could be set up and closed down without recourse to Rome; it could be established in its own building or share space with an already constituted territorial parish (or indeed, although the document doesn't mention it, it could operate in a rented storefront or hall). If the immigrant community moved to a different neighborhood or even to another town, the mission could follow them without the canonical complications that might hinder this move in the case of a parish. In spite of all these advantages, only one chapel along the lines of *Exsul Familia* was set up for Puerto Ricans in the United States; this was the Capilla del Sagrado Corazón in Lorain, Ohio, erected in 1952 and now a flourishing national parish.[46] With this one exception, *Exsul Familia* had no effect on the American Church's policy towards the Puerto Rican migration. The few dioceses, such as Trenton and Camden, whose bishops did not object to national parishes continued to set them up, while the majority of the hierarchy continued with the model of integration. While the *Exsul Familia* model avoided many of the practical objections to the national parish, it still offered the immigrants an ecclesial and sacramental community of their own. This is just what the integrationists avowedly did not want them to have, since it retarded their goal of assimilation and integration as soon as possible into "the Church as it now exists and operates in this country."[47]

The principal "practical" argument for the integrated parish was the claim that, because of the Americanization of the second- and third-generation immigrants, national parishes would soon become white elephants. On closer inspection, however, this argument has no validity in the case of the Puerto Rican migration. The decline of the national parishes which had been established for European immigrants was a result of two combined factors: the Americanization of the later ethnic generations, and the end of massive European immigration after the quotas imposed by the Immigration Laws of 1924. Without this second factor, these parishes would have continued to flourish, since new first-generation parishioners would have replaced those who assimilated into the "American" parishes. But in the case of Puerto Rico we are dealing with a "country" whose language and culture are foreign, but whose inhabitants are American citizens; their entrance into the mainland cannot be legally restricted. Therefore, even granting the speedy Americanization of the second and third generations, Puerto Rican national parishes could have counted on a steady supply of first-generation immigrants to keep them alive and useful long after the grandchildren of the original parishioners had deserted them for "American" parishes. There was no reason at that time, any more than now, to expect an end to the migration of island-born Puerto Ricans to the mainland, or to expect that a general Americanization would take place in the island itself, especially among the poorer classes which constituted the bulk of the migrant population. Since a number of significant factors were present among the Puerto Ricans which tended to retard assimilation, it would seem that the principal practical argument for the integrated as against the national parish was least valid precisely in the case of that ethnic group to which it was first applied.

Finally, we must look at the argument that the national parish is "divisive" and retards integration into the American Church. In fact this argument stems from a concept of unity which is false at the theological level and counterproductive at the practical level. Theologically the notion of unity as uniformity is totally unacceptable; part of the meaning of the Church's catholicity is precisely that its faith can and should be expressed in every human language and in terms of every human culture.[48] For an ethnic group to desire a place where its culture's way of expressing the common faith is not an anomaly or a footnote, but rather the local community's central expression, is not schismatic, but truly Catholic and eminently healthy. As we have seen, context and forms of expression are, at the psychological and sociological level, at least as important as content. From this point of view a local church which holds the same theology as one's own original community, but expresses it in forms that one finds alien, is hardly "one's Church" in any but the most institutional sense. Such an experience is not unifying; it is rather alienating.

At the practical level the spirit of unity is often better served by a mutually respectful separation than by a forced integration, where one group has all the power and expects the other to assimilate to it. As long as the Puerto Rican members of the "integrated parish" cling to their own language and culture, they will have to be given their own liturgy and their own parish organizations. Because these separate services are found within the same parish, and are therefore highly visible, they often grate on American parishioners, who resent the "separatism" of the Hispanics rather more in this situation than when they are "out of sight and out of mind."

At the same time the Puerto Ricans are painfully aware that in an integrated parish the English-speaking parishioners are perceived as "the parish," and their interests and their tastes are perceived as the interests and tastes of the parish, while Hispanics are perceived as a subgroup that ought to subordinate its interests and its tastes to the "common good." Thus, for example, if there should be a conflict of scheduling between the Spanish Mass and some extraordinary parish event—e.g., a concert or a school Mass—it is the Spanish Mass that must be omitted or shortened. The American community would never be expected to make a similar sacrifice for the sake of the Hispanics, since that would subordinate the "common good" to a "particular interest group." On Christmas and Holy Week, when the Puerto Rican soul most craves to express itself in its own traditional ways, parish unity must be expressed by a single united liturgy which is of course in English and in the American style—with a reading and a hymn in Spanish as a concession to the Spanish-speaking parishioners. Such efforts at enforced unity are frustrating and counterproductive, especially to the group which is always expected to do the integrating. And this frustration—which is rarely expressed at the conscious level, but which does affect attitudes and behavior—is especially dangerous to the Church because of the historical factors which lead the Puerto Ricans to identify with their cultural expressions of Catholicism more than with the Church as an institution.

In its desire for visible unity and its commitment to its self-image as the Americanizer of the immigrants, the archdiocese of New York—and its archbishop, Cardinal Spellman—forgot the axiom that "one integrates from a position of strength, and not from a position of weakness." It was in their national parishes that Italians, Germans, and Poles acquired the confidence which enabled them to eventually come out into the mainstream, feeling that they had much to offer as well as much to gain. It was in the national parishes that these and other groups gradually formed a process of collective and often unconscious discernment about what to keep, what to discard, and what to modify in their ethnic heritages, and so were able to integrate into the American Church and American society on terms which they found acceptable, and at a pace which they found comfortable. By denying this experience to the Puerto Ricans—and to later groups of Hispanic immigrants, to whom the same policy was in turn applied—the American Church has, with the best intentions, deprived them of a most useful tool for healthy integration and has deprived itself in their case of the good will and loyalty which the national parishes created in earlier ethnic groups.

6

Implementing the Vision

It is, of course, one thing to decree the integration of the Puerto Ricans "into the existing pattern of archdiocesan life"[1] and quite another to implement this vision on a citywide scale, especially when the migration became massive and overflowed the confines of Spanish Harlem. In the long run the decision to integrate the Puerto Ricans into the territorial parishes where they lived turned out to necessitate something close to the integration not of one or two parishes, but of the archdiocese itself.

The archdiocese, in fact, was not equipped to integrate or assimilate such an overwhelming number of Puerto Ricans, since hardly any of its priests were fluent in Spanish. Even fewer of them had any understanding of the cultural presuppositions or religious ethos of the newcomers. Among the first to realize the need for the archdiocese to enter into a serious program of self-adaptation if it were to effectively serve the Puerto Ricans without recourse to the national parish model were two young priests, one a religious and the other a priest of the archdiocese, but an outsider by origin and training: Joseph Fitzpatrick, S.J., and Ivan Illich.

Father Fitzpatrick, an Irish American from Bayonne, N.J., had just joined the faculty at Fordham in the fall of 1949 after obtaining a doctorate in sociology at Harvard with a prize-winning dissertation on the organizing of white-collar workers in Wall Street. He came to Fordham with the intention of founding a labor management institute under the auspices of the university, which he expected to be his life's work.[2] In the very year in which he graduated and began to teach, however, the Puerto Rican migrants began to attract his attention both as a sociologist and as a priest. As a sociologist he was blessed with a rare gift of empathy, which allowed him to enter into the minds of the "objects of his research" and see the situation with their eyes; as a priest he had a tremendous amount of natural *simpatía*— a charm which quickly won the hearts of the Puerto Rican community, whose experience of New York priests up to that point had all too often been of cold and rigid authoritarianism. Fitzpatrick began to study the sociological and religious problems encountered by the Puerto Ricans in an alien environment—not "the Puerto Rican problem," therefore, but rather the "American problem" which the Puerto Ricans had to deal with—and within a couple of years was bringing it to the attention of both the Church and the academic community.[3] Both as priest and academic Fitzpatrick had found his real life's work; eventually he would be recognized as the foremost authority on the sociology of Puerto Rican migration. But to the New York Puerto Rican community he has always been much more than that: a real *padre* and a warm friend.

In 1952, the same year in which Fitzpatrick gave his first public conference on Puerto Ricans, another young priest arrived in New York and was assigned to Incarnation parish in Washington Heights, an Irish neighborhood which was fast turning Puerto Rican. His name was Ivan Illich, and his background was exotic by New York archdiocesan standards. Born in Vienna to a minor Dalmatian noble and his Jewish wife, he was an alumnus of the historic *Collegio Capranica*, had a doctorate in the philosophy of history from the University of Salzburg, another doctorate in science from Florence, master's degrees in philosophy and theology from the Gregorian University, and had just been accepted by the *Accademia dei Nobili Ecclesiastici*, the training school for the papal diplomatic service and the Vatican Secretariat of State. He had supposedly come to New York on a dare, being teased by some American fellow-seminarians to the effect that with all his brilliant talents, he wouldn't be able to survive in a parish in a New York changing neighborhood.[4] Be that as it may, it is certain that he came "highly recommended to Cardinal Spellman" by the latter's Roman contacts,[5] and that Illich's own connections in Rome as well as his diplomatic skills were useful to the cardinal on more than one occasion.[6] Spellman eventually came to admire and trust Illich to such an extent that, even after Illich had become a *bête noire* to many bishops on the cardinal's side of the ecclesiastical spectrum, he stood behind him unreservedly.

Within three months of his arrival at Incarnation Illich had added Spanish to the list of languages he spoke fluently and was working to understand the Puerto Rican ethos by spending as much time as possible listening to the people in his parish, and going out into the streets to get input from those who did not go to the rectory. Aware that one could not understand New York's Puerto Ricans without understanding their roots, he spent his vacations in the island, walking and hitchhiking up and down the country districts and learning to know and appreciate the Puerto Rican peasants' approach to life.

In this endeavor his aristocratic European background was a definite asset. As a product of a cosmopolitan education he was much less culture-bound than New York's priests and had little difficulty adding one more worldview to the many with which he was comfortable. Indeed he seems to have found the culture of the New York rectories rather harder to move in than that of the *jíbaros*, whose values and attitudes were much closer to those of European peasants than the attitudes of the New York middle classes were to those of the European aristocracy or intelligentsia. He also had "the aristocrat's complete trust in the people"[7] which enabled him to value the *religiosidad popular* of people who did not always live by the rules. At the same time he was very firmly grounded in traditional theology and spirituality,[8] and never reduced the Church's mission—as many of his disciples were to do—to its social action component of improving the lot of the less fortunate. Where Fitzpatrick was *simpático*, Illich was intense—a quality which Puerto Ricans find very attractive in a priest or a political leader.

Also in 1952—a bit of an *annus mirabilis* for New York's Puerto Rican apostolate—Monsignor John J. Maguire, chancellor of the archdiocese,[9] asked a young diocesan priest-sociologist, Father George Kelly, to do a scientific study of Puerto Ricans and their relation to the New York Catholic Church. This study was meant to produce a basis of hard data on which to plan the Church's response to the migration, substituting "knowledge for hunches, certainty for guesswork."[10] The document resulting from this study, *Catholic Survey of the Puerto Rican Population in the Archdiocese of New York*,[11] was ready the following year and its findings were a jolt to whatever complacent feelings the archdiocese may have felt about its service to the Puerto Ricans. Almost fifteen years after the decision to integrate the Puerto Ricans into the existing territorial parishes, there was still "almost a reluctance on the part of the pastors of diocesan parishes to plunge into Puerto Rican work wholeheartedly, or to have their parishes known as Puerto Rican, even when a large minority of the Catholics, and in some places a majority, are Puerto Rican."[12]

Using membership in parish societies, and especially holding office in them, as an index of "the extent to which Puerto Ricans are integrated in the parish structure,"[13] he found that even in parishes where Puerto Ricans had a high proportion of Mass attendance their membership in the societies was negligible; only in the national parishes with a strong Puerto Rican identification did they join or hold office in significant numbers. "Either Puerto Ricans are not sought out," he concluded, "or they find barriers raised against them, or believe such barriers exist."[14] There was a fourth possibility which Kelly did not consider: the Puerto Ricans themselves may not have wished to cross the inherent barriers of language and culture; they may have had no wish to join the societies as they existed, even if they were sincerely wanted. But in view of the cardinal's avowed wishes it was easier to blame pastors and parishioners for the fact that the integrated parishes were not really integrating than to consider the possibility that the supposed beneficiaries of the policy had no wish to integrate. It is significant that in his introduction Kelly proposed to himself the task of discovering if there were significant differences between Manhattan and the Bronx, between religious and diocesan parishes, between various districts within each borough . . . but *not* between national and integrated parishes.

The clearest and most indisputable finding of the *Catholic Survey* was that in terms of priests and women religious qualified to work with Puerto Ricans the archdiocese of New York was in no position to deal with the already massive and still increasing numbers involved in the Great Migration—especially if these numbers were to be served from the territorial parishes in which they lived. Only seventy-seven full-time priests in New York City could speak Spanish functionally, and of these only twelve were incardinated in the archdiocese. Sixty of these seventy-seven were stationed in Manhattan (one to every 2,300 Puerto Ricans in the borough) and seventeen were in the Bronx (one to every 3,600 Puerto Ricans).[15] Thirty-four more priests were learning Spanish. The situation among teaching Sisters was even worse. Only thirty-two Sisters (less than 2 percent of the total in the two boroughs) could speak Spanish, while only 4.3 percent were learning it. In Southern Manhattan, which had 20,000 Puerto Rican residents, not one Sister spoke Spanish, and not one was studying the language; in the "Spanish Bronx" only three spoke it, and sixteen were learning.[16]

According to Kelly, "if the Archdiocese was geared to provide care for the Puerto Ricans commensurate with the service it gives to non–Puerto Ricans it would presently have at least 200 Spanish-speaking priests and 500 Spanish-speaking Sisters."[17] If migration trends continued, by 1960 the archdiocese would need 500 Spanish-speaking priests and 1,500 Spanish-speaking Sisters in its parishes, not counting the need for Spanish-speakers in the marriage tribunal, Catholic charities, and other archdiocesan agencies.[18] In view of this, Kelly concluded, "it does not seem that a voluntary system of training future priests in Spanish for work in the New York Archdiocese will meet the demand. It would almost seem imperative that every priest being ordained speak Spanish, and that his training in that language be compulsory."[19]

Cardinal Spellman had opted for the integrated parish model in the first year of his episcopate (1939). But this decision, at the time it was made, was directed at an increasing but not overwhelming migration and presumed that a number of territorial parishes turned over to religious orders with Puerto Rican or Latin American experience could deal with the situation. It was the data and the recommendations in Kelly's 1953 *Catholic Survey* that led to another step, usually combined with the first in people's minds, but which was actually taken fourteen years after the decision to integrate: the massive education of diocesan priests in Spanish, so as to make feasible the ideal of a Spanish-speaking priest in every parish that had a significant percentage of Puerto Ricans within its territorial boundaries. With Kelly's data in hand, Maguire was able to make Spellman realize that the integrated parish solution demanded that a vast majority of the Manhattan and Bronx parishes be in a position to integrate, and that superhuman efforts at educating the New York clergy would be needed to make this a reality.

In the process of conducting his survey, Kelly came in contact with a number of Puerto Rican groups, such as the civic clubs composed of people from the same hometown, which were beginning to articulate a Puerto Rican community independent of the Church's leadership. While these and similar groups had no desire to be subsumed under clerical leadership, they were by no means anticlerical and were aware of the advantages to be gained from an alliance with such a powerful entity as the archdiocese—powerful not only in its political connections but in its capacity to give moral legitimacy to an ethnic group which was still perceived rather negatively by most New Yorkers. In Kelly they saw something which up to then seems to have been rare: "a representative of the Archdiocese concerned with Puerto Rican and Hispanic interests,"[20] and they gave every indication of desiring such a liaison. As a result "it was decided to create a new office

within the Archdiocese with the responsibility of representing the
interests of the Archdiocese within the Hispanic community, and
of advocating Hispanic interests within the parishes and other
institutions of the Archdiocese."[21]

The Office of Spanish Catholic Action in the Archdiocese of
New York was created on March 24, 1953 "to integrate the work
being done for New York's Puerto Rican people by Catholic religious, educational and social agencies, and to develop the scope
of the present program to provide more extended facilities for our
newly arriving co-religionists."[22] In order to impress the Puerto
Rican community with the importance which the archdiocese gave
them, and in order that the office's projects should not be disregarded by pastors and chancery officials, it was imperative that
its head be a diocesan priest of some prestige, and with personal
influence among the clergy. The choice fell on Monsignor Joseph
F. Connolly, a respected priest and former faculty member at the
major seminary; he was also in residence at Incarnation parish and
was on close terms with Illich.[23]

Monsignor Connolly spent much of his energy on the preparation of a *Suggested Basic Plan of Coordination of Spanish Catholic
Action for the Archdiocese of New York*.[24] This included a coordi-
nating council of representatives from the various archdiocesan
departments (such as education, Catholic charities and vocations)
which would arrange for each of these to serve Puerto Ricans
in its own sphere without the Hispanic office having to set up
a parallel Spanish-speaking service for each of those spheres.[25] It
also included a layman's committee, whose principal purpose was
not lay participation in the planning or decision making (no one
dreamed of such a role for the laity in the 1950s) but rather for public relations. Connolly saw the office's need for high visibility in the
Puerto Rican community, but felt that this visibility necessitated attendance at conferences and other meetings "which are essentially
unimportant and unproductive . . . but which accidentally become
important" because the archdiocese's absence could be interpreted
as lack of interest in the concerns of the community. The main
purpose of the laymen's council seems to have been to free the
clerical members of the office from such necessary but wasteful
engagements by enabling them to send a"delegated layman of
prestige" to represent the office.[26]

The role of the office itself is seen in the plan as basically referring the needs of Puerto Ricans to the appropriate departments of
the archdiocese, and keeping in touch with all agencies, within and

without the archdiocesan structure, concerned in matters affecting the Puerto Rican community.

The plan itself was approved by the cardinal, but was never implemented; its importance lies in the glimpse it affords us into the mentality of Connolly and of the inner circles of the archdiocesan curia on the issue of the Puerto Rican apostolate. The paternalism evidenced by the comments on the laymen's council is also present in the central idea of the plan, which was to adjust the structures and procedures of the archdiocese to the needs of the new situation "to the extent that is necessary—and only to that extent,"[27] in order to integrate the Puerto Ricans "into the existing pattern of Archdiocesan life," so as to "avoid the unhappy and undesirable evolution, in effect, of a separate diocese within the Archdiocese."[28] From these statements it can be seen that while the archdiocese was willing to go to great lengths in order to minister to the Puerto Ricans, it had no intention of budging one inch from its self-image as an American and Americanizing institution, with a unified structure into which the interests and wishes of the Puerto Ricans had to be subsumed. The archdiocese was willing, and in the person of its coordinator, even zealous to serve the Puerto Ricans, but only on its own terms.

Within a few weeks of his appointment Connolly took two steps which were practical, but also symbolic. They were intended to impress not only on the Puerto Ricans but on the New York diocesan clergy the idea that "a whole new era was beginning as far as the archdiocese and the Puerto Rican community were concerned."[29] These were the institution of the Fiesta of St. John the Baptist and the sending of a number of seminarians to Puerto Rico to learn the language and familiarize themselves with the ethos of the island. Both of these decisions were to acquire increased importance in future years, and in both we detect the imaginative creativity of Ivan Illich, who was to be deeply involved in their development.

The decision to celebrate the Feast of Saint John the Baptist as a patronal feast for the "Spanish-American Catholics of New York" was announced in a press release dated May 29, 1953, and further details were given in a later press release on June 23, the eve of the feast.[30] That year it took the form of a pontifical Mass at St. Patrick's Cathedral, celebrated by Bishop McManus of Ponce, with Cardinal Spellman presiding from his archiepiscopal *cathedra*, and Bishop James Griffiths, an auxiliary bishop in the military vicariate, preaching the sermon in Spanish. The mayor of New

York and a number of civic leaders were present at the ceremony, as well as a congregation of 4,500.[31]

To understand the enormous turnout for a pontifical Mass at a location far removed from any Puerto Rican neighborhood, a turnout which actually increased every year until St. Patrick's could no longer hold the congregation, we must realize that up to that point there had been no public manifestation of the Puerto Rican presence in New York in a positive context and under the auspices of a respected institution which would give the Puerto Ricans some legitimation in the eyes of the rest of the city.[32] As Monsignor Stern notes,

> in its day the San Juan *fiesta* was a very important thing. It corresponded to a deeply held Puerto Rican value: *respeto*. At that time all of what the public at large thought they knew about Puerto Ricans in New York was that they were poor, they didn't speak the language, and they were the ones who were ruining the city. . . . The *fiesta* offered an opportunity for a public demonstration of the religious and cultural values of the Puerto Rican community, for until then they had no special expression of their culture or language or dignity. It was the first city-wide event that gave presence to the Puerto Ricans; there was nothing else. For several years it remained the main Puerto Rican event in New York.[33]

In Illich's mind, the fiesta should do for Puerto Ricans what the St. Patrick's Day parade had done for the nineteenth-century Irish immigrants; it was to serve as a catalyst for and manifestation of their pride in being who they were, as a chance to see themselves as having something to offer the city and the archdiocese, and of saying this to both their fellow New Yorkers and their fellow Catholics in a dignified and upbeat way. A decade before such slogans became widespread, the fiesta was meant to be immediately a focus for "Puerto Rican Pride" and eventually also for "Puerto Rican Power," as attending city officials became aware of the community's voting potential.

This, or something close to it, seems to have been Illich's vision when he presented his idea to Connolly and to Spellman. But the significance of the event was diluted, at least in the mind of the clergy, by the constant use of the term "Spanish-American" instead of "Puerto Rican" in discussions and press releases,[34] in spite of the fact that St. John the Baptist is the patron saint of Puerto Rico, and not of Latin America, and thus held no attraction for other Hispanics.

While the fiesta was always a *de facto* Puerto Rican event, this reluctance on the part of its sponsors to accept and reinforce its specifically *Puerto Rican* nature, would in the long run weaken its appeal. What the New York Puerto Ricans instinctively wanted was an event that would both foster and express their sense of being a people; a celebration of Puerto Rican-ness as the St. Patrick's Day parade is a celebration of Irishness. The fact that the fiesta was controlled by a non–Puerto Rican clerical establishment which was ambivalent about the creation of a strong Puerto Rican Catholic community in New York carried with it, therefore, an implicit contradiction. Unconsciously, the sponsors of the fiesta and its participants were at cross-purposes. Furthermore, by this time a significant and vocal minority in the Puerto Rican community iden-tified as Protestant and were not willing to participate in such an overtly Catholic celebration, or to accept a vision of Puerto Rican identity which was centered on the island's Catholic tradition. The archdiocese used the fiesta to foster an image of Puerto Rican identity as centered on Catholicity, and to foster among Puerto Ricans a sense of unity with other Spanish-speaking Catholics, and ultimately with all Catholics in New York. But by the 1960s the Puerto Ricans would come to see religion as a divisive rather than a unitive factor in their efforts at building community; they needed an event that would be purely Puerto Rican in its emphasis and which would exclude no Puerto Rican. In that same decade the new leadership of the Spanish-speaking apostolate began to downplay the aspects of the fiesta which appealed to Puerto Rican popular religiosity and popular culture, and to use the event as a "teaching opportunity" to expose the Puerto Ricans to their renewed vision of Church and society—again fostering an agenda which was not shared by all Puerto Ricans at the expense of those elements which were common to the people's ethos. This combination of factors finally made the fiesta vulnerable to competition from the purely civic, and purely Puerto Rican controlled, Puerto Rican Day parade, which has replaced it as the central expression of the community's identity and pride.

But all this was still far into the future, and the best was yet to come. In 1955 the St. John's Day Mass had been sung to an overflow congregation at St. Patrick's, and on the basis of this Illich convinced Spellman to hold the 1956 Mass outdoors, in the main quadrangle of Fordham University. This enabled him, with the help of Father Fitzpatrick and doña Encarnación de Armas, a lay Catholic activist with experience in city politics, to prepare a new version of the fiesta in which, as in the Puerto Rican tradition of *fiestas patronales*, religious events (High Mass, processions, etc.) combined with picnicking and secular amusements such as fireworks, dancing, and games to create a holistic celebration in which the sacred and the secular interpenetrated and complemented each other.[35] Cardinal Spellman, of course, would preside at the outdoor Mass, but a civic/cultural program would follow, whose great "catch" was the extremely popular mayor of San Juan, doña Felisa Rincón de Gautier, a populist grande dame whose presence symbolized the union of the *Puertorriqueños ausentes* with their brothers and sisters in the island. After the formal events, civic and religious, were over, the rest of the day would be spent on a picnic featuring the traditional *lechón asao*, roast suckling pig.

The success of the fiesta's new format exceeded all expectations. The police had expected five thousand to attend and had disregarded Fitzpatrick's calculations of thirty thousand; in fact thirty-five thousand Puerto Ricans showed up at Fordham, some arriving at dawn although the events were scheduled for noon.[36] The unexpected climax of the day came when Spellman broke a four-foot *piñata* and the crowd rushed to grab the gifts that spilled from it. The cardinal, of course, had been told what to expect and took the mob scene in stride, but the police rushed to protect him, assuming that the unpredictable Puerto Ricans had suddenly turned vicious and were attacking him. The garbled story made front-page news all over the nation, and Spellman, who loved publicity, was confirmed in his admiration for Illich, as well as totally convinced of the superiority of the new format.[37]

While the fiesta was a most effective symbolic gesture, the second step taken by Connolly—the sending of diocesan clerics to Puerto Rico for training—was eminently practical, and was meant as a response to the crying need for Spanish-speaking priests which Fr. Kelly's *Catholic Survey* had pointed out. Up to that point there had been little or no formal study of Spanish by the diocesans; those who learned it did so at their own choice, and often picked it up informally from their parishioners. In June 1953 the cardinal assigned two of the priests in that year's ordination class to temporary service in a parish in Puerto Rico; six of the major seminarians were also sent to spend the summer as unordained assistants in the island's parishes, with the hope that they would not only have "total immersion" practice in Spanish, but also the opportunity to gain some firsthand knowledge of Puerto Ricans in their "natural habitat." Here again, although the initiative officially came from the cardinal through Connolly, we can detect the influence of Illich's experience during his vacations in Puerto Rico, where he had tried to immerse himself in the worldview of the country people.[38]

Two priests and a number of seminarians were sent again to Puerto Rico in 1954 and 1955, but it soon became clear that an increase of two new Spanish-speaking priests a year was nothing when compared to the yearly growth of New York's adult Puerto Rican population. By 1956 the cardinal had become aware that drastic measures would have to be taken if his vision of an integrated service to Puerto Ricans was to be truly effective. That year he sent half his ordination class to Georgetown University for two months of intensive, total immersion language training according to the latest methods developed by the State Department for the quick training of diplomatic personnel. The following year half the ordination class took the same training, but in Puerto Rico, where they could also be exposed to the people's culture and be trained in intercultural communication skills. Under Illich's influence—still to a great degree behind the scenes—the archdiocese's vision of integration was being modified into some sort of acceptance that Puerto Ricans were really different, and that the integrated parishes would need priests who would not only know the language ("until we can cancel the Spanish services") but who also understood and empathized with the cultural presuppositions and expressions of the Puerto Ricans. This new approach would indeed attract and keep many Puerto Ricans who might have otherwise been lost to the Church. But implicit in this new approach was an unspoken compromise of the older ideal of integrating the newcomers as soon as possible and not allowing them to become "a parish within the parish or a diocese within the Archdiocese."

The final achievement of Connolly's tenure was the Conference on the Spiritual Care of Puerto Rican Migrants, held in San Juan on April 11–16, 1955. This was ostensibly convened under the auspices of Bishops Davis of San Juan and McManus of Ponce, and officially organized by Father Gildea of the Redemptorist parish of San Agustín in Puerta de Tierra, a barrio of San Juan. The original idea may have in fact come from Gildea,[39] but it was Spellman who took on the financing of the whole project—including the travel expenses of all the priests who attended from the mainland and the publication and distribution of the proceedings[40]—and the actual planning was done by Fathers Fitzpatrick and Illich. Thus while the polite fiction was preserved that the conference was an activity of the Church of Puerto Rico, under the auspices of its two bishops and presided by the rector of its Catholic University, in reality it was very much a project of the archdiocese of New York.

The conference was attended by thirty-five priests representing sixteen U.S. dioceses (of whom eleven were from New York)[41] and a further thirty-five priests—some American, some Spaniards, and some Puerto Ricans—from the two island dioceses. The aim of the conference was to get priests from all sides of the Puerto Rican situation together to discuss that situation in a comprehensive way: the religious situation in the island, problems of migrant farm workers, problems of immigrants to the cities, and problems of the mainland dioceses in responding effectively to them. Thus the knowledge, experience, and outlook of priests working in each aspect of the situation would throw light on the other aspects; the mainland priests would have a better idea of the cultural and spiritual background of the immigrants they served, and the island's priests would have a better idea of what they should be preparing the potential migrants in their flock to encounter in the mainland. To allow for free discussion and honest statement of participants' opinions the sessions were closed; at the same time it was made clear to all participants that the purpose of the conference was purely the sharing of information and outlook, not policy making or even the making of recommendations.[42] The importance of the conference, therefore, does not lie in its occasioning any major policy changes, but in the fact that its discussions exposed a number of influential mainland priests to the experience and insights of priests working with Puerto Ricans in their own environment—and especially to input from native Puerto Rican priests, who explained aspects of the Puerto Rican mentality and religious ethos. The proceedings of the conference spread this input to bishops and priests who had not been present.

By 1956 Monsignor Connolly had come to feel that he could not give Spanish Catholic Action the care that was needed; in November Father James J. Wilson was appointed acting coordinator and in May 1957 became coordinator in his own right, holding this post until July 1963. Three years before, when Connolly had been appointed, he had not even been fluent in Spanish.[43] While this may sound shocking, it makes more sense when it is kept in mind that to a very great degree the post of coordinator had been created to impress New York pastors with the idea that Spellman was serious about ministry to the Spanish-speaking, and expected *them* to be. From that angle the coordinator's standing with the priests of the archdiocese, his being perceived as a man with clout in the chancery, and his capacity to manipulate the clerical "old boy network" for the benefit of Hispanics were more important qualifications than the capacity to communicate in Spanish. This is part of the reason why Illich, who was immensely popular with the Puerto Ricans but very much a "new boy," and who never was on comfortable terms with the pastors' establishment, was never made coordinator, but always played the role of *éminence grise*, privately suggesting ideas which were then officially proposed by others.[44]

Wilson, in contrast with his predecessor, had already become fluent in Spanish while on assignment to the Philippines, where it was spoken by a significant minority; his seven years there had also given him an appreciation for cultural diversity. One of his principal tasks was to try to instill such an appreciation in the territorial parishes of the city, where Puerto Ricans still tended to meet a chilly reception from clergy and people. He often enough had to struggle with pastors to obtain equal treatment for the Puerto Ricans in the parishes into which they were supposedly integrated, but which were openly reluctant to offer them Spanish Masses or to hold these in the main church. On this issue he more than once had to contend with the cardinal himself who, while committed to integration in principle, was not willing to take on certain vested interests or antagonize influential pastors.[45] One of the ironies of the integrated parish model was that the archdiocese was in a position to keep Puerto Ricans from having their own parishes, and even to refuse to find out if they wanted them, as became manifest at the 1955 conference, but it was not always in a position to impose a real and fair integration on the American pastors and parishioners, whose cooperation the cardinal might need on other issues. Wilson also struggled to convince pastors to learn Spanish themselves, and not to relegate the Puerto Ricans exclusively to a curate—as was already becoming the custom—since he felt that this latter course invariably resulted in the creation of two parallel communities within the same parish.[46] In his efforts to get the Puerto Ricans accepted in the parishes, Wilson went so far as to produce a movie, *The Other Side of the Coin*, about the sufferings of Hispanic families in New York, and how they met nothing but discrimination when they turned to the Church for help or comfort. The movie, whose cast included Ricardo Montalbán, was shown in parish halls in an effort to sensitize American Catholics to the deep faith and Christian values of Puerto Ricans, and to their need for acceptance.[47]

The new coordinator—soon raised to the rank of monsignor—continued with enthusiasm the two great programs begun by his predecessor, the *Fiesta de San Juan* and the training of clergy in Puerto Rico. Indeed, it was during his tenure at the office that both of these reached their apogee. The 1956 *fiesta* had been a resounding success, but it had strained the resources and spatial capacity of Fordham's campus, and there was good reason to expect an even greater turnout in 1957. Wilson therefore rented the stadium and park at Randall's Island from the city, and for the next eight years—its period of greatest success—this was to be the *fiesta's* location. There it also crystallized its classic format (already adumbrated in the 1956 Fordham celebration) which closely approximated the traditional style of the Puerto Rican *fiestas patronales* and fulfilled many of that celebration's religious, civic, and psychological functions. This format consisted of a procession, in which the lay sodalities and confraternities marched behind their respective *estandartes (processional banners)*, leading to a solemn outdoor Mass with a Spanish sermon by a guest preacher and concluding remarks by the cardinal. The religious celebrations would be followed by a civic ceremony with the participation of local and island politicians and leaders, which culminated with the awarding of that year's San Juan Medal, and by a cultural celebration featuring Puerto Rican music, theatre, and other forms of entertainment. Finally there followed an organized recreation period, which gradually moved into informal non-programmed picnicking, card playing, etc. in small groups all over the grounds of the park for the rest of the day.[48] During the years of Wilson's tenure, attendance at the *fiesta* averaged 55,000 or more,[49] who came not only to pray and to have a good time (in varying proportions), but also to affirm their identity not just as Puerto Ricans or as Catholics, but as Puerto Rican Catholics. As such they wanted to express their faith in ways which did not fit in the average New York parish, so that at least once a year they could express themselves free of constraints, and in space which was "theirs," even if only for a day.

The program for training priests in Puerto Rico was also expanded well beyond its previous parameters. In the later part of 1956 Cardinal Spellman and William Ferree, S.M., Rector of the Catholic University of Puerto Rico agreed on having Father Illich sent on loan to the diocese of Ponce to be Vice Rector of the Catholic University; a year later, at the age of twenty-nine, he also became a domestic prelate—the youngest monsignor in the US. Church. His principal assignment in Ponce was the creation of the

Institute of Missionary Formation under the official sponsorship of the University, so as to place the informal training program on a solid basis. While this institute was ostensibly a program of the Catholic University, in reality it was very much Illich's project; it was financially underwritten by Cardinal Spellman and was specifically geared to the needs of the archdiocese of New York. In 1959 it changed its name to Institute of Intercultural Communication—a change which reflected Illich's priorities—and was incorporated, not in Puerto Rico, but in the state of New York. "The incorporation placed full control of the institute in the hands of the archdiocese."[50] While it still appeared on paper as a program of the Catholic University of Puerto Rico, it was in reality a program of the New York archdiocese which used the facilities of that university. Its director was appointed directly by the archbishop of New York, and the archdiocese spent some $100,000 a year on it.[51] The cardinal continued the already established policy of sending half his ordination class each year for training, which now took place at the institute.

Under Monsignor Illich's direction the aims of this training were as follows. First of all, the acquisition of a fluent command of conversational Spanish at as rapid a rate as possible; eight weeks were allowed for priests, and six for nuns and brothers, using the Georgetown Foreign Service Institute methods of language training. In the minds of most priests and religious who came to Ponce, and probably in the mind of Cardinal Spellman, this was the institute's principal service. But other aspects of the program were equally, if not more important in Illich's mind; these were later described by him as the "de-Yankeefication" of the American clergy who were to serve the Puerto Ricans in New York.[52]

These other aspects included the theoretical and practical study of Puerto Rican culture, sensitivity to the values of Puerto Rican popular Catholicism, and a frank awareness of where and how these values differed from those of American culture and American Catholicism—as well as a realization that in a good number of cases the values of this style of Catholicism were actually humanly superior and more truly Catholic than those of the religious culture to which Puerto Ricans were expected to assimilate. This, it was hoped, would produce in the American pastoral agents a respect for the Puerto Rican not just as "human being," but as "other," with a historically rooted "otherness" which could not be ignored or denied if the pastoral contact was not to do more harm than good. While it could not be denied that American Catholicism had values which could enrich the Puerto Ricans, and which Americans could and should be willing to share, they needed to be made aware that Puerto Rican Catholicism also had values which it could offer the American Church for its improvement, and values to which Puerto Ricans should cling even if they were incompatible with the American ethos.[53] This was a very different position from Spellman's enthusiastic statements about the providential encounter by which Puerto Ricans would be led by the archdiocese of New York to a true understanding and full practice of their ancestral faith.[54] In the language of Clara Rodríguez's *The Ethnic Queue*, Illich was trying to move the young priests of the archdiocese from an ideal of "one-way integration" for Puerto Rican migrants to one of "two-way integration," in which the Church of New York, if it did not want them to become "a separate diocese within the Archdiocese," would have to change its own ideals and methods as much as it expected the Puerto Ricans to change theirs. It remained to be seen whether the archdiocese was willing to pay that heavy a price for the integration of the Puerto Ricans.

In order to get this across to his students, Illich sought to create in them a theoretical and experiential "understanding of the process of transition from one culture to another."[55] One of the more conventional ways of doing this was to send them on weekend assignments to help out at a local parish, where they would have to use the skills they had acquired and meet real people. It was one thing to "practice your Spanish" on the Puerto Ricans as a minority in an American parish, and quite another for the American priest to have to adapt himself to a parish which was Puerto Rican, and thus where it was *he* who had to integrate. At the end of the eight weeks' training, a priest had the option of spending a further four in such an arrangement.

Realizing that the Puerto Ricans, due to their sense of hospitality, might let the students off too easily during these assignments, Illich purposely became a "monster" to them, in order to break ingrained cultural habits, as well as to let them realize what it felt like to have to assimilate to an alien culture. He himself slept on a cot on the floor, and during the training period ate only Puerto Rican food as cooked and eaten by the poor; he imposed the same diet on the trainees. He inspired them to imitate his hitch-hikes across the island, totally dependent on the charity and hospitality of the poor peasants, as well as on their own city-boys' legs and their beginners' Spanish. This would put them in a truly helpless position, where they would come to appreciate values such as unquestioning kindness to strangers and a spirit of sharing the little that one had—values rare among middle class Americans, but taken for granted among the "religiously ignorant," "nominally Christian" *jíbaros*. Most irritatingly, he gave up his natural punctuality and would more often than not arrive late for class or for appointments, to get them used to the very different sense of time of the Latin cultures.[56] This, he said, was particularly important, since "many Puerto Ricans failed to attend Mass in the United States because it started on time."[57] If the Puerto Ricans were to feel at home in the American parish, its priests would have to be broken—brutally if need be—out of the mental habit of thinking that all parish events must start and end on schedule.[58] What Americans considered the virtue of efficient punctuality, Puerto Ricans perceived as the vice of rigidity, of considering clocks more important than people.

Illich stayed in Puerto Rico directing the institute until the fall of 1960. By this time his disagreement with Bishop McManus's position with regard to Governor Muñoz Marín had become well known in clerical circles. In October Cardinal Spellman, who had come to the island to consecrate the present Cardinal Aponte (first native bishop since the death of Arizmendi in 1814) as auxiliary of Ponce, was prevailed upon to have a well-publicized lunch with the governor, thus breaking the image of Muñoz as an "enemy of the Church" which the Puerto Rican hierarchy was trying to project.[59] McManus forbade the priests of his diocese to attend, but Illich, being incardinated in New York, did not feel McManus could forbid him to accompany his own archbishop. He was, however, also the vice rector of McManus's university, and the times were strained; the bishop also suspected Illich—erroneously—of having arranged the lunch in the first place. The next day he wrote a letter to Monsignor Illich ordering him to leave the island.[60]

Although the institute could not replace Illich's charisma and creativity, it did continue for more than a decade along the lines which Illich had set for it, coupling intensive Spanish classes aimed at quick conversational fluency with classes and practicums aimed at producing an understanding of the cultural differences between Puerto Ricans and Americans, as well as a positive appreciation of the values of Puerto Rican culture, even when these went counter to American values. By 1970 the New York archdiocese had more that 200 diocesan priests who could speak Spanish, working at 130 parishes that offered Spanish services,[61] and was justifiably proud of this fact. But it should also be noted that in an archdiocese that often has as many as ten auxiliary bishops, not one of them was at that time functional in Spanish. After twenty-five years of the policy which had produced the 200 Spanish-speaking priests, it was still impossible to hold a Confirmation in Spanish. It is also worth noting that none of these Spanish-speaking American priests was in the inner circles of archdiocesan policy making.[62]

It is impossible to exaggerate the importance of the Ponce institute, and especially of Illich himself as its founding director, not only on the Spanish-speaking apostolate but on the archdiocese of New York as a whole. In the words of Monsignor Stern,

> the Puerto Rican experience profoundly influenced a generation of New York priests. Standing outside their own culture, however briefly, they acquired a critical perspective of it. The contact with Hispanic Catholicism helped them to discern the Irish quality of New York's church. The experience of pluralism stood them in good stead as the whole church began to change in the days of Vatican II. The Puerto Rican trained clergy became the pastoralist vanguard of the Archdiocese.[63]

While the chancery may have remained a stronghold of traditional New York Irish values and methods, Illich's influence was acting as a leaven throughout those 136 parishes and, in the second half of the 1960s, this influence would be found at the top of the newly renamed Office of Spanish Community Action in the person of Wilson's successor, Monsignor Robert Fox (coordinator 1963–1969).

But Illich's success, while spectacular, was only partial. His aim had not been merely to give his disciples a critical perspective on New York Catholicism, but to create a generation of priests who, while American by birth and upbringing, would be able to think and feel like Puerto Ricans, and so would serve the immigrants in terms of their own cultural style. Illich was well aware that, while an educated person may be able to move—with effort and pain—from one culture to another, this could not be asked of simple people. Therefore, rather than assimilating Puerto Ricans into American culture, what was needed was an assimilation, albeit not uncritical, of their priests into Puerto Rican culture. This stepping out of ingrained worldviews, and relativizing of one's cultural identity, was a sacrifice that could be realistically and ethically asked of educated men who were strongly motivated to serve and had freely responded to a vocation. But it was neither ethical nor realistic to expect this difficult process from simple peasants, adrift in a strange city whose cultural presuppositions they did not understand.

Spellman's response to the Puerto Ricans had been based on St. Paul's dictum that "in Christ there is neither Jew nor Greek," which in terms of his American patriotism was understood as meaning that in the American Church there is neither Irish nor Italian nor Puerto Rican; we are all Americans and all Catholics.[64] Illich himself preferred another Pauline dictum, that an apostle must be willing to become "a Jew with the Jews and a Greek with the Greeks." In a 1956 article he clearly stated this principle, as well as the importance he, in a most un-American way, gave to a person's roots and culture:

> [If an individual] misunderstands St. Paul's instructions to make himself Jew with the Jews and Greek with the Greeks by an exegesis such as 'We are all Americans', he again denies your right and his to have a background, to be human, with roots reaching down in history to times before you both were.[65]

Unfortunately Illich seems to have had much better success in "deYankeefying" a generation of New York priests and religious than he had in Hispanicizing them. In the wake of Vatican II, when "tradition" became for many Catholics a negative value and roots were often perceived as hindrances to forward movement, the Ponce-trained priests and religious became indeed "the vanguard of the Archdiocese," and Hispanic ministry became a most attractive alternative ministry for those who found less and less meaning or satisfaction in the traditional parameters of the parish or the parochial school. But, in criticizing their own culture and freeing themselves from the hampering effects of their own roots, they did not see why Puerto Ricans should cling to *theirs* and so they ended by trying to transform both the traditional American Catholics and the Hispanics into a new creation, oriented to the future rather than the past. Just as Spellman translated "in Christ there is neither Jew nor Greek" into *we are all Americans* so did Monsignor Fox during his tenure as coordinator translate the same text into the idea that in Christ there is neither American black nor Puerto Rican; we are all one in our oppression.

The generation trained in Ponce tended to understand their vocation in terms of social action, and of building a community of the oppressed on the periphery of the official Church; a community which would leave behind the trammels and divisions of the past and move on to create a liberated future. This, together with the desire to qualify for funding under the War on Poverty, led to a very serious downplaying of both the denominational Catholic aspects and the culturally Puerto Rican aspects of the Spanish apostolate. Indeed by the late 1960s its work had become avowedly non-denominational and avowedly integrated—i.e., working at once for Hispanics and American blacks, whose differences of language and culture were regarded as irrelevant or divisive in comparison to their shared neighborhood and shared oppression.[66]

This approach was excellently suited to the needs of the new generation of priests and religious, who sought in the Secular City a liberation from ecclesiastical traditions which they found increasingly meaningless and oppressive. Unfortunately it was rather less suited to the ethos of its supposed beneficiaries. To them the new American Catholicism of the 1960s was at least as alien as the kind of Catholicism which Spellman had tried to impose on them in the 1940s and 1950s. We have mentioned earlier that preconciliar American Catholicism was marked by a strong sense of authority, sin, ritual, and supernaturalism, and that while the Puerto Ricans' version of Catholicism did not share the first two, it did share, although in its own way, in the latter two. In the late 1960s the vanguard of American Catholicism was understanding the spirit of Vatican II as a mandate to deemphasize all four. While this vanguard was attracted to working with Hispanics by their easygoing attitude to ecclesiastical authority and their lack of "Catholic guilt," it tended to be frustrated by their continued attachment to traditional rituals and by their stubbornly unsecular worldview. Being in power, the new generation of clergy simply changed the forms of Spanish ministry by *fiat*, in order to bring the Hispanics into the Church of the Future, and wean them from the habits of the past.

Thus, to give but one example, the *Fiesta de San Juan*, whose format from 1956 to 1964 had so well corresponded to traditional Puerto Rican culture by its interpenetration of the sacred and the secular *under the aegis of the sacred*, was taken apart and rebuilt in 1965 into a new format, "viewed by the clergy as a means to 'educate' the Hispanic people."[67] The Mass was moved to 5 A.M. in order to make it an event for the "truly committed," separating it from the larger *fiesta*, and the local and Puerto Rican political leaders were discouraged from attending by the definitely countercultural and antiestablishment tone given to the program by its organizers. At the same time that they made the *fiesta* a forum for "controversial" issues with which Puerto Ricans did not identify (and whose connection to religion they could not see) the organizers avoided any clearly Puerto Rican issues, as well as the kind of fun and games with no "serious" content which had formerly characterized the parts of the *fiesta* which were not overtly religious.[68] As a result of these changes the *fiesta* lost popularity; by the time these experiments were given up its role in the life of the community had been taken up by the Puerto Rican Day Parade.[69] The *fiesta* still survives, but its role as the premier event in the New York Puerto Rican community was lost irretrievably.

This and many other efforts to convert or educate the Puerto Ricans into post-conciliar American Catholicism were met with the same passive resistance which had been shown to earlier efforts to turn them into Irish Catholics. This resistance was all the harder to detect in that the architect of the renewal, Monsignor Fox, was a man of great personal charm, eminently *simpático.* whom Puerto Ricans found impossible to dislike as a person. Practically everyone in the community loved him, even if one also loved the things he was trying to dismantle, and even if one kept on doing them. Ironically, but significantly, Fox's greatest triumph was the "Peace Procession" by which he defused the 1967 riots in *el Barrio,* which neither Mayor Lindsay nor Herman Badillo, the best known Puerto Rican in city politics, had been able to stop. But in order to achieve this, he had to resort to the very things which he and his followers considered superannuated: a procession carrying candles and holy images and singing the Rosary to the traditional Puerto Rican tune of the *Dios te salve, salve María* through the riot-wrecked streets. Where the "Secular City" approach failed, the Sacred came to the rescue.

Two factors had entered the life of the New York Puerto Rican Catholics before 1965 which helped to sustain their traditional attitudes and to keep them in the Church during this time. The first was the presence of a good number of Spanish and Latin American priests in many of the archdiocese's parishes. They often came to New York to study at one of the city's universities and were given lodging at rectories in exchange for doing the work of a Spanish-speaking curate; others were religious assigned there by their Provinces. Many of them were quite conventional in their approach to ministry, but while this meant that they did not go out in search of the lost sheep, it meant at least that the parishioners knew where they could find them, and could expect from them the kind of services they were used to, and in a style with which they were familiar. While the *avant garde* was looking for new and creative ways to present the Gospel to a world which supposedly found the Sacred irrelevant, the Puerto Rican people kept seeking the Sacred, and found it—even if at times in lamentably uncreative forms—in the hands of these priests.

The second factor was the *Cursillos de Cristiandad,*[70] a movement founded in Spain in the 1950s with the purpose of overcoming the indifference of the average Spanish male towards the Church. It sought to counteract the generally held attitude that the Church was the concern of priests, women, and children, and to get men emotionally involved with Christ and with the Christian community. Since peer-pressure would make any such efforts hopeless if they were directed at the individual in his normal environment, the *Cursillo* took a group of men away from that environment for a long weekend, and during those days strove to present to them a different and more attractive version of Christianity: "a life of conscious and growing grace" rather than the practice of *beatería* ("pious old lady-ism") which they found ridiculous, and which, as it turned out, the priests and lay leaders of the *Cursillo* could mock with the best of them. Besides presenting this vision, which was reinforced by much joking, singing of popular songs, and manly camaraderie, the *Cursillo* was geared to produce, before the weekend was over, a strong emotional experience of having personally encountered Christ.

The powerful experience of the *Cursillo*—which is supposed to be a once-in-a-lifetime experience—was designed to change the individual man's attitude to religion and the Church. Since it was obvious, however, that upon returning to their normal environment both routine and peer-pressure would almost certainly wear off these new attitudes, the movement developed a system of weekly small group meetings, as well as formation groups (*Ultreyas, Escuelas de Dirigentes*, etc.) which would effectively create a new peer-group for the *cursillista*. The dynamics of this new group would be geared to help him persevere in the new lifestyle, and to integrate him into the regular Christian community.

Although the original intention of the movement was to reconquer the Hispanic male for the Church, the religious vision which it offered was so new and so attractive that it eventually proved impossible to limit the experience to men. *Cursillos* for women were authorized by the founder of the movement in 1960,[71] and while the movement does not run youth *Cursillos*, a number of youth retreat and movement formats have arisen which closely imitate

the *Cursillo*. In the early days of the movement, and especially in
Spain and Latin America, the *Cursillo* appealed just as much to the
professionals and the middle class as to the popular classes, and
the men participating in any given *Cursillo* were supposed to be
a microcosm of the local society. But among the Hispanics in the
United States there was no elite class, and so the Spanish-language
Cursillos[72] became a popular movement to an extent unparalleled
elsewhere. Since the membership was almost exclusively from the
popular class, and the running of the movement on a day-to-day
basis was by design almost exclusively in the hands of the lay
membership, the Hispanic *Cursillo* movement took on the style
and flavor of the popular class. This in turn made it the Church's
beachhead into the world of this class, and especially of its male
population. Its importance to the community may be gauged by
the fact that in the 1988 Survey of Hispanics sponsored by the
archdiocese of New York, 43 percent of those surveyed said the
Cursillo was important to them, while only 25.9 percent thought
the Second Vatican Council was important; conversely, 59.8 percent
had never heard of the Council while only 31.2 percent had not
heard of the *Cursillo*.[73]

After an early and unsuccessful try, the first *Cursillo* in New
York took place in September 1960, directed by a team from Laredo,
Texas; in December of the same year a team from Ciudad Real,
Spain—the see of Bishop Juan Hervás, founder of the movement—
gave the second and third *Cursillos*.[74] These were held at Tagaste,
the seminary of the Spanish Augustinian Recollects in suburban
New Jersey; this order is still very strongly involved with the movement. In December 1961, at the recommendation of Monsignor
Wilson,[75] the archdiocese established St. Joseph's *Cursillo* Center in
West 142nd Street, staffed by the Recollects, but under the direction
of the Office of Spanish Catholic Action. This would obviate the
need for a trip to Tagaste, which Wilson felt was too costly for poor
men, and would also allow for more frequent *Cursillos*.

By March of 1962 a diocesan secretariat for *Cursillos* had been
set up in the archdiocese along the movement's recommended
lines. While the clerical members of the secretariat—Spanish Augustinians—were ultimately in control, the lay members had a
great amount of real power; certainly much more than had been
envisaged in Connolly's plan for a laymen's council in the Office
of Spanish Catholic Action. The *Cursillo* movement thus presented
the Puerto Rican laity with both leadership training, in the *Ultreyas*
and School for Leaders, and the opportunity to exercise leadership

in the *Cursillo* itself, where most of the talks were given by lay members, and in the secretariat. Furthermore, both the training and the exercise of leadership were in their own language, and in a style and mentality with which they could identify.

In the words of Monsignor Stern, "perhaps one reason for the rapid spread, great popularity and considerable impact of the *Cursillo* among New York's Hispanics is that this diocesan-wide, city-wide movement provided a framework and community to the individual Hispanic immigrant otherwise submerged in New York's dominant non-Hispanic culture and in danger of losing his identity as Hispanic and Catholic," giving him "great opportunities for recognition and leadership."[76] Since the movement never really caught on among Americans, it was totally Hispanic rather than "integrated"; it was led by Hispanic laymen, and its resource clergy tended to be Spanish, since a great number of the "forward looking" American clerics found its emphasis too "churchy" and preconciliar and did not choose to get involved with it.[77]

While the integrated parishes treated the Puerto Ricans like poor relations, and the archdiocesan office, after 1963, drifted farther and farther away from their religious ethos and continually strove to "educate" or "enlighten" them into an ethos they found even less attractive than old-style American Catholicism, the *Cursillo* movement gave them that "diocese within the Archdiocese" which they so needed and which the chancery so feared. The *Cursillo* movement was the one important entity in the archdiocese of New York that was, *de facto*, Hispanic owned and operated. For this reason it won the loyalty of the people and became the main instrument that kept alive a Hispanic Catholic community and a Hispanic way of being Catholic throughout the 1960s.

7

Beyond New York

Up to this point this essay has concentrated on the city and Archdiocese of New York for a twofold reason. First, as late as 1970, more than half the Puerto Ricans in the United States mainland lived within the New York city limits,[1] and in the period before 1965 the proportion was closer to seventy or eighty percent. Second, and as a consequence of this, by the time the Puerto Rican presence began to be significant in other cities, both the city and the archdiocese of New York had established policies on how to deal with them, and other cities and dioceses found it natural to imitate these. New York was especially influential at the ecclesiastical level because of the prestige of its archbishop, Cardinal Spellman. Thus before 1965 the history of Puerto Ricans in New York is in fact the history of the great majority of Puerto Ricans in the United States, and the analysis of the decisions which determined New York's approach to the Puerto Rican apostolate is also to a great degree the analysis of the decisions which determined the approach taken to this apostolate in many other dioceses. Spellman's influence was particularly important in securing the general abandonment of the national parish model for the integrated parish, and the concomitant policy of Americanization as soon as possible—a policy which had to be modified by the early 1950s, and which has not yet succeeded in its avowed goals, but which has effectively hampered the development of a strong and ecclesially-centered Puerto Rican Catholic community.

It is necessary, however, to look also at the development of Catholic pastoral approaches to the Puerto Rican presence outside New York City. First of all we shall look at the efforts of a number of dioceses—New York included—to minister to those Puerto Ricans who did not settle in the urban centers, but who came to the mainland as seasonal farm workers. Then we shall study a selected number of dioceses, some of which followed the New York example and centered their efforts on having Spanish-speaking priests in territorial parishes, but a few of which insisted on the validity of the national parish model or, in one case, utilized the model of the ethnic chapel as proposed in *Exsul Familia*. Finally we shall look at the one other mainland location where the Puerto Rican presence reached massive numbers before 1965: the city and archdiocese of Chicago.

Starting in the 1940s, a great number of Puerto Rican farmworkers came to the farms of Central Pennsylvania, New Jersey, and Upstate New York as seasonal workers. This seasonal migration was particularly attractive because the crop season in the Middle Atlantic states coincided with the *tiempo muerto* or "dead season" of sugar cane growing, a time in which the cane requires no care and during which the majority of cane workers are therefore without work or wages. A similar situation existed in the coffee plantations, where most of the work was concentrated between December and May. Traditionally, therefore, the months between June and November were the time for the peasants to tighten their belts, and so the opportunity to do farm work in the mainland and return home in time to cut cane or pick coffee beans was quite attractive. By 1955 some 12,000 to 15,000 men—in most cases leaving their families at home—were recruited each year under government supervision, were flown to the mainland, and worked under contracts which the Puerto Rican government inspected in order to keep them from being exploited. More than 70 percent of them returned home each year, but a significant minority either settled in the rural areas where they had been working or drifted to the urban zones and took non-agricultural jobs.[2]

Those migrant workers who came directly from the coffee-growing mountain districts had a strongly Catholic religious background and came from a society in which daily family prayers and other forms of devotion were normal, but those who came from the coastal cane-growing areas were from a much less religious social environment. Their situation presented peculiar difficulties to the dioceses in which they worked. Their stay was brief and they did not necessarily remain in the same place throughout their stay, since they had to move from one area to another as one crop's season ended and another began. They sometimes lived in small, widely scattered groups, two or three to a farm. While Protestant farmers sometimes tried to proselytize them, Catholic farmers did not share this zeal for the souls of their temporary employees.[3] The priests were sometimes unpopular with the employers because they protested subhuman conditions in the camps and pressured the Department of Health to intervene.[4]

In spite of these difficulties, the different dioceses appointed bilingual priests to work with the seasonal farmworkers, and some of these did truly heroic work. The diocese of Camden, which claimed to have "the largest number of seasonal farmworkers in any district on the mainland,"[5] assigned Father Pasquale di Buono to this apostolate; during the season he would visit the central camp—at which 100 new men arrived each day—three times a day. There he tried to have a personal meeting with each man and gave out literature, rosaries, medals, and other religious articles. Mass was said at the main camp every Sunday morning and the Rosary on Wednesday evenings. These were attended by about half the camp's population; a much better percentage of attendance than the island's average, especially for males. Such a high attendance may have been due to the presence of large numbers of men from the more traditional mountain farm areas, as well as the lack of other sources of distraction. Small Puerto Rican groups were settling permanently in some of the rural towns in this area, and eight of these parishes had bilingual priests assigned to them. A similar phenomenon was occurring in the diocese of Trenton; there the Claretian priests who took care of the growing Puerto Rican community in Perth Amboy drove out to the villages to take care of the scattered Spanish-speakers in the rural areas, and eventually set up a number of permanent chapels for their service.[6]

In the diocese of Harrisburg Father Anthony Kane worked for ten years on the apostolate to migrant workers while also serving as full-time pastor in rural parishes. At the height of the season he would be helped by a Redemptorist, Father Charles Sullivan, who had worked in Puerto Rico. Neither of them limited his work to the purely spiritual, and they became vocal advocates of the Puerto Ricans. Father Kane especially "was known among the migrants as their own 'defender',"[7] and many stories were told of his forceful defense of Puerto Ricans in trouble. His sudden appearances, whether to preach an impromptu sermon or to get a judge to reduce a sentence, earned him the nickname of "Robin Hood." After 1955 he was made director of the Migrant Apostolate and was able to recruit more helpers; by 1959 he had also been appointed to the Governor's Committee on Migratory Labor, where he served for ten years. In Harrisburg, too, a significant percentage of the migrants eventually settled in the area, where they are now served by a number of Hispanic parishes, chapels, and "centers."

In the diocese of Buffalo an average of 2,500 seasonal workers arrived every year from Puerto Rico; most of them came with their families and returned home at the end of the season. Three bilingual priests and three seminarians cared for them, assisted by

twenty lay volunteers. Eleven Masses a week were offered in nine
locations; because of the work situation they had to be offered
either at dawn or in the evenings. Average attendance was 500.
Religious instruction was also offered on week nights, with an
average attendance of 900. There was also intensive visitation of
the families. The attendance was particularly impressive since the
men had to work from dawn to dusk seven days a week and there
were serious transportation problems; in fact the priests and their
helpers were "amazed and inspired" by their attendance under
such adverse circumstances. Since the workers were constantly
being moved from camp to camp, it was very difficult for the same
persons to attend Mass or instructions every week, which caused
difficulties especially in regard to the continuity of instruction.[8]

The personality of the individuals engaged in this ministry
could make a great difference to its success, as is shown by an
example from the rural section of the archdiocese of New York. In
July 1954 a Spanish-speaking priest from the area began to work
with a group of some 300 Puerto Rican migrant workers in the
Kerhonkson Valley, west of Kingston, N.Y. These workers had been
approached in previous years by other priests from the area, as
well as by Protestant clergy, but had been unresponsive because
neither the priests nor the ministers were fluent in Spanish. The
new priest (no names are given in this particular report) arranged
for an evening Mass on Sundays, after the men had returned from
twelve hours in the fields and had been served supper in five
shifts; on Thursdays he had the Rosary, a Novena, and a sermon,
followed by a sports program. For the three weeks in which he
was able to do this, the turnout was progressively 200, 270, and 300
(100 percent) for Sunday Mass, and 100, 170, and 275 for Thursday
devotions and sports.

In September, however, a Redemptorist with experience in
Puerto Rico was put in charge for the rest of the season. "His
opinion, after two months there, was that it was a waste of time,
because attendance fell practically to the zero point, the dining
hall [where the Masses were held] dirty, there was listlessness
(religious) on the part of the congregation, a long distance to be
traveled to reach the place, etc."[9] The priest presenting this part
of the report comments, with no trace of sarcasm: "This priest's
opinion is not to be taken lightly since he is a veteran of many
years on the Puerto Rican Mission."[10] The Redemptorist's distaste
for the work comes through clearly, however, and must have also
come across to the farm workers, who then responded in kind

to his ministrations. But their rate of attendance while the other priest was in charge had been nothing short of amazing by island standards, demonstrating that the negative results had more to do with the replacement's personality than with the workers' supposed religious indifference—a more *simpático* approach had produced abundant results.

The dioceses of Camden and Trenton not only had a large amount of seasonal farm workers, but also a growing urban population of Puerto Rican origin. Both dioceses were frankly and firmly committed to the national parish model although this went against the agreed policy of the majority of the U.S. hierarchy. In the early 1950s the city of Camden had approximately 3,000 Puerto Rican residents, and in 1953 Bishop Bartholomew Eustace opened the church of Our Lady of Fatima as a Puerto Rican national parish, with one priest and some 300 regular attenders.[11]

In the diocese of Trenton the Puerto Rican population was concentrated not in the see city, but in Perth Amboy, which since 1981 has belonged to the newly erected diocese of Metuchen. In 1948 some 300 Puerto Rican industrial workers settled there and increased at a slow rate, but in 1953 their numbers suddenly increased to 1,500, and two years later had risen to 2,500. In that same year of 1955 the city of Trenton had 1,500 Puerto Ricans, and 2,000 farm workers had settled permanently in the rural areas of the diocese.[12] In 1948, "in order to prevent problems arising where migration was left unattended for some time, the Bishop of Trenton admitted the Claretian Fathers to care for the Puerto Rican migrants throughout the Diocese."[13] Two Claretians settled in a house provided by the diocese in Perth Amboy, but drove around the whole diocese serving the scattered Puerto Rican rural population, in a model of ministry which seems to have anticipated the directives of *Exsul Familia*.

By October 1949 the Claretians had remodeled part of their house into a chapel, dedicated to Our Lady of Fatima, and were offering five Masses every Sunday; in 1950 the diocese bought the adjacent lot, where the "Fatima Social Center" was opened within a year. During this time the Claretians also became involved in civic affairs as advocates and representatives of the Puerto Rican community; one of them was a member of ten city, county, or state welfare agencies. Thus the sudden increase in Perth Amboy's Puerto Rican population which occurred in 1953 found a Puerto Rican Catholic community already in place and ready to welcome them; its priests already accepted in the area as resource persons and spokesmen for the Puerto Ricans not only on religious issues but in all areas of life. Fatima—formally erected as a national parish in that year—was perceived in Perth Amboy as the "clearing agency for anything Puerto Rican,"[14] and had become the localized focus for the city's Puerto Rican community. The strength of the parish was demonstrated in 1954 when, in order to free the priests to spend more time on the time-consuming rural apostolate, a number of Puerto Rican public school teachers organized themselves as the "Fatima Catholic Teachers" to do religious instruction in their free time, since the parish had not been able to obtain Sisters. The Puerto Rican laity of Perth Amboy was, at this early date, already willing and able to take this kind of responsibility.

By 1957 the Puerto Rican population of Perth Amboy had risen to 5,000, of whom 1,050 were regular attenders at Fatima or at La Asunción chapel, which had been set up in another part of town as a chapel of ease.[15] The southern part of the diocese had at that point 6,000 Puerto Rican residents, and two rural chapels had been set up—San Juan Bautista in Lakehurst and San Antonio María Claret in Cassville—which offered Sunday services exclusively in Spanish.[16]

In northern New Jersey the archdiocese of Newark began to attract Puerto Ricans in the early 1950s. They first settled in the central part of the city, where by 1954 two Spanish Benedictines from Newark Abbey, Fathers Genadio Díez and Plácido Alvarez began to minister at St. Patrick's Pro-Cathedral. A Spanish Mass was scheduled, confraternities and societies whose meetings were held in Spanish were founded, and a number of social events were used to create a sense of community.[17] Although the archdiocese had served earlier Spanish-speaking immigrants (the Spaniards who settled in Elizabeth and in the Ironbound section of Newark) according to the national parish model, and even upgraded the Spanish-Portuguese mission in Elizabeth to the status of national parish as late as 1967,[18] the Puerto Ricans were served along the lines of the integrated parish. The reason given was that the "revolving-door migration" made possible by citizenship and inexpensive air travel made the permanence of a national parish doubtful.[19] However, the integrated parish at St. Patrick's had the advantage of having Spaniards rather than Americans to care for the Puerto Rican community. These Benedictines had no Americanizing agenda, and so they fostered separate Spanish-speaking societies, social events, and other services with the avowed intention of creating and strengthening a Puerto Rican community within St. Patrick's. This work was encouraged by the pastor of the Pro-Cathedral, and so, to a degree, the Puerto Ricans in Newark were allowed from the beginning to form at least a "parish within the parish."

By 1956 the Puerto Rican population had spread to the neighboring parish of St. Bridget, where the model established at St. Patrick's was imitated. In 1957 St. Bridget's also began a bilingual catechetical program, staffed by the Missionary Servants of the Blessed Trinity. Because of this community's early ties with Puerto Rico, where their founder had served for some time, they were able to have at least one Sister with first-hand experience of the island in the parish at any given time, and on occasion were able to assign native Puerto Rican Sisters.[20] St. Bridget's priests and the *Trinitarias* also started a food pantry and an employment office, and the Sisters also emphasized their community's tradition of home visitation.

In Jersey City work with the Puerto Rican community was begun in 1954 by two Jesuits, Father James Carmody and Father Joseph Faulkner, who started with social action and moved on to more overtly spiritual services.[21] They founded the Centro Católico de Información, which served as a clearing house and referral service for all sorts of problems encountered by Puerto Ricans in their new environment—principally employment and housing, but also "legal difficulties, police troubles, medical aid, rent gouging, exploitation, burial, food and clothing, scarcity of furnishings, etc."[22] As in other cities, the civil agencies came to rely primarily on the Centro for problems involving Puerto Ricans.

The Centro also sponsored social events, especially a monthly dance, and a men's club. These were in part intended to deal with an intercultural problem peculiar to the encounter between Caribbeans and North Americans: people from the tropics are used to "hanging out" in the streets, and in summer nights in U.S. cities this clashed with local norms, so that all too often confrontations with the police occurred.[23]

But this social action was not an end in itself; "all of El Centro's activity [was] aimed at reaching the Puerto Rican through his needs, and keeping him close to the Faith thereby."[24] In connection with the *Centro's* work a Spanish Mass was started at the students' chapel of St. Peter's Prep, whose attendance rose in a year from 20 to over 550; the usual confraternities were started and a Spanish Jesuit was invited to give a parish mission, which was a great success. St. Peter's parish is still a pillar of the Hispanic Catholic community in Jersey City, although four other area parishes have also offered Spanish Masses and social services since the early 1960s and the area has undergone some gentrification. Although an integrated parish, St. Peter's at the present time offers Spanish-language services, such as CCD and First Communion, which many integrated parishes offer either only in English, or in joint bilingual format. As a result many Puerto Rican parishioners continue to attend there even after they move to other neighborhoods.

In Boston, too, the ministry to Puerto Ricans began with a strong social action emphasis. In the 1955 Conference on the Spiritual Care of Puerto Rican Migrants, the archdiocese's representative had reported that there were only a little more than 300 Puerto Ricans in Boston, and that nothing special was being done in their regard.[25] In 1957, however, Cardinal Cushing assigned Father Frederick O'Brien, a young priest just returned from getting a Doctorate of Sacred Theology at Salamanca, to Holy Cross Cathedral, and asked him to work with the small but growing Puerto Rican community which was clustering in that neighborhood. Father O'Brien said the first Spanish Mass on Low Sunday of that year before a congregation of six to eight persons, and by the end of the year had some sixty or seventy regular worshippers.[26]

Father O'Brien had heard negative reports about the New York approach to the Puerto Rican apostolate, and therefore went to Chicago instead for orientation. The idea he got there was that the Puerto Rican problem was primarily a social rather than a religious problem—the real issue was that the Puerto Ricans found themselves in a social situation which was demoralizing.[27] He therefore started the Cardinal Cushing Center for the Spanish-speaking, better known as El Centro del Cardenal, first in the cathedral's premises, then in a small building which he and his people renovated. Finally, when urban renewal closed that building, the center moved to a converted bank building across from the cathedral which the cardinal bought for $50,000. As in Jersey City, the Boston Centro served as a focal point for English classes, youth activities, employment counseling, and social events, as well as serving as a liaison between the Puerto Rican community and the various city agencies, since in Boston at the time "there were no government employees, hospital workers or other service people who understood Spanish."[28] The center also served as a location for religious instruction, and of course attracted people to Father O'Brien's Spanish Mass in the cathedral.

The archdiocese of Philadelphia also began ministry to Puerto Ricans with social services, but its archbishop, John F. O'Hara, C.S.C., was adamant that this ministry should begin and end with social service, since he felt that any kind of special religious services in Spanish would retard assimilation. It was O'Hara who had suggested to Spellman the idea of replacing the national parish with the integrated parish in New York and as archbishop of Philadelphia his clear ideal was immediate integration, which he and his priests did not hesitate to call by its proper name of "assimilation." Thus the report of the archdiocese of Philadelphia in the 1957 Interdiocesan Meeting of Priests Concerning the Apostolate to the Spanish-Speaking of the East opens with the frank statement that the Spanish-Speaking Apostolate in that archdiocese "has for its objective the assimilation of some 18,000 Puerto Ricans into normal parish life without the formation of any so-called national Puerto Rican Parishes."[29]

Although a small but growing Puerto Rican presence became noticeable by 1950[30] no particular efforts were made to serve them at the ecclesial level until 1953, when the Catholic Interracial Council became involved with the "Puerto Rican problem." This was a lay people's organization, "unofficial and tacitly recognized but not encouraged" by the Philadelphia church authorities.[31] Its moving forces were Robert Callaghan, a prominent and well-connected lawyer with a strong interest in civil rights, and Mrs. Anna McGarry, a dynamic and dedicated widow who was "beginning to emerge as the outstanding lay Catholic in the history of the Philadelphia Archdiocese,"[32] and who had earned the esteem of the city's black community.

When the subhuman conditions of the Puerto Rican barrio were brought to her attention by an Argentinian doctor who was doing research in a Philadelphia hospital, Mrs. McGarry had a meeting with Father Juan Clot, C.M., pastor of the Spanish national parish in the city,[33] to see if that church would be able to institute or sponsor some form of outreach to the Puerto Rican community. Unfortunately she found Father Clot "disillusioned, cynical and uncooperative,"[34] expressing contempt for Puerto Rican religiosity and flatly refusing to discuss any efforts in that direction. In this he probably represented the attitude of "the well established Spanish-speaking citizens of the older generation" who were not from Puerto Rico, and who "were probably embarrassed by the uneducated, rude, former agricultural workers who seemingly were bringing discredit to the entire Spanish-speaking body of

Philadelphians."[35] While his attitudes were not shared by his two curates—one of whom, Father Pedro Masdéu, would in fact succeed him in the pastorate within the year—his negative position effectively closed the door of the city's one Hispanic national parish to any form of Puerto Rican apostolate. By the time Masdéu became pastor it was too late for this, since at that point a different approach had become the official policy of the archdiocese.

On February 15, 1954, about a month after the fruitless interview with Father Clot, Mrs. McGarry and Mr. Callahan visited Archbishop O'Hara and impressed him with tales of Puerto Ricans being lured into Protestant churches by the social services these provided. The archbishop, whose experience in Latin America had left him with the impression that Hispanics were indissolubly wedded to Catholicism by their culture, was quite shaken by this report and agreed to subsidize the setting up of a settlement house in the Puerto Rican barrio, along the lines of Casita María in Spanish Harlem. O'Hara had been in residence at St. Cecilia's in New York at the time of Casita María's foundation and was still a financial supporter of its work. He considered the type of social services provided by such a center more compatible with his ideals of assimilation than national parishes or even a special ministry to Puerto Ricans (taking into consideration their language and culture) in the territorial parishes. As a result of this attitude, when the house which became Casa del Carmen was bought and its use of space was being planned, the archbishop vetoed the setting up of a chapel on the premises. He "envisioned the center as serving only the temporal needs of the Puerto Ricans, who were expected to remain subject to the usual parish structure for their spiritual care."[36]

Archbishop O'Hara resisted any efforts to extend the specific care of Puerto Ricans beyond the purely social service approach of Casa del Carmen for another two years; it was only in 1956 that he began to assign Spanish-speaking priests to parishes with a significant Puerto Rican population and to send some of his seminarians to acquire experience in the island.[37] Rather than in Spanish-language parochial ministry, he placed his faith in the capacity of the Catholic schools to assimilate the next generation and turn them into American Catholics, since "he firmly believed that education could negate domestic influences and parental example."[38] In 1959 he was to say to Mrs. McGarry: "We have 50% of the Puerto Rican children in our parochial schools and in another two years we will have 100%; then their troubles will be over."[39] This

kind of wishful thinking about the prompt Americanization of the
Puerto Rican community seems to have been prevalent in Philadelphia during O'Hara's episcopate. In 1957 the archdiocese's report
at the Interdiocesan Meeting of Priests engaged in the Spanish-
Speaking Apostolate referred hopefully to "a number" of inter-
marriages of Puerto Ricans in the Reading area as a sign of quick
assimilation, and gladly reported that in that town Puerto Rican
Mass attendance was "good" in spite of the fact that the only
concession made to their presence was the reading of the Gospel
in Spanish, which was interpreted as "another indication of feeling
at home in an American parish."[40] Four years later, when Allentown was made a separate diocese from Philadelphia, a parish
in Reading and another in Allentown began to offer services in
Spanish, and in 1965 both were officially designated as "Spanish-
speaking" parishes.[41] The authorities of the new diocese obviously
did not share Philadelphia's sanguine appraisal of the effects of
such integration in their territory. Similarly, whatever percentage
of Puerto Rican children may actually have gone to Philadelphia's
parochial schools, the Puerto Rican community in that city has not
assimilated any more effectively than in any other U.S. city.

West of the Alleghenies the diocese of Youngstown, Ohio, also
chose to respond to the Puerto Rican presence by setting up a
center for social services. Youngstown was a major center for the
iron and steel industry and labor was in great demand and short
supply, since only workers desperate for jobs were willing to put
up with the unavoidably unpleasant conditions, however good the
pay might be. When the 1924 Immigration Laws cut off the supply of European immigrants, the metal industries of Youngstown
turned to black migrants from the South, and when this migration
slowed down around 1950, they turned to Puerto Rico, where many
unemployed men were attracted by the idea of steady work and
good pay. By late 1951 the Puerto Ricans in Youngstown amounted
to two or three thousand.[42]

The Puerto Rican workers became members of the United Steel
Workers of America, which used Spanish-speaking organizers, and
so were not exploited at the workplace. But they were exploited
in other contexts, especially in the field of housing, which was
acutely scarce in Youngstown. Tiny apartments had incredibly high
rents, and even when a man was settled in one of these, he had to
go looking for something larger—and proportionately more exor-
bitant—if he wanted to bring his family over from the island. The
Puerto Ricans' ignorance of English and their unfamiliarity with

the bureaucracy which in America accompanies anything from going to the hospital to paying one's income tax led to a great amount of otherwise avoidable problems.

Since the growth in the steel industry which had attracted the Puerto Ricans to Youngstown was occasioned by the expansion of the national defense program, Bishop Emmet M. Walsh of Youngstown requested the National Catholic Community Service, which was an agency of the United Community Defense Services, to set up some form of program for the Puerto Rican defense workers. As a result of this, the NCCS established a center for Puerto Ricans in Youngstown in August 1952, in a building purchased for this purpose by the St. Vincent de Paul Society and provided rent-free to the center.

The center offered recreational facilities of various types from 10 A.M. to 10 P.M. seven days a week, as well as practical help with issues of housing, health, translation, and English classes. Since it also received funding from secular sources, and its board purposely included not only Catholics but also Protestants and Jews, whites and blacks, it was officially non-denominational. Social problems brought to the center were referred to the competent agency, with the center providing a translator if one was needed, while spiritual problems were referred to a clergyman of the individual's denomination. Along with its initiation and co-sponsorship of the center, the diocese had one full-time Spanish-speaking priest, Joseph Richter, M.S.C., assigned to the needs of Hispanics throughout the city.

It is significant that objections were voiced against the center on the grounds that it resulted in an "undesirable segregation" of the Puerto Ricans from the rest of Youngstown society.[43] The ideal of "integration at once" blinded some persons to the simple fact that the needs of the Puerto Ricans were different from those of other groups, and thus could not be properly met in an integrated milieu. The proponents of the center themselves shared in the common attitude of their time and assumed that its existence would be of a transitory nature. Its purpose was "to help Puerto Ricans to adjust themselves to the manners and customs of the community"[44] rather than to help them preserve their identity or create their own community. "With its objective accomplished, it [would] have no reason for continued existence."[45]

The Puerto Rican community did in fact make itself at home in Youngstown and outgrew its need for the center. But it did not assimilate. In a city where national parishes outnumber the territorial ones, ecclesial integration was simply not practical. By 1959 a regular Spanish Mass was scheduled in the basement of the cathedral, not for the Puerto Ricans of that parish, but for those of the whole city. In 1961 the diocese purchased an old Protestant church on Himrod Avenue and designated it as St. Rose of Lima Spanish-speaking parish. Due to Father Richter's age and declining health, he was not able to be the pastor, and the assignment was given to Father James Channel. Having moved to a different location in 1976, St. Rose's still serves a flourishing Hispanic community.[46]

Also in Ohio, but in the Diocese of Cleveland, is the city of Lorain, whose Puerto Rican colony "is often hailed as the most organized and stable in the United States."[47] Its origin lies in the efforts of the National Tube Company to stabilize its work force by recruiting labor in Puerto Rico, starting in 1947. The recruiters chose to concentrate on the mountain areas, especially the rural barrios of the municipalities of Lares, Utuado, Caguas, and Jayuya because in their opinion "the men we get from there are superior in almost every respect to those available in the coastal towns."[48] This area coincidentally, is also much more devout than the coast, although often rather in terms of traditional religious practices than of institutional regulations.

The workers who were selected had to pass rigorous physical examinations, receive a certificate of good conduct from their local police, and be able to read and write at least in Spanish, since otherwise they would have been unable to read safety signs in the steel mills. Many of them, in fact, were high school graduates.[49] Some of these requirements may seem offensive by our standards, and there probably was a certain amount of racism involved in the decision to recruit in the mountains rather than in the more racially mixed coastal plain.[50] Still, the selectivity of the recruiters certainly contributed to the stability of Lorain's Puerto Rican community. Lorain's distance from the great centers of migration also helped; it meant that most of its community's increase would be either in the form of further recruits or of the relatives of those already there, so that the community would be well-knit to an unusual degree and the least common denominator of skills and education would also be higher than usual.

By 1951 the Puerto Ricans in Lorain had reached about 3,700 and were more than the city's industries could absorb, so that Lorain actually had to place advertisements in the island's press announcing that its factories were no longer seeking workers. The city even asked the Puerto Rican government's Office of Migration to direct Puerto Ricans to other areas. At this time the Ohio Employment Services relocated 1,524 Puerto Rican men from Lorain to places like Youngstown and Cleveland,[51] thus beginning the Puerto Rican communities of those cities.

By the mid-1950s the Puerto Ricans in Lorain were building a stable community with a 98 percent employment rate, and an average salary almost double that of the average New York Puerto Rican's: $66.80 a week compared to New York's $36.28. Lack of adequate housing forced many of the men to leave their families in Puerto Rico for years, but eventually many of them bought vacant land just outside the city limits and began to build houses or else bought and renovated dilapidated houses. At the same time, they began to establish cultural, religious, and social institutions for their community. The first church to serve the Lorain Puerto Ricans was Templo Bethel, founded by Pentecostal members of the Puerto Rican community who pooled their resources and bought an old Baptist church near their lodgings.[52] The Catholic majority of the community had tried to join one or another of the nearby Catholic churches. St. Louis's church, known locally as "St. Lass" (*Szent Lajos*) was a Hungarian national parish and was naturally reluctant to accept a large non-Magyar contingent, which would destroy its character as a center for the Hungarian community. Although it was the church of choice for the majority of the Puerto Ricans, who found it convenient to their lodgings, it was not a territorial parish, and so was under no obligation to minister to people simply because they lived near its buildings. St. John's church, on the other hand, was a territorial parish, and a good number of the 500-strong Lorain Mexican community worshipped there. But there too the Puerto Ricans got a definite feeling that they were not really wanted.[53] Integrating the Puerto Ricans into the existing parochial structures did not seem very promising. At the same time the diocesan authorities disliked the idea of setting up a national parish for fear that "this would hinder the assimilation process."[54] Finally it was decided to set up an ethnic missionary chapel after the pattern offered by the just promulgated Constitution *Exsul Familia*, with the presupposition that its Spanish-speaking staff of Missionary Servants of the Most Holy Trinity "would leave in several years after its mission was complete."[55] On Sunday, September 7, 1952, Father Paul Fredericks, M.S.Ss.T., celebrated the first two Masses at the Capilla del Sagrado Corazón, withan attendance of 121 persons.

By 1955 the chapel was staffed by two Trinitarian priests and four Trinitarian Sisters, of whom two were native Puerto Ricans, and sponsored a Holy Name Society, a Ladies' Altar Guild, and a chapter of the *Hijas de María*, the traditional Puerto Rican confraternity for unmarried young women. Two daily Masses were celebrated, with an attendance of 15 to 20 persons, and four Sunday Masses attended by over 500. About 25 to 75 persons attended the Rosary said in the chapel every evening. The Sisters were engaged in constant house to house visitation—a central apostolate of the *Trinitarias*—and taught religious instruction to adults and children; they also set up a missionary cenacle, by means of which lay persons become involved in the apostolate of this congregation. The chapel also sponsored sports and social activities.[56] While the Puerto Rican Pentecostals had a head start on the Catholics in Lorain, the presence of what *de facto* amounted to a national parish made it the spiritual heart of the Puerto Rican community, to the point that even non-religious historians tend to forget that there are Lorain Puerto Ricans whose lives do *not* revolve around the Capilla.[57]

Sagrado Corazón now celebrates the Liturgy in its own beautiful Spanish-Colonial church built in 1975 by the joint efforts of the Trinitarians and their parishioners. The "temporary" ethnic chapel has been a national parish since 1982, although at the people's insistence its official name remains La Capilla del Sagrado Corazón. With an attendance of about 1,000 families at its five Sunday Masses, it recently celebrated forty years of service to Lorain's Puerto Rican community, and neither the church nor the community it serves give an sign of "melting" into their surroundings.[58]

Some of the Puerto Ricans displaced from Lorain in the early 1950s, when that city's factories stopped hiring, found employment in Cleveland, where they began a community which by the early 1980s would number some 25,000 persons. They settled at first in the east side of the city, "attracted . . . because of their proximity to Our Lady of Fatima Catholic Church and St. Paul's Shrine, where Spanish-speaking Trinitarian priests were located."[59] An unusual number of Trinitarians were fluent in Spanish because of their founder's connections with Puerto Rico, and so it was not surprising that Spanish-speaking priests should be found in some of their parishes which up to that point had no Hispanic population. It is possible that the Trinitarians at Lorain, after the foundation of the Capilla there, may have directed Puerto Ricans leaving for Cleveland to their confreres in that city. Other Cleveland parishes did not welcome the new arrivals and often opposed the celebration of "Spanish Masses."[60]

By the late 1950s the area near St. Paul's and Fatima was deteriorating, and the Puerto Ricans began to move away from it to an area closer to the steel mills and other factories where most of them worked. From that period on, the Trinitarians held Spanish Masses at a number of non-Trinitarian parishes in the new Puerto Rican neighborhoods. This arrangement had obvious drawbacks, but it was not until 1975 that, "as a result of determined and sustained efforts by many of Greater Cleveland's Puerto Ricans,"[61] the national parish of San Juan Bautista was established by the newly arrived Bishop James A. Hickey. One of its former pastors, Father Domingo Rodríguez, has recently been elected General Custodian of the Missionary Servants of the Most Holy Trinity, the first time a Puerto Rican has headed an American congregation.

While its numbers could never compare with New York's during the period discussed in this essay, the Puerto Rican community in Chicago was without doubt the second largest in the mainland.[62] At the religious level the importance of the archdiocese of Chicago and its reputation for creative approaches to ministry gave Chicago's Puerto Rican apostolate an importance quite out of proportion with the number of Puerto Ricans in that city.

The Puerto Rican community in Chicago numbered about 240 persons in 1940.[63] By 1946 the community began to grow as a result of contracted labor recruited by the Castle, Barton, and Associates contracting company; some of these contracts were for foundry work, as in the other Midwestern cities we have covered, and others were for domestic service. In both cases, as it turned out, the terms and the actual implementation of the contracts were of an exploitative nature. As these persons began to realize that there were other employers in the city who were willing to give them better salaries and better treatment they often broke their contracts and moved on to these more attractive factories. They were helped in their plight by members of the small colony of Puerto Ricans already established in Chicago, and by a number of Puerto Ricans of the elite classes who were students at the University of Chicago; among these were Muna Muñoz Lee, daughter of the governor of Puerto Rico, and the future sociologist Elena Padilla.[64]

The Church also came to their help in the persons of Monsignor Peter Meagan and Auxiliary Bishop Bernard Sheil, founder of the CYO. This organization started a Puerto Rican project to deal with housing, employment, and health problems, as well as providing recreational opportunities (such as a weekly dance) which helped to break the individuals' isolation in a strange city.[65] By 1947 a *Sociedad Católica Puertorriqueña* had been founded in Chicago under the auspices of the CYO.[66] Indeed, the CYO club house at Congress and Wabash streets became so important that the Puerto Ricans began to move into the area so as to live near it.[67] Manuel Martínez sees this incipient concentration as the beginnings of a first Puerto Rican neighborhood, but Sheil saw it as the beginning of a Puerto Rican ghetto, and great efforts were made to spread them around in different parts of the city.[68] Once again, as so often happened in that period, the ideal of integration, which socially conscious American Catholics transferred to Puerto Ricans from their work with blacks, tended to work against the Puerto Rican desire for community building.

In the early 1950s, as relatively small but increasing numbers of Puerto Ricans began to look further afield than New York City, the Chicago community began to grow significantly. At first these migrants lived dispersed among the other ethnic and racial groups in the city, wherever they could find apartments. However, according to Felix Padilla, "in the majority of the cases Puerto Ricans lived in segregated ethnic enclaves within these communities. . . . The fact that Puerto Ricans might have shared certain communities in the city with other groups does not mean that they lived in integrated communities."[69] It is probable, of course, that this lack of integration was in part a result of prejudice on the part of the non–Puerto Ricans among whom they lived. But it certainly had just as much to do with the Puerto Rican preference for mixing with people who also spoke their language, and who approached life, on both trivial and important issues, from the same points of view as they.

As a result, and in spite of the wishes of their American bene-factors, a number of Puerto Rican neighborhoods began to emerge. Among these the area around Division Street became during the 1950s and 1960s the "headquarters" of the Puerto Rican commu-nity; the Chicago counterpart of New York's el Barrio. This was per-ceived by Americans as a ghetto, and in many ways it was; housing and facilities were substandard and the city's services were not delivered as promptly and efficiently as in other neighborhoods. It was also a ghetto insofar as the racism of the more established ethnic groups made it hard for Puerto Ricans to move out of the area except to other Puerto Rican neighborhoods. But it should be kept in mind that there were also many reasons for Puerto Ricans to choose and prefer to live in the barrio even if they had been welcome elsewhere. Here was a neighborhood where everyone spoke Spanish, where the *bodegas* sold their kind of products and the restaurants served their kind of food. It was a place where they felt at home in the middle of an alien city, and the territorial base which every community needs in order to develop and conserve its identity.

At the same time, a number of civic and recreational organizations, hometown clubs and newspapers began to develop, which struggled to preserve and reinforce Puerto Rican identity and values, and to serve the peculiar needs of the Puerto Rican community. At this point an organization was founded which marked a turning point in the history of the relationship of the Church in Chicago with that city's Puerto Rican community: the Caballeros de San Juan. This group originated in 1954, when Father Leo Mahon, a recently ordained priest who had volunteered to work in the mainly black neighborhood of Woodlawn, was approached by a number of Puerto Rican men from the area, who asked him for help in organizing a program to improve their conditions in the area.[70] Father Mahon became more and more involved with this group, and eventually they decided "to form an organization that would do for Puerto Ricans what other social agencies and religious organizations had done for European immigrants—to help with work and wages, health and housing, the difficulties of adjustment of an essentially rural population to the conditions of a city environment and of modern life."[71]

As the name they chose for their organization indicates, the model—although not slavishly followed—was the Knights of Columbus, an organization at once solidly Catholic, but not primarily devotional. Thus it would seek to attract the "unchurched" Puerto Ricans by social, fraternal, and other secular advantages, on the assumption that one could not became a "practicing Catholic by *American* Catholic standards"[72] until one had developed "good social values."[73] Setting up Puerto Rican councils of the Knights of Columbus or integrating Puerto Ricans into existing ones was considered impractical because this organization presupposed the "social values" and Catholic practice which had to be instilled into the Puerto Rican community. While the Caballeros made no bones about being a Catholic organization, by design they admitted to membership men who did not attend Mass regularly or whose marital situation did not meet official Catholic standards.[74] Once they had come under the influence of the Church, they could slowly be attracted to Mass, the sacraments, yearly retreats, and other religious practices. This attraction, especially in the case of the group's leaders, could reach the point of arm-twisting. Padilla reproduces a letter from Father Mahon to the manager of one of the sports teams sponsored by Los Caballeros which, while decrying the idea of *forcing* the team members to attend a certain retreat, exhorts him vehemently to do "everything in your power to get them all out there." The recipient of the letter, however, was given no free choice: "It goes without saying that you as the manager should make the retreat. I expect you to lead your men on the right road and I can hardly think of a reason that would excuse you from making the retreat."[75]

In 1954 the new organization fulfilled an important need in the Puerto Rican community, and did so under the auspices of an entity—the Catholic Church—which was highly respected both in the community and in the wider American milieu, and under the leadership of a young man of no mean talent and charisma. Within a year it was also able to employ a number of organizers trained in the methods of Saul Alinsky, whose salaries were paid by the archdiocese. As a result the Caballeros de San Juan experienced a very rapid growth: by 1957 they had five councils in Chicago and two more in process of formation; by 1964 they had eleven and eventually came to have thirteen.[76] From 1955 to the early 1960s the Caballeros were practically synonymous with Puerto Rican leadership in Chicago. The organization provided "the primary means by which Puerto Ricans began to structure a self-conscious community for ethnic advancement and betterment."[77] It was in Los Caballeros that a whole generation of Chicago's Puerto Rican leaders acquired both leadership skills and a group following. "In fact," says Padilla, "this 'elite', the founders and leaders of the organization, went on to dominate Puerto Rican life well into the 1960s; they ran the social affairs, organized the civic ventures, and acted as spokesmen for Chicago's Puerto Ricans in matters of group concern."[78]

A year after the foundation of the Caballeros de San Juan, in the fall of 1955, Cardinal Stritch set up the Cardinal's Committee for the Spanish Speaking in Chicago. In spite of its title this committee concentrated almost exclusively on the Puerto Ricans since the Mexicans, who were at least twice as many as the Puerto Ricans, had been for decades served by three national parishes under the care of the Claretian Fathers, and it was feared that any efforts in this direction would be perceived by them as interference.[79] Under the chairmanship of the archdiocesan chancellor, the committee consisted of twenty-one priests and lay persons "who set the policies for [Hispanic] work in the archdiocese."[80] The executive staff consisted of Father Gilbert Carroll as coordinator, Father Mahon as executive assistant, Nicholas Von Hoffman and Lester Hunt as full-time organizers for the Puerto Rican community, and another organizer (a Mexican layman) for work among the Mexican community, as well as a secretary.[81]

The first decision of the Cardinal's Committee was to rule out the national parish for ministry to the Puerto Ricans. The only two reasons given in any account of this decision are that "Puerto Ricans did not and could not bring their priests with them from the Island" and that they "were spread too thinly through the city for this to be practical."[82] Carroll adds that "of course there were other reasons," but does not specify them; Mahon simply says that the decision was taken "for reasons too complicated to explain here."[83] It is pretty clear from other statements made in the sources that the unexplained "other reasons" were firstly, the desire to mold the Puerto Ricans as soon as possible into the image of American Catholicism, which goal would be retarded by the national parish, and the committee's preference for the community organization model already started by the Caballeros de San Juan, which was perceived as both more creative and more compatible with the goal of integration. This was, of course, expressed and perceived by the Americans involved in terms of "welcoming the Puerto Ricans" to share the life and ethos of what they considered the most vital form of Catholicism in the Universal Church; to be left out of this would be a tragedy. Thus *America* reported that Cardinal Stritch "inaugurated a policy of helping Puerto Ricans to 'integrate themselves religiously, socially and economically' into the life of the city. . . . 'We are making all our institutions available to them. We are encouraging them to go to churches and schools in their neighborhoods. There will be no special churches devoted to them.' "[84]

The "Chicago approach" to the Puerto Rican apostolate, therefore, consisted of a firm commitment to the integrated parish model, combined with community organizing and a heavy social action emphasis. It was through the latter two that the "unchurched" Puerto Ricans—i.e., that great majority which was perceived by the Chicago pastoral agents as "hardly Catholic" because they lived their faith by their old cultural traditions rather than by institutional involvement—would be first attracted and then socialized into the American Catholic ethos. Thus the Chicago approach was, just as much as New York's, basically assimila- tionist. Just as Cardinal Spellman hoped to be able to discontinue the Spanish Masses and other special services within one gener- ation, so Father Mahon, when speaking or writing to American clerical audiences, openly expected the Caballeros de San Juan to fade away after the goal of integration had been achieved. This organization, like anything else which in any way represented a concession to the differences between American and Puerto Rican cultures, was by its very nature provisional and temporary.[85]

In this attitude, which was central to the Chicago approach, the archdiocese was unwittingly at cross purposes with the instinctive but persistent aspirations of the Puerto Rican community, which wanted rather to consolidate and preserve its identity and heritage. Thus the archdiocese insisted on perceiving the Puerto Ricans' situation as a social justice problem, in which Puerto Ricans were the victims of discrimination, and it therefore saw integration/ assimilation as the ultimate solution. It did not see, or did not approve, their desire for the creation of a *permanent* community which would relate to the American community, but not be ab- sorbed into it. In Padilla's words, "the Church could not, due to its own relationship with American society, help the Puerto Ricans resist the violation of their culture and personal identity."[86]

As a result in the 1960s the Church lost its position of leader- ship in the Chicago Puerto Rican community. The very approach which it had taken of starting from secular needs in the hope of attracting the people to religious practice eventually backfired; other groups, often more identified with the Puerto Ricans' aspira- tions to identity, arose in competition to the Caballeros, or became rivals to the clergy in influencing their membership. Thus in 1964 Fathers Carroll and Headley (Mahon's successor in the Cardinal's Committee) complained about the influence of the local office of the Commonwealth of Puerto Rico on some of the councils. This influence, in their mind, "tends to confuse the community rather than unite it"[87] because the office has "managed to maintain the 'Expatriate Citizen' point of view in the people."[88]

The very leaders of the Caballeros, who had been trained in leadership and community organization, moved on to other groups and causes, and often used their skills to perpetuate that Puerto Rican solidarity and distinctness out of which the group's clerical leaders had hoped to ease them—although they always retained an outspoken love and admiration for Father Mahon. While leaders primarily attracted by the secular aspects of the Caballeros were dropping out for yet more secular pursuits, those attracted to the more spiritual aspects had formed, under Father Mahon's direction, a lay community called Los Hermanos de la Familia de Dios, whose principal work was catechizing in the parishes, but who also were committed to a more intense spiritual life, with frequent reception of the Sacraments and daily Scriptural reading.[89] This was to a certain degree modeled on the Puerto Rican Hermanos Cheos, a community of lay preachers who had spontaneously arisen in the *campos* of the island at the beginning of the century and had eventually been approved by the bishops,[90] but it also anticipated groups such as the *Comunidades de Base* and RENEW. However, just as the more secularly oriented element in the Caballeros moved on into purely secular pursuits, so by the late 1960s many of the Hermanos moved on to the permanent diaconate, to the disgust of some of the early founders, who at first had encouraged the diaconate "as that which could take clericalism out of the Church," but in the end came to believe that it merely turned good laymen into ersatz clerics.[91]

Ultimately the decline of the Caballeros de San Juan—which now survives only as a credit union—was a result of the organization's commitment to "the elusive but ultimate goal of equality by means of accommodation."[92] In the 1950s this was the only acceptable approach, and while it did not really capture the Puerto Ricans' enthusiasm, they went along with it in order to improve their situation—although whenever they were left alone to start their own programs or clubs these tended to emphasize what united the community and gave it its identity (*Puertorriqueñismo*) rather than what united them to the wider community (*Americanismo*). As we mentioned in an earlier chapter, while they were not willing to see themselves as anti-American, neither did they have any real wish to assimilate and become *Americanos*. With the arrival of the 1960s—which as a cultural rather than chronological phenomenon lasted not from 1960 to 1969 but from 1965 to 1975—it became for the first time respectable to question the universal validity of the American Way, and to consciously and overtly desire to retain one's own culture, rejecting the ideal of integration/assimilation. At that point the program of the Caballeros de San Juan, to which its clerical leaders were unshakeably committed, came to be out of touch with the community's now conscious aspirations and "its ability to speak for the Puerto Rican community faded."[93] The liberal and creative approaches of Mahon and Headley in Chicago ultimately had no more success than the conservative approach of Cardinal Spellman in New York precisely because of what both approaches had in common: the desire to transform the Puerto Ricans into American Catholics, whether of the pre-Conciliar or post-Conciliar stamp, and the refusal to wholeheartedly accept and cooperate with the U.S. Puerto Rican community's unyielding desire to remain Puerto Rican.

Conclusion

Central to the relationship between the American Church and the Puerto Rican people in its midst has been the issue of *Identity* Over the nineteenth century the Puerto Ricans had come to identify themselves as a distinct people. With the change of sovereignty in 1898, this identity came to be centered on the Spanish language, and on the culture and ethos of the island, which were basically Spanish, although modified by history, climate, and the presence of Native American, and more importantly, of African elements.

In the early part of the twentieth century the American government took strong measures to Americanize the Puerto Rican people, primarily by means of a public school system in which English was the compulsory language of instruction. While this effort succeeded in creating widespread functional bilingualism at least in the middle and upper classes, Puerto Ricans as a whole remained Spanish-speaking among themselves, and refused to treat English as anything but a second language.

In 1917, and over the protests of the island's elected Assembly, American citizenship was unilaterally conferred on all Puerto Ricans. Eventually the majority of the people came to accept this citizenship, which brought with it a number of advantages—and to which there was no viable alternative. But the overwhelming majority of the people still identified as Puerto Ricans rather than as Americans. While by the middle of the century only a minority was formally and militantly committed to the independence of the island, Puerto Ricans as a whole saw the United States and Puerto Rico as two countries, each with its own territory, flag, and language. The United States might be a great and noble country, and it might exercise a benign protectorate over their island, but it was not their country. They were *Puertorriqueños*, not *Americanos*. As don Luis Muñoz Marin, the island's first elected governor, once put it, Puerto Rico was "a Latin American country composed of good citizens of the United States."[1] To this day, after close to a century under the American flag, the overwhelming majority of Puerto Ricans quietly but quite stubbornly refuse both independence from the United States—which they have come to perceive as economically and politically dangerous—and Americanization at any but the most superficial levels—which they perceive as a betrayal of their deepest self. Any efforts to deal with the Puerto Rican people which ignore this psychological need to preserve their identity, and the deep-seated loyalty to the language and culture which embody it, is in the long run doomed to failure.

This Puerto Rican culture was strongly pervaded by an Iberian Catholic tradition. But due to historical circumstances this tradition was not centered, for the majority of the people, on the institutional Church, but on a Catholic worldview which had been transmitted from generation to generation by means of images, prayers, and popular customs and devotions. The Mass and the sacraments, as well as the ecclesiastical authorities, were not irrelevant to this popular Catholicism. But the scarcity of clergy, as well as long distances and bad roads, made these elements of Catholicism unusual and extraordinary in the lives of the peasants. On a day to day basis it was the popular religiosity which sustained them in their trials and expressed their joys, and therefore it was to this traditional religiosity that they gave their loyalty.

Just as the change of sovereignty in 1898 brought a concerted effort to Americanize the Puerto Rican people at the secular level, so the new American hierarchy tried to re-make Puerto Rican Catholicism after the pattern of the American church. The local seminary was closed and candidates for the priesthood were sent to American seminaries, American religious orders were invited to the island, a Catholic school system was set up, and American-style lay societies were encouraged. By the 1950s these efforts seemed to be bearing fruit, but the elections of 1960, which were won by the Popular Democratic Party against the overt opposition of the hierarchy, showed that while Puerto Ricans remained a very religious people, the institutional Church did not control their relationship with God.

The problem of identity became particularly acute when Puerto Ricans began to migrate to the mainland in massive numbers about the year 1945. The overwhelming majority of these immigrants were from the poorer classes, so they did not have articulate leaders to speak for their wishes and interests. Since native vocations in Puerto Rico were at an all-time low, no Puerto Rican priests could be spared to accompany the migrants and minister to them in their new environment, and incidentally to serve as leaders and spokesmen for their people. At the same time the ease with which they could travel to and from the island helped to reinforce their Puerto Rican identity, keeping them in close touch with their language and culture. The very fact that they were already American citizens paradoxically served to retard assimilation, since there was no moment of decision in which they would have had to say "I am no longer a Puerto Rican; I am now by choice an American." Precisely because the American flag waved over their *patria*, and because even there everyone was an American citizen, it was possible to live in New York or Chicago and still consider oneself *Puertorriqueño* rather than *Americano* with no wish to become the latter.

This lack of enthusiasm, indeed this distaste, for the idea of becoming American, or of perceiving the United States as their land, is an important difference between the Puerto Ricans and other immigrant groups. In the early years it led to a general feeling that individuals were there on a temporary basis; that the purpose of coming to the mainland was not to settle there, but to make enough money to return home in a better economic situation. As time went by a significant number of Puerto Ricans began to sink roots in the mainland and to realize at least half-consciously that they were there to stay. But it is significant that they did not then choose, by analogy with other immigrant groups, to call themselves "Puerto Rican–Americans" a term which is to this day practically unheard of.[2] Instead, in the 1960s, they coined the term "New Yorican," as if saying (to paraphrase Gertrude Stein) "Puerto Rico is our country, New York is our home town."

The Great Puerto Rican Migration arrived at a time when Americans were laying a strong emphasis on assimilation and Americanization. Race was also an important issue in American society, with conservatives wanting to keep the society divided along color lines, while liberals insisted on a policy of integration which decried the segregation of Americans, who shared the same values and culture, into separate and unequal compartments. Since Puerto Ricans were a racially mixed group, they were exposed to prejudice along racial lines. But their insistence on dividing people by language and culture rather than by color did not only mean that the lighter skinned Puerto Ricans refused to blend into white America and avoid prejudice. It also meant that both light and dark Puerto Ricans held on to the very values which made them "foreign," and that they were not attracted by integration at the price of losing their identity.

For historical reasons, the Catholic Church in the United States had come to emphasize very strongly its character as a truly American institution, and as the best vehicle for Americanizing the immigrants. These attitudes were particularly forceful in the 1940s and 1950s, and they led the American clergy to desire and promote the Americanization of the Puerto Ricans, and their integration into the American church and society, at the speediest possible pace. This led to the rejection of the national parish model by the archdiocese of New York, a decision which was widely imitated as Puerto Ricans spread to other cities. Especially in the 1940s, concerned clergy tended to discourage the formation of any kind of Puerto Rican community, since such communities would retard Americanization and integration.

These efforts of the American clergy were made in good faith, but they were at cross-purposes with the basic aspirations of the Puerto Rican people. As a result a Puerto Rican community did develop in the United States, but it developed around secular clubs and organizations, and around Protestant storefront churches which were run by Puerto Rican ministers in a Puerto Rican style. Hence, although most Puerto Ricans in the mainland still identify as Catholics, the Church as an institution is to a great degree peripheral to the Puerto Rican community.

Even within the Church, however, pastoral realities dictated a compromise with the Puerto Ricans' need to be served as Puerto Ricans. By the 1950s George Kelly's *Catholic Survey* had demonstrated that Puerto Ricans were not being effectively served in the "integrated parishes," and under the leadership of Joseph Fitzpatrick, S.J., and Ivan Illich an effort was launched to produce a sufficient number of bilingual priests in the archdiocese of New York. Illich especially insisted that functional mastery of Spanish was not enough; in order to serve Puerto Ricans the American priests would have to be able to step outside of their inherited values and worldview, and look at the world through Puerto Rican eyes. This effectively meant that to some degree the bilingual curate in an integrated parish would become the center of a Puerto Rican community: the very "parish within the parish" which had been considered undesirable in the previous decade. Without giving up on the integrated parish model, the archdiocese had to quietly back away from its program of immediate integration and Americanization.

This tacit compromise had two flaws, however. In the first place, the integrated parish was still perceived to be centered on the American parishioners. The Puerto Rican community developing within it felt itself treated as a secondary entity and did not feel that the parish belonged to them. Hence they in turn were not committed to it and tended to give it minimal support. Secondly, the bilingual priests on the whole found it easier to learn Spanish than to really understand the Puerto Rican culture and worldview. In many cases this meant that they still were trying their best to Americanize and integrate their Puerto Rican parishioners, even as the latter were trying to build a Puerto Rican community around them. In other cases, especially in the 1960s, the priests trained by Illich gave up the traditional American Catholic ethos, but did not replace it by a Puerto Rican Catholicism. Rather, they replaced it by the radical, secular, and countercultural mentality of that decade and strove to convince the Puerto Ricans that they, too, should exchange their traditional approaches for the new ones. Both types of priests were often well loved by the Puerto Ricans in their parishes for their personal qualities. But their agendas were at cross-purposes with the need of the community to preserve its identity, and in the long run they did not succeed in attracting the Puerto Ricans to their worldview or to their goals.

An important development in the 1960s was the coming of the Cursillos de Cristiandad. This movement was designed to involve Latin men—traditionally aloof from religion—into a new concept of Christianity, centered on grace and the sacraments rather than on traditional practices of piety. Lay persons had by design an important part in the running of the actual Cursillo weekend and of the movement itself. Because the Cursillos caught on much more successfully among Hispanics than among Americans, and because the priests associated with its direction tended to be Spaniards or Latin Americans, the Cursillo became the one important element in the religious life of the Puerto Ricans in the mainland which was centered on their culture, worked in their language, and where they had an opportunity to exercise real leadership, and to acquire leadership skills. It is difficult to overestimate the importance of the Cursillo movement as a vehicle for the creation and preservation of a Puerto Rican Catholic community in the United States. An idea of its importance in the mind of the community may be gathered from the fact that of the persons questioned in the New York Archdiocesan Survey of Hispanics in 1981, 43 percent said that the Cursillo was important in their lives, while only 25.9 percent thought the Second Vatican Council was important to them. Conversely, 59.8 percent of the Hispanics surveyed had never heard of the Council, while only 31.2 percent had never heard of the Cursillo.[3]

The Second Vatican Council, however, has had a number of results which have affected the life of the U.S. Puerto Rican community to an important degree. Of these, the most influential has been the vernacular liturgy, and the encouragement of inculturation by the Constitution on the Liturgy.[4] This meant that the "Spanish Mass" in the integrated parishes would no longer be a Latin Mass with a Spanish sermon, but a Mass celebrated entirely in Spanish— while the other Masses would be celebrated entirely in English. When inculturation was added to mere translation, the Spanish and English Masses began to differ not only in language, but also in the general flavor of the whole event. As a result going to the English Mass became a much more "alien" experience than it had been in the 1950s. The coming of the vernacular thus raised a serious obstacle to any eventual integration of the Americans and Puerto Ricans in the integrated parish into one worshipping community. It reinforced the sense of being a community with its own identity, and centered around a Eucharistic celebration which was unmistakably its own—celebrated in the community's own language and expressed in terms of its culture.

The Council's theology of the laity opened the door to a much greater involvement of lay people in leadership positions in the Church. This was a special opportunity for Cursillistas, who already had training and practice within their movement, to exercise leadership both in the liturgy and in the community. But on the whole Puerto Rican Catholics have not been responsive to the religious valuation of the secular which was such an important result of *Gaudium et Spes* in the American Catholic community. Efforts on the part of American priests and religious to transmit their theology of secular involvement to the Puerto Rican community were on the whole not successful. For reasons that have not been sufficiently analyzed, Puerto Ricans prefer to pursue secular goals in a purely secular spirit, keeping religion out of them, and to pursue religious experience in frankly "sacral" terms. Efforts to combine the two seem to make them uncomfortable and tend to meet passive resistance. A movement like César Chávez's strikes, which at once sacralizes a secular struggle for better conditions and brings secular concerns into liturgy and prayer seems to be incapable of obtaining a large following among Puerto Ricans. The Theology of Liberation has not only left them indifferent, but is regarded with clear hostility in many quarters—especially among the Charismatics.

The new ecumenical spirit ushered in by the Council has had little impact on the Puerto Rican community, because, unlike the "mainline" Churches, the overwhelming majority of the Protestants with whom they come in contact are bitterly anti-Catholic and not open to mutually respectful dialogue. It has had, however, a very important indirect effect. The Ecumenical Movement made possible the rise of the Charismatic Renewal among American Catholics. In its origins this tended to appeal to educated American Catholics and had no impact on the U.S. Puerto Rican community. But in late 1971 a team of American priests gave a Charismatic retreat in Aguas Buenas, P.R., where many of the participants received the Baptism of the Spirit, and the movement began to spread rapidly in the island, especially among the popular classes. Once it had caught on in Puerto Rico, the renewal spread from there to the Puerto Rican community in the mainland and has attracted a sizeable and enthusiastic following.[5] This movement, too, has contributed to the growth of lay leadership in the community. But as a popular movement with a strong emotional appeal and with many affinities to Pentecostal theology, it is a problematic element in the Hispanic Catholic community. For many it has been a means of enriching their Catholic experience, but for many others—individuals and even groups—it has proved a bridge out of Catholicism into independent Charismatic churches. It has also introduced a strong element of fundamentalism and moral rigidity into the Spanish-speaking Catholic community.[6]

Finally, the Council's restoration of the permanent diaconate has had an important impact on the creation of a Puerto Rican Catholic community. One of the great obstacles to this development had been the great scarcity of Puerto Rican priests in the island itself at the time of the Great Migration, which had resulted in the immigrants' dependence on the ministry of American priests committed to assimilation and integration. While some Puerto Rican vocations arose eventually among the second and third generations, the law of celibacy and the educational requirements for ordination have kept the number of Puerto Rican priests in the mainland pitifully small. The emergence of the permanent diaconate, which has no celibacy rule and whose training is within the reach of persons with only a high school education, allowed many of the leaders who had emerged from the Cursillo and Charismatic movements to seek ordination. In this way the community came to have ordained leaders who had risen from its ranks, who could be seen vested at the altar on Sunday or presiding at Baptisms and other sacraments, but who were also seen in overalls at the factory or shopping with their wives at the local *bodega*. They were married clergy, and clergy which had not been assimilated into the middle class or the American ethos by the seminary experience.

Many American Catholic leaders, and indeed many leaders among other Hispanic ethnic groups, tend to have a negative evaluation of the permanent diaconate, which they perceive as turning good lay leaders into pseudo-clerics. But at least in the Puerto Rican community they serve a most important function. They are canonically, theologically, and sacramentally just as truly ordained clerics as any priest, but sociologically they live a lay lifestyle, and are therefore closer to the people than most priests can be. The Puerto Rican Catholic community has more than enough lay leaders, but it has hardly any priests. The Puerto Rican permanent deacons thus have become their community's "native clergy," a source of pride and validation who represent them at the altar in a way which neither the American priest nor the Puerto Rican lector or cantor can.

As the year which saw the closing of the Second Vatican Council and the beginning of its implementation, 1965 is therefore a turning point in the history of the Puerto Rican Catholic community. In the secular world as well 1965 was the beginning of a new climate of opinion in American society, and this change too impacted the U.S. Puerto Rican community—not only in its relations with American society but also with the American Church.

The assassinations of John and Robert Kennedy, the souring of the Civil Rights movement and the murder of Martin Luther King, the rise of the "counterculture" and the growing disillusionment with the war in Vietnam led to a general questioning of accepted American ideals; of the moral purity of America and the superiority of the "American Way." These developments made possible a resurgence of ethnic identification among ethnic groups which had up to then been considered substantially assimilated; whose members had been busily insisting they were "just American" and had not passed on their language to the next generation. Now these groups began to learn the ancestral languages and to take pride in what made them different from other Americans.

These developments affected Puerto Ricans in a different way. All through the period from 1945 to 1965, the Puerto Ricans had been quietly resisting Americanization; holding on to their language and culture, refusing to self-identify as *Americanos*, and trying to build Puerto Rican communities wherever they settled, rather than integrating into the American community. But in the climate of the 1940s and 1950s all this by necessity had to be done quietly, almost instinctively, while outwardly accepting the assimilationist agendas of the larger society, at least by a silence which could be taken for consent. Before 1965 it is difficult to find a clear statement of resistance to assimilation; to discover how the Puerto Ricans really felt one has to study what they said when they were off-guard, and what they did when they were left to do what came naturally. After 1965 it became possible to say these things explicitly. Groups like the Young Lords became openly anti-American, but the majority of U.S. Puerto Ricans simply went on with their traditional attitude of saying "America is a very nice country, but it is not our country." The first half of that sentence was much more positive than what many Americans were saying at the time, but the second half went far beyond the "ethnic revival." But in both of its parts it did not really represent a change from the attitudes of the Puerto Ricans in the previous decades.

In spite of the new respectability of ethnic identities, however, the American Church did not noticeably change its policies towards Puerto Ricans. The hierarchical Church continued to be committed to the policy of the integrated parish. And the "radical Church" chose to see Puerto Ricans not as a nationality, but as one more oppressed minority, which should unite with all other oppressed minorities in one struggle to change the structures of oppression. They did not perceive that Puerto Ricans felt most oppressed precisely by the expectation that they should give up their most prized possessions—their identity, their language and their culture—to melt into a larger unity, whether it was the mainstream culture or the generic category of "oppressed peoples."

In the 1980s and 1990s the accepted attitude to the plurality of ethnic groups, both in American society and in the American Church, has come to be "multiculturalism." This also presents serious problems for the Puerto Ricans, insofar as they do not so much desire to have the mainstream culture accept or adopt certain parts of their culture as to be allowed to hold on to their own culture without accepting any parts of the mainstream culture which they do not choose to adopt. In terms of the Church, they do not want a fair part in a great multicultural celebration; they want to be allowed to celebrate their own Spanish Mass and to express themselves in terms of their own culture. If the Americans too celebrate their Mass exclusively in terms of their own culture, why shouldn't they? Why should Americans give up their identity, and Puerto Ricans theirs, in order to form one new people? Throughout their relationship with the American people and with the American Church, Puerto Ricans have only asked for one thing: let us be ourselves. This is all they ask. And quietly, without confrontations or declarations, but very stubbornly, they will not settle for less.

PART II

Cuban Catholics in the United States

Lisandro Pérez

1

The Catholic Church in Cuba:
A Weak Institution

> I have come to believe that in this country there has never been a religious base; that is to say, that we Spaniards have not been fortunate, for that which characterizes us and which we have taken everywhere, religion, we did not bring here. . . .
> —Ramón Fernández Piérola y López de Luzuriaga, Bishop of Havana, August 4, 1880[1]

After only eight months on the job, Havana's Spanish-born bishop reached a conclusion that Cuban historians have since consistently espoused: the Church never had as profound an impact on Cuba as it had on the rest of the Spanish colonies of the New World. Foreign observers of the island have long noted the distinctly secular character of Cuban society. During his trip to Cuba in 1859 the American writer Richard Henry Dana noted that

> there existed, naturally enough, a vast amount of practical infidelity among the people, and especially among the men, who it is said, scarcely recognized religious obligations at all.[2]

Robert Porter, sent by President McKinley to Cuba in 1898, made the same assessment with respect to religiosity and gender:

> Generally speaking, the Cuban men . . . do not pay much attention to religious observances, leaving that duty mainly to the women.[3]

Half a century later, another foreign observer of Cuba, the Dominican Juan Bosch, argued that the Catholic Church "abstained from deforming the Cuban soul with fanaticisms and persecutions, so that hedonism has taken possession of the Cubans."[4]

The historian Calixto Masó was direct in his assessment of religiosity in Cuba:

> Cubans have always given scant importance to religious problems, and although they are not atheists, they are not fanatics, and their religiosity, particularly in the practice of their religious obligations, virtually borders on indifference . . . that is why in Cuba religion was never a factor in the political process. . . . [5]

The relative lack of religiosity has been accompanied by the weakness of the Church as a social institution in Cuban society. One indication of that weakness is that the hierarchy of the Cuban Church, even in colonial times, lacked the political clout that its counterparts tended to wield throughout Latin America. Dana observed in 1859 that "the Roman Catholic Church has now neither civil nor political power in Cuba."[6]

At the close of both the nineteenth century and Spanish rule in Cuba, Manuel Santander y Frutos, the successor of Fernández Piérola in the bishopric of Havana, was engaged in a constant—and losing—battle to retain the traditional authority of the Church over a wide range of social matters, especially burials and marriages. The colonial authorities were permitting Protestants to establish cemeteries and they were requiring couples to appear before a civil magistrate in order to be wed. Furthermore, the political and fiscal discretion of the bishop was being continually circumscribed by the island's government.

The correspondence of Santander reveals a man—and a Church—frustrated and under siege. To the papal nuncio in Madrid he wrote: "the pattern here is simply to oppress and vex the Church."[7] To the Minister of the Colonies in Madrid he complained: "I have argued for what I thought just . . . and I have made all possible concessions, and have obtained nothing. The Church is treated as if the [civil] administrators were themselves the Protestants."[8]

The traditional powerlessness of the Cuban Catholic Church was already evident many years before when it lost its financial autonomy to the administrators who represented the Bourbon monarchs.[9] It would also be evident many years later when the Church was totally ineffective in its efforts to influence and mediate in order to prevent a civil war in the closing years of Batista's dictatorship.[10]

The comparative weakness of the Church in Cuba, the relative absence of religiosity, and the scant observance of Catholic practices in the general population can be traced to five interrelated historical phenomena, the combination of which was unique to Cuba among the former colonies of Spain.

THE ROLE OF HAVANA AS A PORT CITY

By the middle of the sixteenth century, Cuba had become an abandoned outpost of the empire as the mineral riches which the Spanish sought were found not in the island, but in the mainland of the new continent.[11] The trade which those riches spurred, however, led to the establishment of the *flota* system. Designed to protect valuable cargo from attacks by pirates, the flota system involved large convoys of ships that sailed to and from Spain and either Veracruz or Cartagena. By the close of the sixteenth century, Havana had become the axis of that extensive trade network, as the large flotas would always make a lengthy stopover there, outfitting themselves for the remainder of the voyage.[12]

Cuba's role—with Havana at its head—as a collection of ports servicing the Spanish flota became established and would remain the island's principal function for Spain throughout most of the remainder of the colonial period. This meant, of course, that Havana flourished while the hinterland languished.[13]

The major Spanish settlements on the American continent were typically established in inland and remote locations on or near Indian settlements. That relative isolation contributed to the firm establishment of the Church from the very founding of those settlements and to the development of religiosity, with an emphasis on the sacred.

In contrast, Havana was a crossroads and developed all the characteristics usually associated with busy port cities.

> Havana early acquired a tawdry appearance and became a city teeming with merchants, vendors, gamblers, deserters, and peddlers. . . . Many passengers arrived weighed down with fortunes made on the mainland, and relieving them of this weight engaged the resourcefulness of *habaneros* of all sectors of society. Lodging and dining facilities increased . . . retail trade expanded. So too did illicit trade and commercialized vice. Brothels early established something of a ubiquitous presence in Havana.[14]

Throughout the early colonial period, clerics worried and complained about the "immorality" of Havana, with so many "mariners and transients."[15] Hugh Thomas described Havana as "unique, easy-going, brilliant but semi-criminal, maritime and cosmopolitan."[16]

The unquestionably secular character of Havana permeated Cuban society. Throughout the seventeenth century, this "immoral" city contained more than half of the population of the island.[17] Cuba would continue, throughout its subsequent history, to have a distinctly urban character, in both demographic and cultural terms. The political and economic abandonment of the countryside, and the contrasts between town and country, have been perennial features of its society and culture. The secularism of the port city has therefore old, deep, and pervasive roots in Cuba.

THE ORGANIZATION AND OPERATION OF THE CHURCH IN CUBA

A second historical condition, related to the first, that has determined the relatively irreligious nature of Cuban society can be found in the organization and operation of church activities in Cuba. If Spain paid little attention to the development of Cuba—other than as the crossroads of the fleet—so did the Church. Throughout most of the colonial period, and especially after the middle of the sixteenth century, Cuba was understaffed by the Church, and the priests were concentrated in the cities, especially Havana.[18] In comparison with the riches of the Church elsewhere in the Spanish empire, the Cuban Church was poor in resources.[19] No Cuban cathedral, for example, could rival those built in the principal cities of Spanish America.

At the close of Spanish rule in Cuba, in the late nineteenth century, there was a critical situation with respect to clerical personnel on the island. José Martín Herrera de la Iglesia, archbishop of Santiago de Cuba, reported in 1885 that fourteen parishes in his archdiocese were without priests. Furthermore, those priests in his service were poorly paid and were subjected to difficult conditions in the attempt to minister to a widely dispersed population.[20] In this situation the quality of the clerical corps deteriorated, since those who accepted posts in Cuba were usually those with few opportunities elsewhere. Bishop Santander of Havana complained that:

> because of lack of resources . . . [the priests] cannot survive. They leave for Spain and I cannot keep them and here there are no vocations. . . . [S]oon there will be no priests at all to send to the towns.[21]

It was a vicious cycle: the weakness of the Church, especially in rural areas, led in turn to a low number of vocations among Cubans. The Church's presence in rural areas was virtually nonexistent.

Nor did the situation improve in the twentieth century. In the voluminous report of the Commission of Cuban Affairs sent to Cuba in 1934 by the Foreign Policy Association there is only one reference to religion, and it is made in a discussion of the social conditions of workers in sugar mills. "There is no religious life at all," concluded the Commission, in what may have been an overstatement.[22] Yet in 1950, a U.S. sociologist, Lowry Nelson, in his comprehensive work on rural Cuba, echoed the Commission in his only observation on the Catholic Church:

> In Cuba the church plays only a minor role among farm people . . . their contact with churches is minimized . . . in rural areas the church is usually nonexistent.[23]

THE SUGAR REVOLUTION AND THE SECULARIZATION OF THE MILL

A third factor that contributed to weakening the Catholic Church in Cuba was the sugar revolution that started in the late eighteenth century and lasted until the middle of the nineteenth.[24] This was perhaps the most significant economic and social phenomenon of colonial Cuba. The island's economy was radically transformed as small agricultural producers were virtually eliminated in western Cuba and a new class of wealthy native-born *habaneros* started producing sugar on a large scale. The small sugar mills, with limited land and relatively few slaves, gave way to huge land holdings where sugar cane was processed in larger, technically advanced mills. The operations that turned Cuba into a world sugar power also required more labor and this resulted in the massive importation of African slaves.

This transformation of Cuba's agriculture was the motor for fundamental changes in the island's society. An entire new elite class—the "sugarocracy"—rose to prominence. Influenced by the Enlightenment in Europe, this class viewed itself as progressive and rational, committed to the development of science and the application of technology to the production of sugar.[25] It was therefore a class with secular values and with a European bourgeois consciousness. It brought to Cuba inventions and patterns of consumption that far outpaced anything in Spain or in Spanish America.[26]

The biggest contradiction of this new Cuban sugar elite, however, was that it was dependent on the primitive system of slave labor. The sugar boom required progressively more slaves, who were treated as mere factors of production.

A new world is created which adds to the barbarism of slavery the civilized torments of overwork. . . . Intensive and extensive exploitation of the Negro made him a costly raw material and required an urgent and expanding process of replacement. To the slaves needed for starting and expanding the factories must be added those daily devoured by the work. Sugar and Negroes grew alongside one another.[27]

The sugar revolution dramatically increased Cuba's population, and especially its slave population. In 1774, prior to the boom and after nearly three centuries of colonial rule, the entire island had only 172,000 inhabitants. Slaves represented 23 percent. By 1841, however, the population of Cuba had grown to 1,007,000 of which nearly 44 percent was categorized as slave.[28]

This new and predominant sugar order was inherently in conflict with the Church, both in ideological and economic terms. With a secular worldview, the sugarocracy was not disposed to making the economic investment to maintain the presence of the Church in the expanding mills. When the mills were small and a semipatriarchal order predominated, the owners would build a chapel and contract for the services of a priest to minister to the slaves. But with an expansion in the size of the mills, both in terms of land and slaves, the economic commitment necessary to maintain the presence of the Church on their holdings also grew. The sugarocrats balked at the expense and refused to go along.

In short order the insoluble contradictions between a merchandise-producing system and the Church's feudal superstructure became obvious. The modern sugarocrat, obsessed with raising production and lowering costs, needed to prune away all expenses which did not contribute to his merchandise-creating mission. The payroll item for "religion" was ridiculous from an economic standpoint and there was a not surprising tendency to suppress it.[29]

In addition to refusing to economically support a religious presence at the mills, the owners were also unwilling to grant slaves the time to practice the sacraments, to receive religious indoctrination, and to observe Sundays and religious holidays.

There were also conflicts with the Church over tithing and the opening of cemeteries at the mills.

These were conflicts which eventually the Church lost, resulting in its gradual disappearance from the mills. Moreno Fraginals has called this the "sugar-secularization process."[30] The impact of this process on Cuban society cannot be underestimated. Its most evident result was the inability to effectively indoctrinate into the faith the large numbers of arrivals from Africa. This made possible the retention and continued vitality of the African beliefs, which blended with Catholic practices and remain a feature of Cuban religious life to this day.

> The Catholic faith in its most rigid form did not penetrate the sugarmill; but when slaves assembled in mill yards, its saints were effectively produced to the muffled sound of drums. . . . The mill came to resemble a demoniac temple where a new faith was being fashioned, with white gods and black gods, with drums beating time to Catholic prayers.[31]

The Importance of Non-Catholic Religions

The beliefs of the African slaves have always represented a challenge to Catholic religious hegemony in Cuba, but in many ways those beliefs were not exclusionary and tended to blend with Catholic practices. While some manifestations of that syncretism tested the tolerance of church officials, the Catholic saints and the Yoruba *orishas* were identified with each other and have coexisted within one religious complex that has been nominally associated with Catholicism.[32]

Therefore, while the influx of African slaves, with their non-Christian beliefs, had an indelible impact on the Cuban religious scene, it did not pose as great a threat to the Cuban Church in institutional terms as did the growth during the nineteenth and twentieth centuries of religions that were historically in competition—or even in conflict—with Catholicism.

In 1896, Juan Bautista Casas, a Spanish priest in Havana, complained of the many factors that undermined the Church in Cuba. Prominent among them was:

> An entire horde of Methodists, Quakers, Anabaptists, Baptists, Episcopalians, spiritualists and others that have flooded the island with temples, schools, and Protestant centers. . . . [33]

Bishop Fernández Piérola believed that in 1880 there were more than fifty masonic lodges in Cuba.[34]

Although the hierarchy of the Cuban Catholic Church may have exaggerated the extent of the non-Catholic, especially Protestant, presence in Cuba, there is no question that the religious heterogeneity of the island's population started increasing markedly during the last two decades of the nineteenth century.

Marcos Antonio Ramos has traced in great detail the origins and development of Protestantism in Cuba.[35] It is a history that starts in earnest around 1883. Although most of the early missionaries were Cuban, the Protestant denominations received a major push with the growing interest of the U.S. in Cuba, the Spanish-Cuban-American War, the U.S. occupation of the island from 1898 to 1902, and the subsequent influx of U.S. capital and influence during the first decades of this century.[36]

Protestant missionaries found fertile ground in Cuba since the rural areas had been traditionally neglected by the Church, and its presence in urban areas was not strong. Furthermore, Protestant proselytism was consistent with the "Americanization" of Cuba espoused by many in the U.S. The economic and political dependence of the new Cuban Republic and the paternalistic nature of U.S.–Cuba relations fostered efforts to spread American values and institutions to the island.[37]

Although their accuracy is questionable, the figures compiled by the Evangelical Foreign Missions Association on the state of the Protestant missions in Cuba in 1961 give some idea of the growth of the Protestant presence during the twentieth century. Ramos uses those figures, and other sources, to conclude that the number of Protestants in the island that year was between 250,000 and 360,000.[38] The population of Cuba at that time was just over six million. A wide range of denominations were represented, with Methodists, Episcopalians, and Southern Baptists leading all others.[39] In 1961 there were 1,416 Protestant places of worship, 1,367 Cuban religious workers, and 225 foreign missionaries.[40]

Besides the growth of Protestantism, there were other causes of the island's religious heterogeneity in the twentieth century. Foremost were the high levels of immigration, aside from the importation of African slaves, which Cuba experienced, especially during the second half of the nineteenth century and the first decades of this century. Although the Spanish represented the largest group among the immigrants, sizable migration flows from China, Eastern Europe, the Middle East, and, to some extent, the Caribbean, served to greatly increase the non-Catholic population. The Jewish presence was evident in the twentieth century, as were communities of Chinese and Arabs, especially in Havana.[41] In eastern Cuba, Haitians and Jamaicans, taken to the area early in this century to work in the sugar cane fields, represented sizable immigrant populations.[42]

All of these immigrant populations served to increase religious heterogeneity in Cuba, and especially in Havana, reducing further the possibility that the Catholic Church would exercise hegemony over religious matters.

THE CHURCH AS AN ENEMY OF CUBAN INDEPENDENCE

A fifth and final phenomenon that contributed to the weakness of the Catholic Church was the perception that the Church was pro-Spanish and an enemy of Cuban independence. There is a solid basis for that perception. Although many Cuban priests contributed to the independence effort, the Church hierarchy in Cuba was clearly aligned with the continuation of Spanish rule in the island. One reason for this is a factor mentioned earlier: the predominance of Spanish priests in Cuba due to the relatively low number of native vocations. It was to be expected that the allegiance of those priests would be with their home country.

But the support of the Cuban Church for Spanish rule also had to do with the political struggles and the relationship between Church and state in Spain during the closing years of the nineteenth century. Traditionalists and liberals were locked in a debate over changes in the political and constitutional order. The Church hierarchy, of course, supported the maintenance of traditional institutions and was "intent on demonstrating to the government the value of the Church as a source of order and respect for authority."[43]

Maintaining the control over the colonies was part of the status quo the Church defended. Maza Miquel argues that one of the great tragedies of Cuban Catholicism is that the struggle for independence coincided with the moment in which the Spanish Church was intent in showing that it was a "key note in Spanish national identity."[44]

The result was that the Catholic Church in Cuba was viewed as an ally of the oppressive colonial power. The Spanish priest Juan Bautista Casas in 1896 bemoaned that "in Cuba, the hatred of Spain and the hatred of Catholicism are always united."[45] One source has even gone as far—perhaps too far—as to suggest that the success of the Cuban independence movement represented a triumph for "nationalism and the ethos of Freemasonry."[46] Indeed, the leading figure of the Cuban independence movement, José Martí, was not a Catholic. Supporting Spain led to the Church's "discredit and lack of popularity after independence."[47]

In summary, it is not surprising that virtually all sources agree that the Catholic Church has traditionally been a weak institution in Cuba and that Cubans in general have been characterized by a lack of religiosity. Five related factors, the combination of which was unique to Cuba, created this situation: 1) the development of Havana as a port city, with its accompanying worldliness and secularism; 2) the relative inattention of the Church to its Cuban flock, resulting in understaffing, especially in rural areas; 3) the sugar revolution, which gave prominence to a new elite and to economic conditions which resulted in the secularization of the mills and a further decrease in the influence of the Church; 4) a growing religious heterogeneity through the immigration of significant numbers of non-Catholics and through effective Protestant proselytism; and 5) the identification of the Church as an enemy of Cuban independence from Spain.

The result of those factors was that modern Cuba, even prior to socialism, was a distinctly secular society. Both constitutions of the Cuban Republic (1901 and 1940) established a strict separation between Church and state. The 1901 Constitution, in Article 26, specifically prohibited the government from subsidizing any religion.[48] Article 55 of the 1940 Constitution explicitly defined public education as secular.[49] A 1918 law made civil marriages compulsory, eliminating official recognition of marriage ceremonies performed by religious authorities.[50] Furthermore, the lawmakers of the Cuban Republic apparently had no qualms about enacting social legislation inconsistent with Catholic principles. The most notable example was a law, enacted more than half a century ago, in 1939, that added "mutual consent" to the list of valid grounds for divorce and permitted the granting of divorces simply upon the request of both parties.[51]

In 1954, a Catholic student organization conducted a study of religious attitudes in Cuba. It found that although nearly 97 percent of Cubans expressed a belief in the existence of God and 73 percent claimed to be Roman Catholics, only 24 percent of

Catholics indicated they regularly attended Sunday Mass. Among non-Catholics, 17 percent said they regularly attended services.[52]

It was in this modernized and secular society, where the influence of the Church was traditionally weak, that the waves of Cuban migrants to the U.S. originated. The religious conditions in the home country cannot be emphasized enough in any attempt to understand the presence of the Church among Cuban-Americans.

2

The Nineteenth-Century
Cuban Experience in the U.S.

Since the bulk of the present-day Cuban-origin population is composed of persons who have departed Cuba since the advent of the Revolution (about 70 percent of all Cuban-origin persons currently residing in the U.S. were actually born on the island),[1] by far most of the literature on the Cuban presence in the United States has focused on the recent postrevolutionary migration and the dynamics of the Cuban communities that have been established since 1959.[2]

Until recently, there was a dearth of studies about the earlier Cuban communities in this country. One notable exception was José Rivero Muñíz's lengthy article in the *Revista Bimestre Cubana* on the Cuban community in Tampa, written in 1958.[3]

In the past few years there has been a noticeable increase in the study of those Cuban communities that preceded the current wave, especially those established in the nineteenth century.[4] In part, this growing interest can be attributed to the recognition that the émigrés of the nineteenth century were crucial players in the development of the island's separatist movement, making the study of the U.S. communities an integral part of the work of historians of Cuba. The upsurge in the number of recent works dealing with the nineteenth-century communities has also been fueled by the broader trend towards the development of a body of literature on the history of the Hispanic presence in the U.S., a trend largely initiated by historians of the Chicano and Puerto Rican experiences.

The existing literature as well as the sketchy demographic data available on immigration point to three distinct stages in the Cuban presence in the U.S. during the nineteenth century: 1) the development prior to 1868 of an elite community of intellectual and political émigrés centered primarily in New York; 2) the outbreak of the Ten-Year War for independence in 1868 and the consequent intensification in migration, especially to New York and Key West; and 3) the opening of the cigar factories in Ybor City starting in

1886 and the emigration prompted by the War of Independence that started in 1895.

This periodization is partially supported by the available data on Cuban migration to the U.S. One of the few official sources of statistics on U.S. immigration prior to 1900 is a publication produced by the Bureau of Statistics of the Treasury Department and published in 1903, covering the period from 1820 to 1903.[5] One feature of these figures that limits their utility is that prior to 1869 Cubans are grouped with all persons from the West Indies. Furthermore, in identifying nationality groups, the immigration authorities used the concept of "races or peoples," e.g., "Cuban race or people," and not place of birth.[6]

Table 1 presents the data on the immigration of Cubans since 1869. After 1870, they are grouped into five-year intervals to make their presentation more manageable. The two years immediately following the outbreak of hostilities in 1868 show a relatively high annual level, which decreases after 1870. In the quinquennium that starts in 1886, however, there is a dramatic increase. It was in 1886 that the first cigar factories opened in Tampa. After a decline during

Table 1

Cubans admitted into the United States
as immigrants, 1869–1900

Years (fiscal years ending June 30)	Number of Cuban Immigrants	Annual Average
All years, 1869–1900	58,392	1,825
1869–1870	3,090	1,545
1871–1875	4,607	921
1876–1880	3,614	723
1881–1885	5,501	1,100
1886–1890	16,027	3,205
1891–1895	9,994	1,999
1896–1900	15,559	3,112

Source: Compiled and computed from data in U.S. Bureau of Statistics, *Immigration into the United States, Showing Number, Nationality, Sex Age, Occupation, Destination, etc.* . . . , *from 1820 to 1903* (Washington, D.C.: Treasury Department, n.d.), p. 4351.

the period from 1891 to 1895, Cuban immigration reached new highs between 1896 and 1900, precisely the period corresponding to the War of Independence. It was a period characterized by strife and turmoil, political and economic instability and uncertainties, and the presence of a vibrant economic alternative outside Cuba.

Before 1868: New York's Exiles

While Cuban immigration prior to 1868 was not very significant, at least in terms of numbers, it was important in political terms. In the 1820s the winds of independence were sweeping Spanish America. Many Cubans started contemplating, and working for, a modification in their relationship with Spain. Some were autonomists, others argued for annexation with the United States, and still others dared to speak of total independence. The old empire, on the other hand, retrenched itself, determined not to lose any more of its colonies. Its governors in Cuba sought to curtail any movement to change the status quo.

That general political climate persisted until Spain's departure from the island in 1899. During that period of more than eight decades, exile was the typical response to the repression, and some of the best manifestations of Cuban culture and intellectual work were most evident outside of the island.[7] New York would witness the arrival, activities, and sometimes even the death of Cuba's most prominent separatist figures. It is not an overstatement to say that an important chapter of nineteenth-century Cuban history—and indeed, of Cuban literature—was written in New York.

The epitome of the intellectual-political exile was, of course, José Martí. His writings and organizing activities in the United States, especially New York, are well known. But what is not as well known is that more than half a century before Martí arrived in New York in 1880, notable Cuban exiles had established themselves in the city. The presence of those earlier exiles in New York, almost seventy-five years before Cuba's independence from Spain, is an eloquent testimony of the depth of the historical connections between the United States and Cuba. Those perennial connections, forged by geopolitical and economic conditions, have shaped the character of Cuban society and determined, to this day, the nature of Cuban migration to this country.

One of the earliest exiles was a nineteen-year-old poet named José María Heredia, who had been involved in a conspiracy against Spanish rule in Cuba. Although he eventually settled in Mexico, where he died in 1839, Heredia spent some time in New York, where he composed one of his best-known works, an ode to Niagara Falls.[8]

Another prominent Cuban who lived in New York was the historian and philosopher José Antonio Saco. One of the most influential of the Cuban writers of the nineteenth century, he is perhaps best known for his *History of Slavery*. In the late 1820s and early 1830s Saco edited in New York a Spanish-language weekly, *The Weekly Messenger*.

In the 1840s, Cubans who favored annexation to the United States formed the Cuban Council of New York (Consejo Cubano de Nueva York). The leading figures of that organization were José Aniceto Iznaga, Alonso Betancourt, and Gaspar Betancourt Cisneros (El Lugareño). They met with President Polk in 1848 to secure his indirect support for their efforts to replace Spanish rule with control from Washington.[9]

The annexionist movement was also in evidence in New Orleans in the period prior to the U.S. Civil War. Although not as significant as New York, New Orleans maintained extensive commercial ties with Cuba. In 1858, for example, two-thirds of all vessels arriving in New Orleans from foreign ports were coming from Cuba.[10] Southern planters saw in the Cuban annexionist movement the possibility of adding a slave state to the Union. They heavily supported the armed expeditions to Cuba of an annexionist, Narciso López. The Cuban flag, taken to Cuba by López in his ill-fated 1850 expedition, first flew in New Orleans in front of the offices of the *Daily Delta*, a New Orleans newspaper that strongly supported López and the annexionists.[11]

One important New York Cuban linked to the annexation movement was the novelist Cirilo Villaverde, who for a time served as secretary to López.[12] Although he also lived for some time in Philadelphia and New Orleans, Villaverde spent most of his life as an exile in New York. It was in New York that Villaverde's novel, regarded by many as the most notable Cuban novel of the nineteenth century, was published in its definitive edition in 1882.[13] He later joined the independence effort and died in New York in 1894.

Overall, the Cuban exiles in the U.S. prior to 1869 were known for their political activism and their intellectual and cultural activities. As one might expect, the group was not characterized by religious activism, and there is virtually nothing written about religious life among these émigrés. It is therefore ironic that the most prominent—and in many ways atypical—figure of that early exile community in New York was a Catholic priest who played a significant role in the development of the New York diocese.

Father Félix Varela y Morales arrived in New York on December 15, 1823, aboard the ship *Draper C. Thorndike*, which had sailed from Gibraltar. Varela was seeking refuge from the wrath of a vengeful Spanish monarch, for he had been one of the three Cuban deputies to the Spanish Cortes which had sought to depose Ferdinand VII. Once restored to the throne by the armies of France, Ferdinand dissolved the rebellious legislature and started executing its most prominent members. Varela was especially targeted for revenge. Taking advantage of the mother country's flirtation with liberal reforms, he had been an outspoken advocate for greater autonomy for his island. Varela found himself forced to leave for Gibraltar in a small boat, under fire from a French warship. Unable to return to Cuba, refuge in the United States seemed to be the only alternative.

Regarded as the intellectual father of Cuban independence, Varela arrived in New York at the age of thirty-five, already a veteran political activist, both in Cuba and in Spain, in the separatist cause. Except for a brief initial period of residence in Philadelphia, he would remain in New York for virtually the rest of his life. His first few years in this country were intensively dedicated to political writings, especially in the publication he founded, *El Habanero*, which was first published in Philadelphia in 1824. He was a prolific writer, very influential among many of his contemporaries, who regarded him as teacher, a function he had largely served in Cuba before his departure. Many of his students, including José Antonio Saco, became prominent Cuban intellectuals and later joined him in New York.

Until his death in 1853, shortly after his retirement in St. Augustine, Florida, Varela divided his time between his writings and activities on behalf of Cuban independence and his obligations to the diocese of New York. Although a great deal has been written about Varela's contributions to Cuban independence, somewhat less attention has been paid to his role as a priest in New York, the aspect of his life that is of greatest relevance here.[14]

At the time of his arrival in New York, the Catholic diocese there was little more than a struggling mission. Headed by its first resident bishop, the Irish-born John Connolly, the diocese

> could boast of but two small churches, old St. Patrick's Cathedral in Mott Street and the pioneer chapel of St. Peter's in Barclay Street,

measuring 48 feet by 80. Its 25,000 believers, struggling for survival in an Anglo-Protestant milieu, were served by a shifting handful of priests, missionaries from foreign lands, uprooted, restless, outspoken men. . . . [15]

In such a milieu, the talented and dedicated Varela was destined to distinguish himself and to occupy a position of leadership within the diocese—this despite his humility and his lack of interest in rising within the clerical hierarchy.

Varela's contributions to the development of Catholicism in New York were critical at a time when the Church was facing extraordinary challenges. In the early 1830s there was a vicious and organized revival of anti-Catholicism among Protestant fundamentalists. The sermons and writings of some of the "anti-Papist" Protestants even fueled acts of vandalism and arson against Catholic churches in New York and New England.

As a theologian and philosopher, Varela was a leading defender of the Church against its attackers, although always with a voice of moderation and reason. He wrote extensively in the area's Catholic publications, especially the *Truth Teller,* joining the debate in defense of Catholic beliefs and the Church. His intellectual leadership was critical at a time when the New York diocese was not blessed with aggressive leadership. Varela founded a number of publications to communicate with the area's Catholic population, composed primarily of poor Irish immigrants.

Recognition of Varela's talents led to his appointment in 1829 as vicar general of the diocese. Together with the other vicar general of New York, John Power, Varela led the diocese during the two years that Bishop Jean Dubois was in Europe.

Varela was involved, among many projects, in a battle with the Public School Society, which funneled public education funds to Protestant educational institutions, while explicitly excluding support for Catholic schools. It was a battle that was aggressively taken up by Dubois's successor, Bishop John Hughes.

Institutionally, Varela's most lasting contribution to the New York diocese was the founding of two churches, greatly expanding the number of parishes in Manhattan. In 1827, while a pastor at St. Peter's, he arranged for the purchase of Christ Church, an Episcopalian house of worship on Ann Street. Almost a decade later, in 1837, he founded the Church of the Transfiguration of Our Lord in a building on Chambers Street previously occupied by the Reformed Scotch Presbyterian Church. Virtually the rest of his life would be spent there, occupied primarily as a parish priest, tending to the needs of his predominantly Irish congregation.[16]

Varela's pastoral work was legendary. His biographers have accumulated countless accounts of his selfless work among the poor. Much of his own personal wealth and possessions he turned over to the work of the parish. He established numerous projects to provide work and income among his parishioners. In a letter to Saco from New York, Gaspar Betancourt Cisneros wrote that Varela "was entirely and exclusively devoted to his Church and his Irishmen."[17] Varela's pastoral work was so extraordinary that in 1984 the Sacred Congregation for the Cause of Canonization of Saints gave permission for the establishment of a commission to initiate the process of his beatification.[18]

Even with the responsibilities of vicar general and parish priest, Varela found time not only for his political and philosophical writings, but also for a range of other intellectual pursuits. He translated into Spanish a textbook on chemistry and also Thomas Jefferson's manual of parliamentary procedure used by the U.S. Senate.

Although in the last few years of his life, as Betancourt Cisneros noted, Varela consecrated himself to his pastoral work, he continued to write about the destiny of his native island. As such, he was a consummate exile, concerned about the affairs of the homeland despite thirty years of residence in the United States. That much he shared with the thousands of Cubans who before and after him would take up residence in this country. But among them Varela stands out as an extraordinary figure. He was unique in his religiosity and his devotion to the Church. He was exceptional in the degree to which he made a positive and notable contribution to his adopted homeland.

The Ten-Year War and the Community in Key West

The earliest reports of Cuban cigarmakers in Key West date to 1831,[19] but it was not until 1868, with the outbreak of the first armed insurrection against Spanish rule in Cuba that the Cuban community in Key West grew to a prominent position in relation to the New York community. The ten-year conflict had disastrous consequences for the economy of the island. Cigar manufacturers were among those that found it increasingly difficult to maintain normal business operations, especially since the Spanish government had placed high tariffs on all exported tobacco products.

One of those manufacturers was the owner of the well-known brand "El Principe de Gales," Vicente Martínez Ybor. Despite the fact that he was born in Valencia, Spain, he adopted a pro-Cuban stance in the struggle. Not long after the outbreak of hostilities, Martínez Ybor found himself in a precarious position, not only as a businessman in a deteriorating economic climate, but also, and more urgently, as a persecuted conspirator against Spain. He barely escaped arrest, fleeing in a schooner to Key West.

Martínez Ybor was not alone. The hostilities in Cuba spurred an exodus from the island to Key West, a migration in which cigarworkers were overrepresented. The hot and humid climate of Key West was similar to Cuba's, ideal for the elaboration of tobacco. A stable political situation and favorable tariffs were additional factors that by the early 1870s made Key West a center for cigar manufacturing and a virtual boomtown.

Table 2 presents the trends in the number of immigrants arriving through the Key West customs district from 1861–1900. Until

Table 2

Immigrants arriving in the United States through the
Key West, Florida, Customs District
1859–1898

Years (fiscal years ending June 30)	Number of immigrants arriving through Key West	Annual Average
1859–1863	621	124
1864–1868	808	162
1869–1873	4,207	841
1874–1878	5,120	1,024
1879–1883	4,958	992
1884–1888	15,777	3,155
1889–1893	14,059	2,812
1894–1898	17,229	3,446

Source: Compiled and computed from data in U.S. Bureau of Statistics, *Immigration into the United States, Showing Number, Nationality, Sex, Age, Occupation, Destination, etc., from 1820 to 1903* (Washington, D.C.: Treasury Department, n.d.), p. 4366.

fiscal year 1868 (the fiscal year ends June 30), annual immigration through Key West fluctuated between 100 and 200. The Ten-Year War started in October 1868. During fiscal year 1869, migrants entering Key West numbered 476, and for the year 1870 the figure reached 1,009. The annual figure remained around 900 to 1,000 until 1877, after which there is a slight decline until 1886.[20]

Although these figures are not available by country of origin of the immigrants, there can be little doubt that the increase was related to the situation in Cuba, especially given Key West's location. The trends shown here are consistent with those in Table 1 for all Cuban migration to the U.S.

In addition to showing the impact of the Ten-Year War in increasing Cuban immigration and in the development of Key West, the table also shows the even more dramatic rise in migration through Key West after 1886. That trend, however, is linked to the establishment in that year of the cigar factories in Ybor City, on the outskirts of Tampa. At that time, Tampa was part of the Key West customs district. The founding of that second cigarmaking community signaled a new—and most significant—stage in the history of the Cuban presence in the United States in the nineteenth century.

Ybor City

On the morning of April 12, 1886, the steamship *Mascotte* arrived in Tampa Bay from Key West with fifty Cuban cigarmakers and their families. They were the first contingent contracted to work in the newly established factories of Ybor City. Many of the inhabitants of the town of Tampa showed up at the port that day to watch the foreigners disembark. The events and conditions leading to the arrival of those workers, and of literally thousands more in the following months and years, involved three elements dear to Cubans: politics, cigars, and guavas.[21]

During the 1870s and into the decade of the 1880s, Vicente Martínez Ybor's cigar business flourished in Key West. He had also established a branch in New York, the major distribution and shipping center for cigars. But both New York and Key West had one characteristic that Martínez Ybor found increasingly intolerable: a growing organized labor movement among cigarworkers.

The devastating New York strike of 1877 paved the way for the creation of the Cigar Makers International Union. Martínez

Ybor closed his operations in New York, as did other cigar manufacturers, and concentrated on Key West in the outskirts of the nascent labor movement, resulting in a renewed vitality for the industry there.

Eventually, however, the Key West workers organized and in August 1885 they launched a strike. Martínez Ybor and other manufacturers became convinced that they should relocate elsewhere, where labor was not organized. The creation of a "company town" in a relatively isolated area had proved successful in other industries in limiting union influence.

Martínez Ybor joined forces with Ignacio Haya, of the New York manufacturing firm of Sánchez and Haya, in a search for the most appropriate location for their operations. Pensacola, Mobile, and Galveston were under consideration.

A central figure in the eventual selection of the Tampa Bay area was the Cuban-born Eduardo Manrara, a junior partner of Martínez Ybor. Since Manrara administered the Key West factory and oversaw the firm's New York business office, he traveled frequently between the two cities. Because he would invariably become seasick, Manrara avoided the usual sea route. Instead, he would take the train from New York to its southernmost destination in Florida (Jacksonville, and later Sanford and Cedar Key), subjecting himself to the arduous overland journey to Tampa, and then boarding the unavoidable steamer to Key West. It is probable that Manrara, long before the 1885 strike, had been urging Martínez Ybor to relocate in order to avoid the need to rely exclusively on ocean transportation for shipping goods (and Manrara) in and out of Key West.

Manrara's obligatory stopovers in Tampa undoubtedly gave him a familiarity with the area. On one of his trips to Key West, in November 1884, he was accompanied by two New York businessmen and associates, the Spanish-born Gavino Gutiérrez and the Cuban-born Bernardino Gargol. Part of the prosperous import business of the two men was the shipment to New York of paste, jelly, and preserves made from guava (a tropical fruit) and processed in their Cuban factory. They had heard (possibly from Manrara) that wild guava trees grew in the Tampa area. They accompanied Manrara to investigate the possibility that these tropical fruit trees could be grown in the United States. Upon arriving in Tampa, they combed the outlying areas in search of the guava trees. They did not find even one, and queried inhabitants were puzzled as to what the travelers were talking about.

Although ending up empty-handed on guavas, they were impressed by the picturesque setting of the town and the potential of the bay as a shipping port. It was probably the first time that Manrara himself had taken a thorough look at the area.

The trio arrived in Key West extolling the virtues of Tampa precisely when Haya was visiting Martínez Ybor from New York. The following day the two manufacturers took the steamer to Tampa. Immediately they became convinced of its potential, especially since the port was more than adequate for the importation of the Cuban tobacco leaves, and the upcoming completion to Tampa of the line from Jacksonville (and New York) would provide an excellent transportation route for the distribution of cigars.

Martínez Ybor and Manrara entered into negotiations for the purchase of land near Tampa. Martínez Ybor wanted not only to build a factory, but also houses for the workers and public buildings. He envisioned an entire community of cigarmakers and their families. He favored a tract of land east of Tampa owned by John T. Lesley. Mr. Lesley wanted $9,000 for it, a price Martínez Ybor considered excessive and offered instead $5,000. The newly established Tampa Board of Trade was very interested in attracting the cigar factories and promised to raise the difference, eventually giving Martínez Ybor $700 in cash and land deeds valued at $3,300.

Gavino Gutiérrez, who by now had moved to Tampa, became the construction engineer of the Ybor City Land and Improvement Company and promptly commenced working on the factory and dwellings for workers. Shortly thereafter, Haya and his partner Serafín Sánchez purchased an adjoining tract and started constructing their factory and houses for workers.

By the beginning of 1886 both factories, "El Príncipe de Gales" and "La Flor de Sánchez y Haya" were completed and were scheduled to open on March 26, 1886. Only the factory of Sánchez and Haya opened that day. Ironically, the opening of the Martínez Ybor factory was delayed because the Cuban workers staged a work stoppage to protest the hiring of a Spanish foreman.

By May, the two firms had completed eighty-nine houses and a hotel was nearly finished. Martínez Ybor concentrated all his operations in Tampa after a fire devastated his factory in Key West. Many of the displaced *tabaqueros* flocked to what was now named Ybor City. There was work for all of them as other firms were induced to establish factories there. The number of factories grew rapidly and so did ancillary industries such as the manufacture of cigar boxes.

Ybor City was entering a period of rapid growth and prosperity that continued into at least the first two decades of the twentieth century. The Morrison Act of 1883 was just one of a series of tariff laws that seemed to ensure that prosperity. It placed a relatively high tariff on the cigars imported from Cuba, while lowering the tariffs on the importation of tobacco leaves. This was crucial, for throughout the period of its expansion, Ybor City would continue to depend on the importation of Cuban tobacco.

In summary, the following factors led to the establishment of the cigar industry in Florida in the late nineteenth century: 1) a tariff situation that favored the manufacture of cigars in the United States using Cuban tobacco, giving Tampa manufacturers a competitive edge over the Havana firms; 2) Cuba's unstable political situation; 3) Ybor City's "company town" setting which held the promise of preventing the union activity and labor conflicts that had occurred in New York and Key West; and 4) Tampa's favorable location, combining climatic advantages with accessibility to both water and rail transportation facilities.

As the twentieth century opened, Ybor City was the premier Cuban community in the U.S. The 1900 U.S. decennial census found 3,533 persons born in Cuba residing in Hillsborough County, the county wherein Tampa is located. This figure represented the largest concentration of Cuban persons in the U.S. that censal year, exceeding the number of Cubans enumerated in Monroe County (Key West) and even in New York County. An additional 963 persons living in Hillsborough County that year were born in Spain.[22] The rapid growth of Ybor City is evident in the fact that only twenty years before, the 1880 census found in Hillsborough a grand total of three persons born in either country.[23]

The Legacy of the Nineteenth Century

As the nineteenth century came to a close, the origins and development of these three communities left an important legacy that would shape the nature and character of the Cuban presence in the U.S. during much of the twentieth century. The trends that became firmly established by the end of the nineteenth century are especially important in understanding religiosity and the role of the Church in the development of the Cuban communities since 1900. Those trends are as follows: 1) the establishment of a substantial migration flow across the Strait of Florida, in which the U.S.

became the principal destination of Cuban emigrants; 2) a tradition of exile among Cuba's political, intellectual, and cultural elites; and 3) the importance of the cigar manufacturing industry in shaping Cuban migration.

By the close of the nineteenth century, there was a well-established tradition of migration across the Strait of Florida. The Committee on Immigration of the U.S. Senate reported in 1893:

> There is daily intercourse between the people of Havana and Key West and Tampa, Florida. The number of persons estimated to pass annually from Cuba to the United States and back is between 50,000 and 100,000. Havana is within six or seven hours, by steam, of Key West. . . . [24]

When a subcommittee of that Senate Committee held hearings in Havana in December 1892, Ramon O. Williams, consul-general of the United States in Havana, reported that

> there is no emigration from the island of Cuba, in the European sense of the word; that is, no emigrant class . . . between Key West and Havana people go as between Albany and New York, or as between New York and Boston on the Sound.[25]

Senator Proctor asked Mr. Williams to expand on that point. The consul-general continued:

> They go back and forward as those French laborers go from Canada into New England and work and then go back home. . . . [Y]ou must understand that these people look upon Florida almost as part of their own country . . . very often they come here and say, "I want to go to the Key," just as in Baltimore they would say, "I am going over to Washington."[26]

Insurrectionist conflicts continued to provide New York with Cuban immigrants who were leaders in the island's intellectual and cultural circles and who were exiled because of their pro-independence sentiments.

The outbreak of the Ten-Year War not only increased migration to the United States, but also the exiles' political activities in New York. José Morales Lemus was named to represent the insurrectionists in the United States.[27] The Cuban immigrant community, however, was badly divided and its support was crucial for the rebels. In 1871, Francisco Vicente Aguilera, a man of considerable wealth and prestige from eastern Cuba who was serving as vice-president of the Cuban Republic in Arms, arrived in New York to attempt to unite the émigrés. He died there in 1877, largely without accomplishing his objective and after losing his wealth in the conflict.[28]

The most widely known chapter of Cuban émigré activity in New York concerns separatist efforts before and during the War of Independence that broke out in February 1895. The émigré communities played a crucial role in the conflict: much of the initiative, organization, and money for the insurrection came from Cubans residing in the United States. In fact, a great deal of the literature on the Cuban presence in the U.S. during the past century tends to focus on the political activities of the émigrés.

The central figure, of course, in the political involvement of the U.S. Cuban communities during the 1880s and 1890s was José Martí. He arrived in New York in 1880 and it was there that he would eventually organize the Partido Revolucionario Cubano (PRC) accomplishing what no other Cuban has ever been able to do: a semblance of political unity among Cuban exiles.

Martí's political activities in the U.S. have been well studied, as have been the organization and importance of the Partido Revolucionario Cubano. It is unnecessary to enter here into a description of what is already found in many other works.[29] What is of relevance here, however, is to establish the singular importance of the role that the New York community played in the separatist movement of the period.

One writer has described the Florida communities in the early 1890s, especially Ybor City, as "hotbeds of revolution."[30] A great deal of separatist agitation was taking place there, and Martí's visits to Florida are well documented. But Martí based his political organization in New York. The PRC, while based on a number of local clubs scattered throughout the Cuban diaspora, had New York as its nerve center.[31]

This was evident in the junta that was elected on April 10, 1893 to lead, with Martí, the PRC. They were all New Yorkers: Tomás Estrada Palma, who had briefly served as head of the rebel government in the Ten-Year War, was the director of a private Quaker school for Cuban boys in Central Valley, in upstate New York; Gonzalo de Quesada was at the time a recent graduate of the Columbia University Law School; Benjamín Guerra, who was elected PRC's treasurer, was a prosperous New York tobacco merchant; and Juan Fraga, long active in separatist activities in the city, owned a small cigar shop in Brooklyn.[32]

As in the times of Varela, Villaverde, and Aguilera, this final period of separatist activities still found New York as the center of the action, despite its having lost demographic supremacy to the Florida communities.

The pace of Cuban immigration quickened with the establishment of the cigar manufacturing centers in Florida during the last three decades of the nineteenth century. That trend carried into the twentieth century, as Ybor City continued to grow into the late 1920s.

Immigration data for the period make it possible to assess directly the impact of the cigar manufacturing industry in shaping Cuban immigration in both the nineteenth and twentieth centuries. The immigration authorities compiled statistics on the professed occupations of the immigrants at the time of their arrival. Table 3 shows the number and relative importance of those Cuban immigrants who indicated they were engaged in occupations directly related to the manufacture of tobacco products.

Obviously, in terms of both numbers and percentages of all Cuban immigrants, the figures are highest during the years in which the Florida cigarmaking communities were being established. Although the percentages decline steadily after that, the number of cigarmakers immigrating remained high from 1902 to 1916. Even with those relatively high figures, these data actually underestimate the total impact of the cigar manufacturing industry on the levels of Cuban immigration. They include only persons in occupations directly related to the manufacture and handling of tobacco. Not included are the clerks, accountants, managers, and professionals who migrated in order to work in the cigar industry.

Table 3

Cuban immigrants classified as
"tobacco-related" in occupation[a]
1875–1931[b]

Years (fiscal years ending June 30)	Number of "tobacco-related" Cuban immigrants	"Tobacco-related" Cuban immigrants as percent of all Cuban immigrants
All years, 1875–1931	33,542	25.8
1875–1880	1,132	23.6
1881–1885	3,234	58.8
1886–1890	7,517	46.9
1891–1895	4,832	48.3
1897–1901	2,284	20.6
1902–1906	6,195	27.0
1907–1911	4,919	25.3
1912–1916	2,176	13.1
1917–1921	644	7.3
1922–1926	270	4.6
1927–1931	339	3.8

Source: Compiled and computed from data in U.S. Bureau of Statistics, *Immigration into the United States, Showing Number, Nationality, Sex, Age, Occupation, Destination, etc., from 1820 to 1903* (Washington, D.C.: Treasury Department, n.d.), p. 4351; U.S., Congress, Senate, *Report of the Immigration Commission, Statistical Review of Immigration 1880–1910*. 61st Cong., 3rd sess, Document No. 756 (1911), pp. 90–91; U.S., Commissioner-General of Immigration, *Annual Report* (Washington, D.C.: U.S. Government Printing Office, annual editions for each fiscal year from 1908 to 1932); and U.S. Department of Justice, Immigration and Naturalization Service, *Annual Report* (mimeo, annual editions for each fiscal year from 1942 to 1950).

[a] During the period covered by the table there were shifts in the title of the category used to group those engaged in the manufacture of tobacco products. From 1875 to 1898 the term used was "tobacco manufacturers and dealers." It can be assumed that virtually all Cuban immigrants listed from 1899 to 1903 under the category of "other skilled workers" were in reality tobacco-related workers, for when they were shifted to the category of "tobacco workers" from 1904 to 1910, the "other skilled" category was practically emptied. Starting with 1911 a breakdown was given, as follows: cigar makers, cigarette makers, and tobacco workers. The category of cigar makers was by far the largest of the three.

[b] Except for 1896, a year for which no data are available on the number of "tobacco–related" workers.

3

The Cuban Communities
in the U.S., 1900–1958

CUBAN IMMIGRATION, 1900–1958

The trends in Cuban immigration from the beginning of the century to the onset of the Cuban revolution respond to a variety of changing conditions, resulting in sharp fluctuations in the levels of Cubans entering this country. Table 4 shows the number of Cubans admitted as immigrants into the United States from 1899 to 1958. The high levels of immigration until 1918 reflect the heyday of the cigarmaking communities of Florida, especially Ybor City. Those communities started declining in the early 1920s. Thereafter, until the post–World War II years, Cuban immigration remained at relatively low levels, especially during the years of the Great Depression.

Immigration picked up late in the 1940s and reached high levels during the mid and late 1950s. This was a largely an "economic" migration, as many Cubans from lower socioeconomic origins sought opportunities for employment, especially in the manufacturing centers of the Northeast. New York recaptured from the Florida communities the preeminent position among Cuban communities in the U.S. In the late 1950s, those economic migrants were joined by exiles from the Batista dictatorship, and immigration jumped drastically.

The figures in Table 4 refer only to those Cubans admitted to the U.S. as immigrants. During the first half of the twentieth century a large number of Cubans came to the United States on a temporary basis. The extensive and growing social, cultural, economic, and political connections between the two countries reached their height from about 1920 to 1958. There was a tremendous traffic of people and goods between Cuba and the United States. Cuba became an important market for many U.S. products. U.S. companies established branches in the island. Cuba, and especially Havana, became a favorite vacation spot for U.S. tourists and more than a few hotels owned by U.S. firms sprang up in the capital.

174

Table 4

Cubans admitted into the United States as immigrants
1899–1958ᵃ

Years (fiscal years ending June 30)	Number of Cuban immigrantsᵃ	Annual Average
All years, 1899–1958	171,240	2,854
1899–1902	8,097	2,024
1903–1906	20,605	5,151
1907–1910	15,509	3,877
1911–1914	13,707	3,426
1915–1918	11,451	2,862
1919–1922	4,900	1,225
1923–1926	5,147	1,286
1927–1930	8,240	2,060
1931–1934	1,709	427
1935–1938	1,307	326
1939–1942	2,253	563
1943–1946	5,124	1,281
1947–1950	10,165	2,541
1951–1954	13,465	3,366
1955–1958	49,561	12,390

Source: Compiled and computed from the data in U.S., Commissioner-General of Immigration, *Annual Report* (Washington, D.C.: U.S. Government Printing Office, annual editions for each fiscal year from 1908 to 1932) and U.S., Department of Justice, Immigration and Naturalization Service, *Annual Report* (mimeo, annual editions for each fiscal year from 1942 to 1958).

[a] From 1899 to 1948 the figures refer to persons admitted as immigrants who were classified as of "Cuban race or peoples." After 1948, data refer to persons admitted as immigrants who were born in Cuba.

Many upper-income Cuban families sent their children to be educated in this country as learning English and U.S. cultural patterns was highly regarded. Furthermore, many Cubans in certain occupations, especially in sports and music, came to develop their careers here.

Data on the temporary movement of persons from Cuba to the U.S. is available for selected years from the Immigration and Naturalization Service. In 1948, for example, passenger travel from

Cuba to the U.S. amounted to 203,532 persons, the largest number of arrivals in the U.S. from any country in the world. That figure represented 20 percent of all U.S. passenger arrivals that year. Of those, 78,110 were "aliens," most of which, we can assume, were Cubans.[1] For fiscal year 1958, 72,618 "Cuban non-immigrant aliens" entered the United States. Of those, 55,850 were "temporary visitors for pleasure," 5,366 entered for business purposes, and there were 3,477 students (the rest were in miscellaneous categories).[2]

The presentation here of this period, from 1900 to 1958, is divided into its most important stages: 1) the religious life of the Ybor City community, the principal center of Cuban-American life during the first decades of this century; 2) the causes and consequences of the decline of the cigarmaking communities; and 3) the migration, permanent or temporary, of persons in the worlds of politics, sports, and music.

RELIGION AND THE CHURCH IN YBOR CITY

> We consider that we are safe in making the statement that the sociological force of religious influences in Ybor City has been, is and apparently will be in the future, of negligible value.
> —Federal Writers' Projects,
> Tampa staff, writing about Ybor City in 1935[3]

> Let me say right out: Ybor City was a radical, trade-union town.
> —José Yglesias, writer,
> and Ybor City native[4]

Given the origins and characteristics of the Cubans who established and developed Ybor City, it is not surprising that all sources agree that religion and the Church did not play significant roles in the social life of that community. The most eloquent testimony to the lack of importance of the religious institutions is that less than a handful of the references in the fairly extensive bibliography on Ybor City even mention religious activities, churches, or the presence of the Catholic Church. From the early testimonies and oral histories of the founders and residents to the more recent scholarly literature, the topic of religion is simply absent.[5]

This omission is much less a case of oversight than it is a reflection of the social reality of the place. Ybor City was built by cigarmakers who were politically conscious and active, a community where trade unionism, despite Martínez Ybor's wishes, was strong, and where liberal, secular, and even radical ideas flourished. Pérez notes that "during the early decades of the twentieth century, Tampa workers embraced a variety of radical ideologies, including communism, anarchism, and syndicalism."[6] Poyo has characterized the political culture of the Cuban cigarmakers of Florida as follows:

> Latin workers in Florida stimulated labor organizing. . . . [they were] socially aware and politically active. . . . [T]heir strong class identification (stimulated by an activist tradition and radical ideals) and group consciousness . . . encouraged the emergence of independent immigrant unions that usually looked to Havana rather than New York. . . . Latin workers preferred the socialist and anarchist ideas dominant in the labor movement in Cuba to the relatively conservative concepts espoused by their North American counterparts.[7]

The origins of those ideological characteristics are many, but one tradition among Cuban cigarmakers, which was continued in Ybor City, greatly served to reinforce and maintain that political culture: the practice of the reader or *lector* in the cigar factories. Paid by a pool of money donated by the workers themselves, the reader would read while the workers rolled cigars. Thus, while most cigarworkers were probably functional illiterates they were well educated and informed.

Since the cigarworkers paid the reader, they would also choose the readings. Pérez indicates that usually the readings "served as a disseminator of the proletarian tradition."[8] The *lector* that Pérez interviewed in 1974 recalled his experience during the 1920s, indicating that he worked one of four daily shifts. One shift was dedicated to national news stories, a second to international political developments, another shift was devoted exclusively to news from the "proletariat press," and the final shift was devoted to reading a novel in installments.[9] Readings were in Spanish, and sometimes translations done by bilingual readers from the English-language press were also read. In addition to newspapers from Ybor City, Cuba, and Spain, the international proletarian press would frequently include, for example, New York's *Daily Worker*.[10] Among the novels, the works of Zola, Balzac, Dickens, and Tolstoy were favorites.[11] It is important to note that, not surprisingly, in the accounts of the *lector* system, there was never any mention of religious or church literature among the readings.

The implication of these readings for religiosity were not lost on a critic of the *lector* system:

> [T]he readings in the cigar factories which was [*sic*] always of the most radical kind. . . . [T]he workers in the factories had to vote and the author receiving the majority of the votes had his novel read in the factory. So we can better understand the influence this reading had over the working masses. Hence affiliation with the Catholic Church was next to impossible.[12]

It is not surprising that in a community with this political ideology, there were many secular organizations established to collectively promote the welfare of the workers and their families. The history of Ybor City cannot be written without emphasizing the social clubs and the mutual-aid societies. The latter included the precursors of today's health maintenance organizations whereby families are entitled to medical care through the payment of membership fees.

The clubs and mutual-aid societies were the backbone of the social life in Ybor City. In the accounts of these organizations from the 1890s to the 1920s there is, once again, an absence of religious or church organizations. Even in the traditional areas of the Church's community involvement, charity and education, the first and foremost private institutions established in Ybor City to serve those functions were not religiously affiliated.[13]

Despite the evidently weak religiosity among the Cubans of Ybor City, there was some Church presence there and two sources provide with some depth the details of that presence. The memoirs of one of the first settlers of Ybor City, Antonio del Rio, represent one of those sources.[14] Apparently, del Rio was a Catholic who had firsthand experience with the Church in Ybor City.

The other source, far more significant than the first, is the collection of essays and reports that were commissioned and compiled from 1935 and 1936 by the Federal Writers' Project. The Jacksonville office gave their staff writers in Tampa the task of producing a study of Ybor City. Each writer was given a set of topics to explore. The resulting reports were anonymously and haphazardly assembled, with no editing and little coherence, into an unpublished, typed manuscript. A hardbound carbon copy of that manuscript is in the P. K. Yonge Library of Florida History at the University of Florida. Despite their shortcomings, many of the reports contain invaluable and unique details about life in Ybor City.[15] The description that follows of the Catholic Church in Ybor City is primarily derived from this source, with some reference to the memoirs of del Rio.

In October 1888, more than two years after the arrival of the *Mascotte* in Tampa with the first Cuban cigarmakers, a Jesuit priest, Father Phillipe de Carriere, arrived in Ybor City with the purpose of establishing a church in the new and growing community. His arrival was a response to a request for assistance from the bishop of the diocese of St. Augustine to the Jesuits in New Orleans. The new outlying community of immigrants was not being adequately served by the three diocesan priests in St. Louis (later Sacred Heart) Church, the only Catholic church in Tampa.

Father de Carriere had previously served in Cuba and was fluent in Spanish. He was joined a year later by Father John Quinlan, S.J. With Bishop John Moore of St. Augustine, they negotiated with the Ybor City Land and Improvement Company for the purchase of a tract of land at the corner of Tenth Avenue and Seventeenth Street. The agreed price was $5,000 and Bishop Moore advanced a $1,000 check for the down payment. Since Mrs. Martínez Ybor was instrumental in facilitating the terms of the transaction on behalf of the priests, the new church would bear the name of her patron saint, *Nuestra Señora de las Mercedes* (Our Lady of Mercy).

Until the completion of the new church, Mass was held in private homes. The first official Mass of the new parish was held on March 16, 1890 by Father Quinlan, who gave the sermon in English, in the home of a Mrs. Tissier. The following Sunday, in the same house, Father de Carriere celebrated Mass and preached in Spanish.

Our Lady of Mercy Church was inaugurated with a High Mass on the 19th of April of 1891. The altar had been donated by Mrs. Martínez Ybor.

For more than thirty years, Our Lady of Mercy apparently served the needs of all the Catholics in Ybor City, for it remained the only Catholic church in the community, despite the rapid growth of its population during those three decades. During that period the Jesuits were replaced by the Salesian Fathers. After years of staffing the parish, the Salesians decided to concentrate on an orphanage that they had opened in 1928, and in 1934 they turned over the parish to the Redemptorist Fathers who were sent there from Puerto Rico.

The opening of a second Catholic church in Ybor City in 1922 apparently responded to ethnic considerations and not to the number of parishioners at Our Lady of Mercy. That number had probably not increased greatly, nor was it likely to do so in the future. The second church, Most Holy Name Catholic Church, was established by an Italian-born Jesuit, Father Vincent M. Dente, in response to an invitation from the bishop of St. Augustine, Rev. Michael Curley, to serve the growing Italian population of Ybor City.

In the area of education, there was a parish school at Our Lady of Mercy since 1891. In 1935, the Sisters of St. Joseph established a commercial school, probably for young women only. Total attendance at both schools was about 800 in 1935. At about that time, the Salesians' orphanage was already in operation, with about seventy-five boys. Most of the Catholic charitable work in the community was apparently conducted through the St. Vincent de Paul Society.

Figures on church attendance provided in one of the papers of the Federal Writers' Projects consistently show relatively few practicing Catholics in Ybor City. In 1935, there were a total of 10,456 persons who had declared themselves members of either Our Lady of Mercy or Most Holy Name. Estimated active attendance was 1,500. In comparison with Spaniards and Italians, Cubans had the lowest number of church members. Most revealing are the data on marriages performed by priests. From 1915 to 1934 the number of marriages involving Cubans officiated by priests did not exceed eleven percent of all marriage licenses issued to Cubans.

One of the writers in the Federal Writers' Projects was direct in his assessment of the religiosity of the Cubans in Ybor City. That assessment is reminiscent of the statements quoted much earlier regarding religiosity in Cuba:

> Of the Cubans there is very little to say, since they, as a whole, do not attend church. Yet those who attend are very ostentatious in the outward display of their Catholicity, but very lacking when it comes to practice. . . . [T]hey will wear medals around their necks and invoke the Divine in name when in trouble and tribulation, but they very seldom attend church services. . . . Cubans who never go to church will have a picture of Our Lady in their homes, with a votive candle burning before it. They will pray for favors and what not, yet they ask them to go to the church, and they will give all kinds of excuses . . . that they are busy, that they work all week, and Sunday they must devote it to housework.[16]

And that description only applies to those who profess to be Catholic. The origins, traditions, and culture of Ybor City, as we have noted, were not favorable to the development of a strong Catholic presence there. That same observer noted, for example, the importance in Ybor City of what he labeled "secret societies." He identified three. One was "Masonic," which exerted a strong influence in the creation of many of the social clubs and mutual-aid societies. The other two, he argued, were "socialist" and "anarchist" societies.[17]

In another section of the manuscript of the Federal Writers' Projects, considerable attention is paid to another non-Catholic religious practice, labeled in the report as "Ñañigo (voodooism)" and the "superstitions and customs of Cuban Negroes."[18] As has been traditionally the case in the island itself, it is clear that in Ybor City not only was the Church a weak institution, but it had plenty of competition from non-Catholic religions and cults.[19]

THE DECLINE OF THE FLORIDA CIGARMAKING COMMUNITIES

The Florida cigar factories grew and prospered because they arose out of a combination of specific economic and political conditions. Their decline resulted, very simply, from the elimination of all the conditions that had led to their establishment and growth.

The first blow to the continued prosperity of the Florida cigar industry occurred early in its history and was in a crucial area: tariffs. The McKinley Tariff passed in 1890 imposed fairly high duties on tobacco imported into the United States.[20] This and subsequent measures antagonistic to the Florida cigar industry (such as the 1897 Dingley Tariff Act) were largely enacted through the efforts of the U.S. Tobacco Trust, whose members were U.S. tobacco growers and cigar manufacturers that used domestic tobacco. The Ybor City firms were seen as a great threat to the Trust, for the Tampa product was a competitive cigar made with fine imported tobacco. While the increasingly unfavorable tariff situation was not a death blow to the Florida cigar industry, it did remove the competitive edge that Tampa cigars had enjoyed over the Cuban-made product, as well as over other cigars made in the U.S.

An additional problem, if only a temporary one, arose in May 1896 when Spain prohibited the exportation of any tobacco from Cuba. Ostensibly done to protect the Cuban manufacturers, the prohibition was designed more to drain the substantial support the Cuban insurgents were receiving from the émigré cigarmakers. The U.S. declaration of war on Spain in 1898 further depleted the tobacco stocks of the Florida manufacturers as Cuba was blockaded by U.S. warships. Cigar production dropped drastically. The tariffs and the war showed how the dependence on imported tobacco made the Florida manufacturers vulnerable to the vagaries of the domestic and international political climate.

The end of the conflict in 1899 brought a renewal to the community as the factories were again able to operate at full capacity. But that very year ushered in a new problem: labor conflicts. The war effort had served to unite the manufacturers and cigarmakers in a common political cause. The return to normalcy, however, allowed long-standing labor-management grievances to come to the forefront. A three-month strike and a subsequent lockout that lasted for five weeks in 1899 had devastating results for the manufacturers.

There would be other strikes. For the manufacturers, Ybor City was no longer a place where the isolation of the "company town" guaranteed a compliant and unorganized labor force.

The two U.S. occupations of Cuba, the second of which ended in 1909, and the growing neo-colonial relationship between the U.S. and Cuba made explicit and formalized by the Platt Amendment ushered in an era of U.S.-guaranteed political stability in Cuba. This undoubtedly made for a more favorable climate for business than what had existed previously. Political instability, a factor that compelled Martínez Ybor to leave decades earlier, must have seemed a thing of the past during the first decades of this century.

In short, most of the factors that gave rise to the Florida handmade cigar industry were no longer present around the dawn of this century. The Depression, mechanization of cigar production, and the growing popularity of cigarettes dealt the final death blows to the manufacture in the U.S. of fine cigars handmade from Cuban tobacco. All the conditions favored the return of that industry to Havana. The Cuban capital thereby regained its position as the undisputed center for the production of handmade Cuban cigars. By the 1920s there was little reason for a Cuban cigarmaker to leave his homeland.

In the long history of Cuban migration to the U.S., Ybor City occupied a very significant, yet temporally circumscribed, place. It rose rapidly and then declined: a "heyday" that, in comparison with most ethnic communities, was short-lived.

Table 5 further substantiates that point. It lists the percentages of all Cuban immigrants arriving in the U.S. from 1908 to 1931 who

Table 5

Cuban immigrants intending to reside in Florida, 1908–1931

Years (fiscal years ending June 30)	Percent intending to reside in Florida
1908–1911	51.1
1912–1915	30.3
1916–1919	26.5
1920–1923	21.2
1924–1927	26.7
1928–1931	18.8

Source: Compiled and computed from the data in U.S., Commissioner-General of Immigration, *Annual Report* (Washington, D.C.: U.S. Government Printing Office,
annual editions for each fiscal year from 1908 to 1932).

indicated, in response to a question asked by immigration officials
at the time of entry, that they intended to reside in Florida. At the
height of the Ybor City community, more than half of all Cubans
entering the U.S. were going to Florida. By the late 1920s, that
percentage had dropped to about 19 percent.

There is direct evidence of a substantial return migration of
cigarmakers to Cuba. From 1908 to 1931, U.S. immigration authorities compiled a surprisingly detailed set of figures on those
persons it classified as "emigrant aliens," defined as "departing
aliens whose permanent residence has been the United States who
intend to reside permanently abroad."[21] The annual immigration
reports for those years present figures on those emigrant aliens by
"race or peoples," the same concept used to identify the country
of origin of the immigrants.

Table 6 presents the figures on "Cuban emigrant aliens" departing the U.S. between 1908 and 1931. It is evident that there
was a substantial amount of "return migration" (the use of that
term assumes that most of the emigrants departed for Cuba). The
table contains the total number of Cuban emigrant aliens as well
as the number of "tobacco-related" Cuban emigrant aliens. The
table also presents the net migration figures, that is, the difference
between the immigrants and the emigrant aliens for each four-year
period. A negative figure indicates, of course, a higher number of
emigrants than immigrants.

Table 6

Emigration of all Cubans and Cubans in
"tobacco-related" occupations, 1908–1931

Years (fiscal years ending June 30)	All Cuban emigrants[a]		Tobacco-related Cuban emigrants	
	number	net[b]	number	net[b]
Total, 1908–1931	33,637	+20,559	8,471	−2,091
1908–1911	7,122	+6,826	2,538	+898
1912–1915	6,710	+6,485	2,142	−434
1916–1919	5,888	+3,330	1,361	−845
1920–1923	4,317	+761	869	−625
1924–1927	4,515	+1,204	857	−612
1928–1931	5,085	+1,953	704	−473

Source: Compiled and computed from the data in U.S., Commissioner-General of Immigration, *Annual Report* (Washington, D.C.: U.S. Government Printing Office,
annual editions for each fiscal year from 1908 to 1932).

[a] "Cuban emigrants" are defined as those persons of Cuban "race or people" who are
not citizens of the U.S. but who had permanent residence in the U.S. before departing
with the intention of residing permanently outside the United States.

[b] The difference between the number of Cuban immigrants (not shown in this table)
and the number of Cuban emigrant aliens.

Whereas the general figures show a positive net migration
in each time period, the figures on the cigarworkers show, for
each period after 1911, a negative net migration, i.e., more Cuban
cigarworkers were leaving than entering the United States. This
table also substantiates what was presented in Table 3: the amount
of migration, in or out, that is related to the cigar industry declines
rapidly after 1911.

POLITICIANS, MUSICIANS, BOXERS, AND BASEBALL PLAYERS

Although Cuban immigration was relatively low during the
1920s through the early 1950s, those arriving represented a human
barometer of the increasingly close political and cultural connections between the U.S. and Cuba. The U.S. became the principal

destination and refuge for ousted political leaders. The U.S. also was where prominent figures in various fields, most notably music and sports, went to develop their careers.

The vagaries of the Cuban Republic resulted in political dislocations which required exile in the U.S. for those who fell from power. In 1933, when Gerardo Machado, Cuba's first dictator, was overthrown, he left the island for Miami, where he died in 1939. In 1944, when General Fulgencio Batista turned over the presidency, he took up residence in Daytona Beach, Florida. When the general decided to go back to Cuba in 1952 to lead a military takeover of the government, the president he ousted, Carlos Prío Socarrás, left for Miami. During Batista's dictatorship, many of his opponents, following the nineteenth-century tradition, carried out political activities and fundraising in the U.S. Fidel Castro was one of them.

In addition to political leaders, there were other Cubans, prominent figures in their respective fields, who repeatedly visited the U.S. during the first half of this century, many of them developing their talents and careers in this country. This was especially true in music and sports, fields in which Cubans made significant contributions in the U.S.

In music Cuban culture has had a clear impact on popular culture in the United States.[22] That impact was made by the many Cuban musicians who performed and recorded in the U.S., especially in New York. In fact, performing in the U.S. and signing a contract with a American recording firm were considered important achievements in the career of a Cuban musician. The *habanera*, the *son*, the *rumba*, the *chachacha* and the *mambo* were all related Cuban musical styles that were brought into the United States by Cuban musicians.

In the late 1920s there were already a number of New York bands with resident Cuban musicians. The most prominent example was the flutist Alberto Socarrás, who arrived in the U.S. in 1928 and later started his own band. Many had a recording contract with Columbia, which was developing its Latin American market. Cuban bands started performing in the U.S., especially in New York hotels.

During the 1930s and 1940s there was virtually an explosion in the popularity of Cuban music and Cuban musicians in the U.S. Many of the songs of Ernesto Lecuona, a prodigious composer, became well known in this country. Lecuona himself performed in New York and served in 1943 as Cuba's honorary cultural attaché in the U.S.

What became known as the "Rumba Era" of Cuban music in the U.S. started on April 26, 1930 with a concert in New York's Palace Theater by Don Azpiazu's Havana Casino Orchestra. It introduced authentic Cuban dance music to the U.S. with its rendition of the "Peanut Vendor," which would become the best-known Cuban tune in this country. From that date on, a number of Cubans, many with their own bands, would bring Afro-Cuban tunes, most with *rumba* and *conga* rhythms, to the U.S. The most well known were: Desi Arnaz, who helped to popularize Cuban music in this country; Alberto Iznaga, the leader of the Siboney Orchestra; Frank Grillo ("Machito"), an innovative band leader and singer; and Mario Bauzá, a musical director who collaborated with Machito.

Cuban music, whether played by Cubans or by U.S. interpreters, was increasingly being heard in Broadway and Hollywood. Many of the popular big swing bands incorporated Cuban songs into their repertoire. Glenn Miller, Artie Shaw, Cab Calloway, and Woody Herman all had popular "Latin" numbers.

The late 1940s saw a fusion of Cuban melodies and rhythms with American jazz, producing what was called Afro-Cuban (Latin) jazz, also referred to as "Cubop." The leading U.S. exponents of the new style were Dizzy Gillespie, Stan Kenton, and Charlie Parker. Their most influential Cuban collaborators were Mario Bauzá, Machito and His Afro-Cubans, and, most notably, Luciano ("Chano") Pozo. The latter, a Conga player with deep roots in the Afro-Cuban tradition, for a time was a member of Gillespie's band.

The stream of Cuban musicians entering the U.S. and playing in bands continued with the maturing of Latin jazz in the 1950s. Percussionists were in special demand. Two of the most notable ones of the era were Ramón ("Mongo") Santamaría and Patato Valdés. The 1950s was also the decade of the *mambo*, a Cuban musical form associated almost exclusively with Dámaso Pérez Prado. One Cuban musician who took up permanent residence in New York in the 1950s was Arsenio Rodríguez, an important exponent of the more traditional *son*.

Sports is another field in which Cubans in this country have made special contributions. The best Cuban boxers and baseball players would come to the U.S., if only temporarily, to enhance their careers. Both sports enjoyed tremendous popularity in Cuba. They had been introduced into the island almost as soon as they had started developing as sports in the U.S.

Cuba produced a number of world champions in boxing.[23] The first notable one was Eligio Sardiñas (Kid Chocolate). After amassing a record in Cuba of 100 victories (86 of them knockouts), Sardiñas came to the United States in 1928. From that date and until 1931 his boxing career unfolded in the rings of the Northeast, especially New York. In Philadelphia, July 15, 1931, he knocked out Benny Bass in the seventh round to capture the Junior Lightweight crown.

Another renowned Cuban boxer was Gerardo González (Kid Gavilán). He won 106 of the 143 fights of his career, and was never knocked out. He made his U.S. debut in 1946. As with Sardiñas, the most important bouts of his career took place in the U.S. González's two close matches with Sugar Ray Robinson, the first one in New York and the second one in Philadelphia, became legendary. On May 18, 1951, in Madison Square Garden, he defeated Johnny Bratton in fifteen rounds to win the Welterweight title. He successfully defended his crown in seven challenges which took place in New York, Philadelphia, Miami, Chicago, and Syracuse.

Before 1961, Cuba was the largest supplier of foreign baseball players for the U.S. major leagues.[24] In no other Latin American country was baseball introduced as early or as successfully as in Cuba. Reportedly, there was a Cuban playing professional baseball in the U.S. in 1871. It is believed that it was in 1874 that the first baseball game was played in Cuba, a few years before the establishment of the U.S. major leagues.

The history of Cubans in the U.S. major leagues goes back to 1911. From that date and until 1940, a total of twenty-one Cubans played in the major leagues. The most notable of the group was a pitcher, Adolfo ("Dolf") Luque, whose career in the majors spanned twenty-two years, from 1914 to 1935. He won 193 games in his career and pitched in two World Series, in 1919 for Cincinnati and in 1933 for the N.Y. Giants. In 1923, as a starter for the Reds, he posted the best record in the majors: twenty-seven wins and only eight losses.

The participation of Cubans in the major leagues would have been greater during those years had the game been racially integrated. There were a number of Cubans who played in the "Negro leagues."

From 1940 to the present, a total of ninety-eight Cubans played in the major leagues. Their numbers peaked in the 1950s and 1960s, and started declining in the 1970s and 1980s with the restrictions on migration from Cuba. Some of the most notable Cuban major leaguers were: Roberto Ortiz, Orestes (Minnie) Miñoso, Sandy Amoros, Camilo Pascual, Orlando Peña, Tony Taylor, Zoilo Versalles, Mike Cuéllar, Tony González, Leo Cárdenas, Tony Oliva, José Cardenal, Octavio (Cookie) Rojas, Luis Tiant, Bert Campaneris, and Tany Pérez.

Athletes and musicians are not typical of any population. Furthermore, they would also not be representative of the levels of religiosity of the broader society. As such, that special migration of Cubans, particularly to New York, represents a continuation of the long-standing trend of secularism among Cuban immigrants.

4

The Exodus from Revolutionary Cuba
and the Catholic Church in South Florida,
1959–1965

Although the history of the Cuban presence in the United States is a long one, the exodus from revolutionary Cuba has been unprecedented in its magnitude. About 90 percent of all persons of Cuban origin presently living in the U.S. date their presence here, or that of their parents, to the migration flow that started in 1960.

One of the differences between the earlier migrations from the island and the exodus from revolutionary Cuba is that for the latter, Miami has been the prime destination. The religious dimensions of the settlement of Cubans in South Florida during the early 1960s has a very rich and dramatic history, and represents an important chapter in both the development of the Cuban community of Miami and in the history of the relationship between the Catholic Church and America's immigrants. The Cuban case is in many ways unique, given the factors that combined to shape it: the reasons for the exodus, the characteristics of the migrants, and the nature of the diocese that received them.

THE CUBAN REVOLUTION

In the early morning hours of January 1, 1959, Fulgencio Batista, the unconstitutional ruler of Cuba since 1952, fled the island. Eventually, a government headed by Fidel Castro, the leader of the principal rebel movement against Batista, took over complete control of Cuba. Castro's government would engineer a complete transformation of the political, social, and economic institutions of the country.

One result of that transformation was the eventual establishment of a political system that severely restricted individual political freedoms. The Castro government also eliminated private ownership of economic enterprises, instituting a system of state

190

CUBAN CATHOLICS IN THE U.S.

control over the entire economy and implementing a profound redistribution of the country's wealth that realigned the social class system.

In response to that transformation and to the nature of the new order, nearly one million Cubans would leave their homeland over the following quarter of a century. It would be the largest migration ever from Cuba to the United States.

REVOLUTIONARY CHANGE AND THE CATHOLIC CHURCH IN CUBA

The Cuban Catholic Church initially supported the new revolutionary government.[1] Sweeping into power with the promise of extensive social reforms, the new regime had a stated agenda consistent with a long-standing nationalistic and progressive reform movement, one with which the Cuban Church was essentially in agreement.

But it would not be long before the Church started disagreeing with the government and expressing concern over many of its measures. Church leaders were critical of the wave of violent retribution, especially executions, against the collaborators of the previous regime. There were also concerns about the warming of relations with the Soviet Union.[2]

What most concerned the Cuban clergy, however, as well as Catholics in general, were the growing threats to Catholic education. It was evident that the government had launched into a campaign to place all schools under state control, with public education for all.

The bulk of the pastoral letters issued by the Cuban bishops during 1960 and 1961 dealt with that threat to the survival of Catholic private education. Other matters, particularly the growing activism and militancy of Catholic youths against the regime, especially at the university, served to place the state and the Church in direct conflict. Kirk notes that "by the summer of 1960, church-state polarization was complete."

With the failure of the Bay of Pigs invasion and the disintegration of the Havana anti-government underground, the persecution of many priests and lay persons intensified. The greatest blow to the Church would come on June 6, 1961, with the promulgation of a law stipulating that all schools in the country would be public, nationalizing all private schools.[3] In fact, many of the

Catholic schools had already been shut down and nationalized before that date.

Joined with the persecution by state forces, the nationalization of schools forced the massive evacuation of clergy and other personnel from the island. The most notable event of that evacuation occurred on September 17, 1961 when, on short notice, 131 priests were forced to board the ship *Covadonga* in Havana harbor and were sent to Spain. The expulsion was especially directed at the Spanish clergy, who accounted for two-thirds of the priests placed on the *Covadonga*.[4]

Table 7 presents the dramatic decline in the number of priests and nuns in Cuba from 1960 to 1965. This phenomenon would prove to be extremely important, not only for the future of the Church in Cuba, but also for the development of religious institutions among Cuban Americans. When the Cuban exiles arrived in the U.S. they came with their own priests and nuns. The Cuban Church was also in exile.

Table 7

The Catholic Church in Cuba
1955, 1960, and 1965

	1955	1960	1965	Percent change 1960–65
Parishes	206	210	226	+7.6
Inhabitants per parish	29,700	32,300	33,200	+2.8
Total priests	693	723	220	−69.6
Inhabitants per priest	8,800	9,400	34,200	+263.8
Priests in religious orders	464	483	120	−75.2
Diocesan priests	229	240	100	−58.3
Total nuns	2,484	2,225	191	−91.4
Inhabitants per nun	2,500	3,000	39,400	+1213.3

Source: Compiled and computed from Isidore Alonso, "Estadísticas religiosas de América Latina," *Social Compas* 14 (1967): 5–6. Reproduced in Mateo Jover Marimón, "The Church," in *Revolutionary Change in Cuba*, ed. Carmelo Mesa-Lago (Pittsburgh: University of Pittsburgh Press, 1971), p. 402.

THE EXODUS FROM THE ISLAND

The first stage in the exodus from Revolutionary Cuba occurred between 1960 and 1962, when some 200,000 persons left the island. Among them was a disproportionately large number of persons who were most likely to be alienated by the elimination of a system of private enterprise: proprietors, managers, executives, and many professionals.

The United States government welcomed the new exiles. Its relations with the Castro regime were becoming increasingly hostile, especially since Castro was confiscating U.S. property on the island and aligning Cuba with the Soviet Union.[5] President Eisenhower, in one of his last actions in office, severed diplomatic relations with Cuba in January 1961.

The first stage of the exodus ended with the Missile Crisis of October 1962, when President Kennedy demanded the withdrawal from Cuba of Soviet missiles. As a result of that action, all regular air traffic between the two countries was discontinued.[6] For the next three years it was difficult for persons to leave Cuba for the U.S. Many left secretly in small boats and rafts across the Straits of Florida. Not all of them succeeded in reaching Florida.

The economic and political conditions in the island continued to worsen. Virtually all foodstuffs and consumer goods were rationed. Life in Cuba became more and more austere. The number of persons wishing to leave the island increased dramatically.

In the fall of 1965, the Cuban government responded to those pressures for emigration by opening the port of Camarioca, allowing persons from the U.S. to go to Cuba to pick up those relatives that wanted to leave the country. Some 5,000 Cubans left from Camarioca for this country before the U.S. and Cuba halted the boatlift and agreed to an orderly airlift.

The airlift, also known as the "freedom flights," started in December 1965 and lasted until 1973. It involved twice-daily flights between Varadero, on Cuba's northern coast, and Miami. In the eight years it was in operation, the airlift brought 260,500 Cubans to the U.S.[7]

The end of the airlift brought another period when migration from the island was severely restricted. Those leaving were doing so through third countries, especially Spain or Mexico. Once again small rafts, usually made with inner tubes, appeared in the waters off the Florida coast. Sometimes the small crafts were found empty.

The pressures for emigration once again mounted within Cuba. Early in 1980, groups of Cubans were forcefully entering several of the Latin American embassies in Havana in an attempt to obtain political asylum and leave Cuba. One such entry, in the Peruvian Embassy, resulted in the death of a Cuban soldier who was guarding the embassy. As a result of the dispute that followed between the Cuban and Peruvian governments, Castro withdrew the armed guard from the embassy. Within twenty-four hours, on April 4, 10,800 persons flocked into the embassy, seeking asylum as a way out of Cuba.

In response to these events, the Cuban government, as it had done fifteen years earlier, opened a port for unrestricted emigration. The port was Mariel, giving the name to the boatlift that lasted for six months and brought, in a manner uncontrolled by the U.S., more than 125,000 Cubans to this country.

The Mariel boatlift was a dramatic event that focused the attention of the entire U.S. on the Straits of Florida. There were concerns in this country that Castro had placed on the boats criminals and inmates of mental institutions. Such concerns, however, proved to be exaggerated. Of the large number of persons that arrived through the boatlift, only about 3,000 were considered by the U.S. to be criminals, excludable from entry into this country.

In 1984, the U.S. and Cuban governments agreed to renew migration from the island. The U.S. committed itself to permitting the entry of some 20,000 persons a year. For its part, the Cuban government agreed to take back the Mariel entrants that the U.S. government regards as "excludables" and which were held in Federal detention centers.

That agreement, however, was canceled by Cuba in May 1985 when the U.S. started operating a radio station, Radio Martí, beamed to Cuba in an attempt to provide information to the people in the island. In November 1986, however, Cuba reinstituted the agreement, making imminent the deportation to the island of the Mariel "excludables." This action resulted in rioting, lasting several days, in the Federal penitentiaries of Atlanta and Oakdale, Louisiana, where the "excludables" were being held.

Presently, the levels of migration from Cuba do not reach the ceiling of 20,000 largely because the U.S. has not granted enough visas to fill that quota. There is, however, increasing clandestine migration from Cuba, largely in response to the rapidly deteriorating conditions in the island. The loss to Cuba of its major trading partners through the breakdown of socialism in Eastern Europe has greatly increased the hardships of the Cuban population.

Table 8 presents the annual number of Cubans arriving in the U.S. from 1959 to 1966, the specific period under analysis here. The

Table 8

Cubans arriving in the United States, 1959–1966

Year	Number
1959 (1 January–30 June)	26,527
Year ending 30 June	
1960	60,224
1961	49,961
1962	78,611
1963	42,929
1964	15,616
1965	16,447
1966	46,668

Source: U.S., Department of Justice, Immigration and Naturalization Service, "Cubans Arriving in the United States, by Class of Admission: January 1, 1959–September 30, 1980 (mimeo sheet, October 1980).

"first wave," from 1960 to the Missile Crisis in October 1962, is clearly evident, as is the relative decline following the termination of regularly scheduled flights. Those arriving in 1963, 1964, and 1965 did so through third countries. The increase in fiscal year 1966 reflects the establishment of the daily "Freedom Flights."

CUBAN IMMIGRATION AND THE DIOCESE OF MIAMI:
IMPACT AND RESPONSE

In the early 1960s the diocese of Miami received the largest number of Cuban immigrants. The impact of those immigrants and the response of the diocese is a fascinating story. While many aspects of it still await research, there is a source that presents an excellent and detailed overview of that story: Father Michael J. McNally's *Catholicism in South Florida, 1868–1968*. Most of what is presented in this section is derived from Chapters 6 and 7 of that book, which McNally devotes to "The Cuban Challenge."[8]

The sudden and massive entry of Cubans into South Florida posed an unprecedented challenge to the region, and especially to the diocese of Miami. In terms of providing for the spiritual needs of the new arrivals, the diocese did not have enough Spanish-speaking priests and other personnel.[9] In terms of social services,

Federal assistance did not actually start until March 1961. Prior to that time, the diocese and national Catholic organizations represented the principal source of such services for the Cuban refugees.[10]

It is impossible to tell the story of the diocesan response to the Cuban influx without highlighting the role of its principal protagonist, the man who served during those critical years as bishop (and later archbishop) of Miami: Coleman F. Carroll. It was Carroll who made all the critical decisions regarding the diocese's programs and policies towards the new arrivals.

From the very start of the influx, Bishop Carroll was extremely supportive of the Cuban migrants, both spiritually and materially. He used his position to welcome the Cubans, thereby providing an example to American Catholics. He portrayed the new migrants very positively, in an attempt to defuse tensions and resentments over the burdens posed by such a massive immigration.[11]

Materially, the diocese was at the forefront of assistance to Cuban families. McNally indicates that in just eleven months, from December 1960 to October 1961, the diocese of Miami contributed more than $875,000 in goods and services to Cuban exiles. During 1962, the diocese spent nearly half a million dollars on their welfare.[12]

One of the principal vehicles for the distribution of the diocese's assistance was the Centro Hispano Católico, a social service agency created by the bishop in October 1959 to serve the needs of Miami's Spanish-speaking population. The Centro offered numerous services, from medical care and day-care to English classes. It handled some 450,000 cases from October 1959 to June 1968. At the height of the Cuban influx, the Centro was attending to some 300 cases a day.[13]

Although Bishop Carroll exhibited an extraordinary commitment to the welfare of the Cuban refugees arriving in his diocese, he did so with a style and approach that drew considerable criticism. His management style was highly centralized. He was involved in everything, everyone had to report to him, and he made all decisions. According to McNally, this was in many ways one of the strengths of the diocese in dealing with the Cuban challenge. Carroll's personal control and the lack of large structure meant that "Diocesan agencies could move quickly and decisively."[14] On the other hand, such a style created many critics, particularly among priests in the religious orders who sought a measure of autonomy from diocesan control.

Carroll's approach was based in his deep-seated belief in the concept of immigrant assimilation. The bishop was committed to diocesan unity under his control. The basis for the integration of the new arrivals was the territorially based American parish. He opposed the creation of parishes based upon nationality and he discouraged the creation of Catholic organizations or subgroups based upon ethnicity. He stimulated the rapid learning of English, not only among the new parishioners, but among the newly arrived priests from Cuba: "It is hoped that they will learn the language and within six months or so be of some service to the Diocese."[15] In fact, many of the religious who arrived from Cuba were assigned to predominantly American parishes or schools, in many cases outside of Miami, to encourage their assimilation by separating them from the faithful of their own country.[16] These, of course, were not decisions that were appreciated by many in the Cuban community. The praise for Carroll's generous assistance is usually tempered by criticism of his aggressive assimilationist policies.

Nevertheless, the bishop did eventually allow for the establishment within his diocese of two churches that were created exclusively for Hispanics, especially Cubans: St. John Bosco parish and the Shrine to Our Lady of Charity.

St. John Bosco served, de facto, as an ethnic-based parish for Cubans, although technically it was a territorial parish located in the Little Havana section of Miami. Established in 1963, many of its parishioners came from outside the parish boundaries. Its pastor, Father Emilio Vallina, is a native Cuban, and during St. John Bosco's early years it was the most important place of worship for Cubans in Miami. It was the one church where one could have a baptism or a funeral Mass performed in Spanish by a Cuban priest. There was considerable lay involvement, and the parish sponsored classes for children in Spanish on Cuban history, geography, and culture. The parish reached it peak in activity in 1968.[17] As other parishes eventually offered Masses and other services in Spanish, and as the Cuban population moved out of the neighborhood, St. John Bosco's parish population waned. It currently serves the new arrivals to its neighborhood, who are primarily from Nicaragua.

In 1966 Bishop Carroll proposed the establishment of a shrine to Our Lady of Charity, the patroness of Cuba. He donated the land adjacent to Mercy Hospital, facing Biscayne Bay. The following year a Cuban-born priest, Father Agustín Román, was named director of the shrine. It was largely through his efforts that the shrine, or the Ermita, as it is known among Cubans, was built.

Years later, Agustín Román was named auxiliary bishop of Miami, but continues to be the resident director of the shrine and he still says Mass there. The chapel has become the site for Masses marking special events in the Cuban community.

One of the diocese's programs to assist Cuban refugees merits a separate mention here because of its importance and its special nature: the Unaccompanied Children's Program. The Pedro Pan Operation, as the program was also known, was a dramatic episode in this story. Its protagonist was Monsignor Bryan Walsh, director of the diocese's Catholic Welfare Bureau.

The program started when Monsignor Walsh became aware of a growing number of Cuban children who had been sent to the U.S., unaccompanied by their parents.[18] This situation was created by fears about the future of the children in a communist regime. There was a persistent rumor that many children would be sent to the Soviet Union. Walsh established homes, and later entire camps, to house and care for the increasingly large numbers of children who were leaving Cuba alone. In fact, the State Department even gave Walsh the authorization to facilitate the process of departure from Cuba. He could issue letters to any child in Cuba between six and sixteen, waiving the visa requirement for entry into the United States. These visa waivers were distributed in Havana by the Swiss Embassy.

As of September 1963, the Unaccompanied Children's Program had processed 14,156 cases.[19] Most Pedro Pan children were, of course, eventually reunited with their parents in the United States.

Transplanted Institutions

The Cuban exiles of the early 1960s not only brought themselves to the U.S., but they also brought many of their religious personnel and institutions from Cuba. This was especially true for Catholics and it was a situation determined largely by the Church-State conflict discussed earlier. That conflict resulted in a virtual evacuation of the Church personnel and organizations from the island, making possible their establishment among Cubans settling in this country.

Perhaps the most prominent Catholic institutions brought to the United States by Cuban exiles center on education: schools, student organizations, and alumni associations. To this day, attenders and graduates of the various religious schools in prerevolutionary

Cuba continue to hold activities and annual social events in Miami and elsewhere in the U.S. For many Cuban exiles such organizations and activities constitute the principal voluntary associations to which they belong. They provide a continuation and reaffirmation of ties created during childhood in the home country.

In the transplantation of institutions of religious education from Cuba to the United States, the Jesuits represent a singular success story. Beyond alumni associations, no other order or organization has been able to bring and sustain in the United States its Cuban educational institutions. Their experience is presented here in detail for three reasons: 1) Jesuit educational institutions in Miami are the best examples of direct transplantations of religious institutions from Cuba; 2) the process of transplantation of those institutions is one that reveals a great deal about the origins and nature of the exodus from socialist Cuba; and 3) it is a story that has largely not been researched nor told.

Belén Jesuit Preparatory School

El Colegio de Nuestra Señora de Belén (The School of Our Lady of Bethlehem), offering instruction at the elementary and secondary grade levels, was founded in 1854 in Havana by the Jesuits. Since then, and until its closing by the Cuban revolutionary government in 1961, its students included the sons of Cuba's elite families. Its graduates figured prominently throughout the Cuban Republic (1902–1958) in the governmental, economic, intellectual, and cultural spheres of national life. Perhaps its best-known and most influential alumnus is Fidel Castro, class of 1945.[20]

The Jesuits did not wait for the closing of the school on May 13, 1961 to start making arrangements to move their school to Miami. Given the tense relationship between the government and the Cuban Church and the increasing radicalization of the regime, the school's administrators anticipated the nationalization order and their expulsion from the massive school building they had built and inaugurated in 1925. As early as November 4, 1960, Father Richard C. Chisholm, a Cuban Jesuit who at the time was serving as director of a Jesuit seminary in Puerto Rico, wrote a letter to Bishop Coleman F. Carroll of Miami exploring the possibility of moving the school to Miami.[21]

The letter was sent on behalf of Father Ceferino Ruiz, vice-provincial of the Society's Antilles Province, which at that time was based in Havana. Chisholm also made clear he was writing with the approval of the Jesuit Father General in Rome. The letter was specific and to the point:

> The proposition is based on the actual and imminent possibility that the Cuban government will ultimately take over the Colegio de Belén. . . . [I]t involves the establishment in Miami of a school "in exile," branch of "Colegio de Belén" . . . mainly for Cuban boys that have had to leave the nation because of the actual circumstances.[22]

Reflecting the mood of Cuban exiles arriving at the time, the Jesuits viewed the transfer of the school to Miami as temporary:

> This school "in exile" would cease to exist once the conditions in Cuba return to normality and it is possible to return safely. . . . [T]he main reason for this school . . . is that the boys should have the possibility of studying such subjects and following such a curriculum which would enable them to continue their studies in Cuba when they return, without having lost their time, as this curriculum would be in accord with the system followed basically in Cuba.[23]

Belén Jesuit in Miami, therefore, was originally proposed as an "exile" school, that is, only as a temporary arrangement, pending an expected return to the island. Its transfer from Cuba was being negotiated more than six months before the school in Havana was actually closed. That foresight on the part of the Jesuits was a critical element in the successful relocation of the school.

The ability of the Jesuits in Havana to anticipate, and plan for, the political conditions that would adversely affect them can probably be attributed to the order's long history of dealing with expulsions.[24] In the case of several of the Spanish Jesuits in Belén, that experience was also a personal one. They had been expelled from Spain during the Spanish Republic and had already undergone the experience of relocating, initially to Portugal, and eventually to Cuba.[25]

Although other orders attempted to reestablish their Cuban schools to Miami (the La Salle brothers, for example), the Jesuits have had the most lasting success. Belén Jesuit is still operating in Miami, with more than 800 students enrolled in grades six through twelve.

In large measure, that success can probably be attributed to the insistence on the part of Jesuits that the school be established independent of diocesan control, despite the economic hardships that such independence entailed. The proposal to Bishop Carroll made clear that the school would be run essentially by the same

personnel that was in Havana at the time and that the Jesuit Province of the Antilles would be responsible for its establishment and
financing, with the approval of the head of the New Orleans Jesuit
Province.[26] The only thing the Jesuits wanted from Carroll was his
permission to establish the school in his diocese.

Bishop Carroll officially gave that permission on August 29,
1961, in a letter to Ramón Calvo, S.J.:

> This letter is to certify that the Society of Jesus has been invited by
> me into the Diocese of Miami to establish within the Diocese a high
> school for boys to replace their similar high school, known as Belén
> School, at Havana, Cuba.[27]

In accordance with his assimilationist approach, however, Carroll stipulates in his invitation to the Jesuits that the school is to
be established as an "American school," with a curriculum that is
"in accord with the laws of the State of Florida and the standards
required by the office of the Director of Education for the Diocese
of Miami."[28] This, of course, fundamentally modified the Jesuits'
original proposal, presented in Chisholm's letter, that Belén be a
temporary "exile" school that conformed to the standards of the
Cuban educational system so as to ease the return of the students
to the island once conditions there changed. Carroll was also very
clear on a point that had been left vague in Chisholm's letter:
"English is to be the language used in teaching all subjects at
the school."[29]

Perhaps the most interesting provision of the bishop's letter of
invitation is his offer of land for the building of the school. This,
of course, had clear implications for the issue of diocesan control
over the school. Carroll wrote:

> The location of the school will be in South Miami, the property
> consisting of twenty acres of land valued at approximately one hun-
> dred and twenty thousand dollars. . . . [T]he owner of this property
> is Mr. Hardy Matheson . . . he will turn the title of this property
> over to the Diocese of Miami directly.[30]

The diocese was to turn over the title of the land to the Jesuits,
but with the "express condition" that if the Jesuits ever decided to
abandon teaching at the school (as they originally intended to do),
the entire property would revert to the diocese.[31]

But Belén's Jesuits did not accept Carroll's offer. Instead, they
opened their Miami school in August 1961 by borrowing space
in the building of the elementary school of Gesu Church, a Jesuit
parish in downtown Miami. During that first school year, about 170

students were enrolled, almost all of them from Belén in Havana or from Dolores, the Jesuit school in Santiago de Cuba.

The school was staffed almost exclusively by the priests from Belén. The administration of the school was formed by the trio of Jesuits from Havana who made the final arrangements, after their departure from Cuba, for the establishment of the school in Miami: Luis Ripoll, Jesús Nuevo, and Felipe Arroyo. The teaching staff was bolstered with the arrival of three North American Jesuits, who represented part of the assistance the order gave to the relocation of Belén. Although many of the priests from Cuba could teach in English, the addition of the three North Americans greatly enhanced the school's capacity to offer instruction exclusively in that language, as stipulated by the bishop in his letter of invitation to the Jesuits.

The assistance from the order was also critical from a financial standpoint. The students from Cuba, many of them arriving without their parents, were not able to pay tuition. It was not until 1964 that tuition was instituted for those who could pay.

In addition to the aid provided, in various ways, by the North American Jesuits, the Miami diocese also rendered critical assistance. Bishop Carroll reportedly contributed $25,000 to the effort, and Monsignor Walsh of the Catholic Welfare Bureau arranged for two residences to house the students who arrived without their families. The houses also served as residences for some of the priests.[32]

The following academic year, 1962–1963, the school moved to a building on S.W. 8th St. and 7th Avenue which formerly housed a dance academy.[33] Dividers were placed on the large dance floor to create several classrooms. In 1965, a second floor was constructed and the adjoining building was purchased.

It was not until 1980 that the Jesuits moved Belén from that location to a multi-million-dollar school they constructed in the western fringe of metropolitan Miami on land donated by an alumnus. What was originally intended as a temporary "exile" school had become a prominent presence in Catholic secondary education in southern Florida, and an important educational institution of the Cuban-American community.

Agrupación Católica Universitaria

The Agrupación Católica Universitaria (Catholic University Association) was officially established in Havana in 1931. Its founder was Father Felipe Rey de Castro, S.J., a Spaniard who in 1925 arrived in Cuba and served as Prefect of Belén School.[34] The establishment of the ACU responded to Rey de Castro's concern for providing continuity, after graduation, to the spiritual development of Belén students. At the time, there was no Catholic university in Cuba, and Rey de Castro believed that Belén's graduates, almost all of whom attended the public University of Havana, were being "abandoned" and "irretrievably lost" to the world of a secular and liberal university education.[35]

Rey de Castro devised a structured program of applied and intense religious instruction for university students built around the spiritual exercises of St. Ignatius. Originally, *agrupados* (as members were known) started participating in the exercises, and in the work of the ACU, as seniors in Belén.

But the Agrupación soon developed an ethos that encompassed much more than religious instruction. The organization became a close fraternity with a strong value placed on professional success and political involvement. This was a consequence of Rey de Castro's basic operating premise: the best way to carry out the work of Christ was not through preaching or proselytism, but through influence.[36] Consequently, the Agrupación "sought to bring into its ranks those individuals who, through their intellectual capacity, social background, or civic involvement, were destined to exert a guiding influence on the future of Cuba."[37] The ACU was therefore conceived as an elite organization.[38] A strong emphasis was placed on the following characteristics: 1) education and professional advancement, 2) networking and mutual assistance among members, 3) development of leadership skills, and 4) civic and political activism. Those characteristics, combined with strong and charismatic personal direction from the Jesuits, gave the ACU a resiliency that enabled it to develop rapidly in Cuba and to become reestablished in exile.

The political activism of its members would be a feature that would unwittingly shape the history of the organization from its very beginning. Unlike what one might expect from elite organizations, a support for progressive causes and popular social reforms tended to predominate. Many of its founding members became involved in the struggle against the dictatorship of Gerardo Machado, who was finally overthrown in 1933.[39]

That activism surfaced again during the dictatorship of Fulgencio Batista, from 1952 to 1958. By that time, the Agrupación had established a formidable presence at the University of Havana. Operating from a compound of houses only a couple of blocks from the campus, the ACU was not only a center for religious activity, but it was also a place for serious academic, political, and civic work. Agrupados exchanged class notes, helped underclassmen with their courses, and even had expert "reviewers" who conducted sessions on coursework in a variety of fields, especially medicine and law.[40] These activities fostered tremendous fraternity among members and a strong identification with, and loyalty to, the organization. Although the ACU received little support from the order and its membership fees were nominal, it developed a financial base that enabled it to expand its facilities and activities. As might be expected from an elite organization, its principal sources of support, then and now, were a few generous benefactors.

But critical to the success of the Agrupación was the dedication and leadership of its Jesuit directors. Rey de Castro provided that strong direction until his sudden death in 1952. His successor was another Spanish Jesuit who in many ways surpassed him in dynamism, charisma, and total dedication to the Agrupación: Father Amando Llorente. Llorente continued Rey de Castro's total commitment to the Agrupación and the tradition that the director was ubiquitous, devoting himself full-time to the students and living in the ACU house rather than with the other Jesuits.

The young Llorente, later assisted by Father Francisco Barbeito, S.J., of the Belén faculty, faced the turbulent years of the anti-Batista struggle. ACU members were very active in that struggle, and some were killed or imprisoned. When Batista left the country on January 1, 1959, and Fidel Castro and his army marched into Havana, the agrupados were supportive and elated, especially Llorente and Barbeito, who were seeing the rise to power of one who had been their student and close friend at Belén.

However, the directions the new government took soon alienated ACU members. The Castro government moved against the economic interests of the elite, and many of the families of the agrupados were adversely affected. By 1960, the members of the ACU were uniformly opposed to the government and many were actively involved in militant activities and conspiracies against the regime.[41] Some lost their lives or were imprisoned.

The failure of the Bay of Pigs invasion, on April 17, 1961, brought about the collapse of the anti-Castro underground in Havana. The ACU house was taken over by the government and its members were among those targeted for persecution. Llorente sought asylum in the Spanish Embassy and eventually fled the country.[42] In the summer and fall of 1961, virtually the entire membership of the ACU left Cuba for the United States. According to one agrupado, "Father Llorente gave the order to leave and regroup in Miami."[43]

Given the nature and character of the Agrupación, and especially of Llorente, it is not difficult to see how it was able to successfully "regroup" in the United States. With its strong leadership and the high degree of solidarity among its members, it would not take long for the ACU to reestablish itself outside of Cuba.

Before leaving Cuba, Llorente declined the offer from the head of the Jesuit Antilles Province to relocate to Europe and to other duties with these words:

> . . . it would be shameful if, after having lived and worked with the agrupados during the good times, we abandoned them in these most difficult times. It would be an unpardonable sin for me in particular . . . I would feel like a traitor abandoning the Agrupación during this, its most formidable test, to go to Spain or Italy.[44]

While carefully guarding his autonomy, from the order and from the diocese of Miami, Llorente obtained permission from both to reestablish the Agrupación in Miami. Two months after leaving Cuba, in July 1961, Llorente was already conducting spiritual exercises with about seventy-five agrupados in a rented room at the Golden Strand Motel in Miami Beach.[45]

Reflecting on the transplantation of the Agrupación, Llorente recently provided his explanation for the apparent resiliency of the Jesuit institutions in the Cuban diaspora:

> [I]f the ACU had not been directed in Cuba by Jesuits, it would have perished because neither diocesan priests nor those of other religious orders have the mobility to relocate from one country to another. . . . [T]hat liberty that I had to go wherever the agrupados went . . . is a privilege of the Society of Jesus.[46]

One of the features of the Agrupación that proved to be very functional for the economic adjustment of the agrupados in the United States was its tradition for educational and professional advancement and networking among its members. Wherever agrupados relocated and learned of professional opportunities for others, they communicated this through their network to help secure employment for fellow ACU members. In this way nuclei of agrupados arose throughout the U.S., many of them in the most unlikely places. The foremost examples of this were in the medical field. A principal source of employment for newly arrived ACU members with medical training was the relatively undesirable jobs on the staffs of state mental hospitals. Once one member obtained such a position, he promoted the employment of other members, resulting in nuclei of agrupados in far-flung communities throughout the U.S., in states such as Georgia, Texas, and Kansas.[47] The function of the Agrupación in economic adjustment greatly contributed to retaining the members' solidarity and commitment to the organization.

While the ACU would be based in Miami, Llorente early recognized the importance of establishing strong ties and organizing the agrupados throughout the U.S. Before 1961 was over, he had already taken the first of several automobile trips across the U.S. Each night he would stay at the house of an agrupado, and members in the region would flock there in the evening to hear him say Mass and preach a message of unity and continued commitment to the organization.[48]

In Miami, Llorente rented a house for the ACU almost immediately after his arrival in 1961. Members without families in Miami lived there with Llorente, who continued the tradition of the resident director, despite having the option of residing with the Belén Fathers. After a succession of other houses, the Agrupación acquired in 1965 a house on the waterfront in the northeastern portion of Miami. Over the years, the adjoining properties were acquired. Today, the ACU is still on that site, occupying a spacious compound that includes a retreat house. Llorente continues to be its resident director, conducting spiritual exercises and maintaining his ties to active agrupados worldwide. He places their number at about five hundred.[49]

While the ACU is a good example of an institution that was successfully transplanted from Cuba, it has had less success in extending its mission to younger generations of Cuban Americans. Although it is very much alive and functioning today, its membership is almost exclusively composed of Cubans born on the island. The core of the organization are those who were active in Cuba and during the early years of exile, and who continue to have a commitment to the organization.

The failure to renew its membership with younger members may be due, at least partially, to the fact that the ACU never established its house near any of Miami's universities. Furthermore, there are no evident extension efforts to that population that has traditionally been its recruitment base: Belén School. But the fundamental problem may well be Llorente's identification with, and commitment to, that generation of agrupados he first served as director and he shepherded through difficult years in Cuba and in the U.S. Integrating a new cohort, one born and raised in the U.S., required a degree of flexibility and adaptation, especially in cultural terms, that was apparently beyond the possibilities of the organization and its director.

That both Belén School and the ACU have survived to this day is a testimony to the Jesuits' experience and capacity for surviving expulsions. Furthermore, the Spanish and Cuban Jesuits who directed those institutions demonstrated a commitment to maintaining them in the new country. In so doing, they provided Cuban exiles with a continuity in their religious institutions from the homeland, a continuity not typical among immigrant groups, and understandable only in the context of the special conditions of that migration from Cuba. The presence in Miami of Cuban religious and educational institutions has greatly contributed to the creation of a true ethnic enclave in Cuban Miami, that is, a fairly unique, institutionally complete ethnic community.

Other Organizations and Movements

Although those two Jesuit institutions are the best examples of institutions transplanted from Cuba, there are others. Aside from the alumni associations of the Catholic Cuban schools, there is the establishment of St. Thomas University in northern Miami. The precursor of that institution was St. Thomas of Villanueva, Cuba's only Catholic university.

One organization that was not transplanted from Cuba, but which developed in Miami among Cuban exiles, was the Cursillos de Cristiandad, a lay movement. The Cursillos, according to McNally, center on "an intensive weekend short course on basic Christianity."[50] The experience is an emotional one, designed to reaffirm faith and commitment to the Church. The first cursillo was held in Miami, in Spanish, in 1962. Its members were very active, but were not integrated in any way into the official Church.

One of the most important trends in Miami's Cuban community is the challenge posed by popular religious movements. The ones with the most evident influence over the Cuban-American population are those derived from the complex of religious beliefs taken to Cuba by the African slaves. Grouped generally under the rubric of "Afro-Cuban" religions or cults their influence in the religiosity of Cuba was briefly discussed in chapter 1.[51]

The distinctions between Catholicism and the beliefs of African origin are not always clear and distinguishable. A considerable amount of syncretism has occurred between the two. A number of Catholic saints, for example, are especially important in the religious practices of many Cubans who consider themselves Catholic, yet the prominence of those saints is originally derived from having been identified with deities, or *orishas*, in the Yoruba pantheon.

Syncretism aside, African religious practices, exactly as they were taken to Cuba by the slaves, have not only survived in Cuba, but indeed flourished. *Santería* is the most well-known of the various Afro-Cuban cults, but it is not the only one. As is typical with folk beliefs, the Afro-Cuban cults have a tremendous resiliency and appeal because the belief systems address the everyday problems persons face, in health, romance, survival, prosperity, and other personal issues. Many of the rituals hold the promise of resolving a person's problems in these areas.

Traditionally, there has been a relationship between the practice of Afro-Cuban religions and socioeconomic status, a relationship that has, of course, exceptions. That is typical of Cuban culture and society, in which African cultural patterns, not only in religion, but also in music, diet, and even diction, have been associated with lower socioeconomic status.

Since the upper socioeconomic levels were overrepresented in the early wave of migration from socialist Cuba, the incidence of Afro-Cuban religious practices among Cuban Americans was not as evident in Miami prior to 1965. As the successive waves of migrants became increasingly more representative of the Cuban population, Afro-Cuban religious practices became more evident in Miami. The Mariel boatlift was especially important in increasing in Miami the number of practitioners and believers in the various Afro-Cuban cults.

Conclusion

After more than thirty years of socialism, the Cuban nation faces a crisis in the new world order. There is great anticipation that a political change will bring about an improvement in the conditions of the Cubans in the island and also the reconciliation with the homeland that exiles have long awaited. It is not likely that such a change will occur without an intensification of the current crisis.

In this current crossroads faced by the Cuban people, it is not difficult to conceive of a role in the process of change for the Cuban Church and for Cuban Church leaders outside the island. It may well be one of the few times in Cuban history, perhaps the first time in this century, that the Cuban Church finds itself in a pivotal role in national affairs. The basis for such a role is that currently the Catholic Church is the largest, and one of the few, non-governmental independent organizations in Cuba that is organized hierarchically and with strong international connections. It may serve as a vehicle, for example, between the reconciliation of the island and its diaspora.

The history of Catholicism among Cuban Americans is therefore a topic that has an unmistakable relevance to the contemporary Cuban situation. This essay and other research that has been done, or remains to be done, on that history provide a context for that future.

Given the current crisis, and the recent history of suffering and hardship endured by the Cuban people, both inside and outside the island, it can only be hoped that the Church's role follows the spirit of the motto of the Catholic Student Youth (Juventud Estudiantil Católica) of prerevolutionary Cuba: Por Cristo y Para Cuba (For Christ and For Cuba).

Notes

1. Church and People in Puerto Rico

The author would like to express his gratitude to the following persons who shared with him documents and other hard to obtain materials in their possession: Dr. David Badillo, of the University of Illinois, Chicago; Dr. Ana María Díaz Stevens of Union Theological Seminary; Rev. Joseph P. Fitzpatrick, S.J., of Fordham University; Ms. Isa Garayúa, Director of OCHA, Youngstown, Ohio; Mr. Thomas Kelliher, of the University of Notre Dame; Rev. Bernard Pistone, of the diocese of Harrisburg; Rev. William Reilly and Sister Lourdes Toro, M.S.B.T., of the archdiocese of Newark; Rev. Deacon Guillermo Romagosa, of Manhattan College; Msgr. Robert Stern, of the archdiocese of New York; Rev. Lydio Tomasi, of the Center for Migration Studies, Staten Island; Rev. Wendell Verrill, of the archdiocese of Boston; Msgr. James Wilson, of the archdiocese of New York; and Rev. Richard York, of the archdiocese of Philadelphia.

Rev. Joseph Fitzpatrick and Rev. Kenneth Smith were helpful in arranging interviews with persons who had been involved in ministry to Puerto Ricans since the 1940s. The directors of Hispanic apostolate for the dioceses of the Northeast took time to answer a detailed questionnaire, and many of them offered documents or gave further time on the telephone. Mr. Mario Paredes, director of the Northeast Pastoral Center for Hispanics, was very helpful in obtaining their cooperation. Finally, a word of thanks is due to the many colleagues, friends, and students who by their patience and encouragement supported the author in this enterprise.

1. Fernando Díaz Plaja, *Los Siete Pecados Capitales en Estados Unidos* (Madrid: Alianza Editorial, 1969), p. 20. This attitude is one of the recurring themes in Robert Bellah, *The Broken Covenant* (New York: Seabury Crossroad, 1975).

2. The following three paragraphs are taken, with some expansions, from my article "The American Church and the Puerto Rican People," *U.S. Catholic Historian* 9, nos. 1, 2 (winter, spring 1990): 122–123, and are reproduced by permission of that review's editor.

3. A significant proportion of the populations of Mexico, Central America, Peru, Ecuador, Bolivia, etc. is full-blooded Indian, and Nahuatl, Maya, Quechua, and Aymará are still living vernaculars in many parts of those areas.

4. Fernando Picó, S.J., *Historia General de Puerto Rico* (Río Piedras, P.R.: Ediciones Huracán, 1986), p. 47.

5. Bishop Rodrigo de Bastidas to the Council of the Indies, San Juan, March 20, 1544; V. Murga and A. Huerga, *Episcopologio de Puerto Rico*, II (Ponce, P.R.: Universidad Católica, 1988), doc. 142, p. 197. Later it was discovered that a number of Spaniards had hidden their Indian slaves, but upon discovery these too were set free (Picó, *Historia*, p. 57).

6. Juan Melgarejo, "Memoria y Descripción de la Isla de Puerto Rico" in Fernández Méndez, *Crónicas de Puerto Rico* (San Juan: Gobierno de Puerto Rico, 1957), p. 114.

7. Picó, *Historia*, p. 57.

8. For a description of the coffee-centered culture of a mountain town, see Picó, *Libertad y Servidumbre en el Puerto Rico del Siglo XIX* (Río Piedras, P.R.: Ediciones Huracán, 1979). The religious aspects of this work are available in English in his article "Institutional Catholicism and the Alienation of the Working Class: the Religion of the XIX Century Daylaborers in Utuado, P.R.," *Thought* 54 (June 1979): 186–202. It was not until long after the abolition of slavery—indeed, within living memory—that the sugar cane industry "invaded the hill country."

9. This word has been coined by Caribbean scholars by analogy to *mestizaje*, the racial and cultural mixture of Spanish and Indian elements typical of certain parts of Latin America.

10. While *Santería* is now not uncommon either in the island nor among U.S. Puerto Ricans, this presence is the result of the influx of Cuban exiles; it was practically unknown in the island before 1960. For a detailed and sympathetic account of Santería, see Joseph N. Murphy, *Santería* (Boston: Beacon Press, 1988). Puerto Rico did have a number of more or less superstitious practices known as *curanderismo* (folk medicine; quackery) some of which were of African and others of Mediterranean origin. (See Jaime R. Vidal, "Popular Religion among Hispanics in the General Area of the Archdiocese of Newark" *Presencia Nueva*, [Newark Archdiocesan Office of Research and Planning, 1988] p. 291, n. 109.) This and popular versions of Spiritism (ibid., pp. 289–292) have often now syncretized with *Santería;* the popular herbal shops called *Botánicas* (ibid., p. 298) cater to all three.

11. *Criollos* or "creoles" was the name given to persons of pure European blood, but born in the colonies. *Mestizos* had both Spanish and Indian blood; *mulatos* both Spanish and African. In Puerto Rico,

once these admixtures became sufficiently diluted, the descendants of *mestizos* and *mulatos* would rate *de facto* as *criollos*.

12. This is an important contrast with the American experience, where the local churches grew gradually and where certain aspects of normal diocesan organization, such as the Cathedral chapters, never took root, at first because of the American Church's poverty, and later because both bishops and popes found it more convenient to operate without the checks and balances which the existence of a chapter places on both their powers.

13. For the importance of the *Reconquista* and the conquest of the Canaries in creating the mentality behind the structures of the Spanish Empire, see R. B. Merriman, *The Rise of the Spanish Empire in the Old World and the New* (Cambridge, Mass.: Harvard University Press, 1918). Currently there has been a resurgence of scholarly interest in the role of the Canaries and the Canary experience in the conquest and settlement of the Antilles.

14. The Bull of Erection (*Romanus Pontifex*, Aug. 8, 1511) is reproduced in Murga and Huerga, *Episcopologio*, I: 366–369.

15. The decree of erection, dated in Seville, Sept. 26, 1512, is reproduced in Murga and Huerga, *Episcopologio* I: 363–380. Being the first decree of erection for a cathedral in the New World, copies and translations of it were kept handy at the Council of the Indies as models for new dioceses to follow (ibid., p. 363).

16. Canon Diego de Torres Vargas, "Descripción de la Isla y Ciudad de Puerto Rico," *Crónicas de Puerto Rico* I: 205. Torres Vargas should know, since he had been offered more lucrative posts elsewhere, but chose to remain in his native Puerto Rico for family reasons; he died as dean of the Cathedral.

17. Roughly equivalent to a modern college professor in philosophy or theology.

18. One exasperated Viceroy of Mexico is said to have commented that if death came from Spain, no one would die in the Indies.

19. A reading of the episcopal list in J. L. Vivas's *Historia de Puerto Rico* (New York: Las Américas, 1962), pp. 314–315 yields some twenty-one years of *sede vacante* for the diocese of Puerto Rico in the seventeenth century and twenty-six more in the eighteenth. But this is deceptive, since some of the bishops in his list died or resigned before leaving Spain, so that the effective vacancy would be longer, and also the episcopal reigns are counted from the date of appointment, while sometimes a bishop would not arrive in the island until a year later. Adding to this the time spent visiting the islands of Margarita and Trinidad which were "annexed" to the diocese until 1791, one could

calculate that the island was without a resident bishop for at least one third of each century. Communications and travel improved in the nineteenth century, but the death of Bishop Pedro Gutiérrez de Cos just before the breakdown of relations between the Vatican and the Spanish government at the time of Isabella II produced a record-breaking vacancy of thirteen continuous years (1833–1846) at a time when the Church could little afford it.

20. Indeed Juan Ponce de León, grandson of the conqueror of the island, resigned his secular posts, was ordained, and became a canon of the cathedral.

21. Fray Manuel Mercado to King Philip II and the Council of the Indies, Aug. 14, 1575. Murga and Huerga, *Episcopologio* II, 292.

22. "Descripción de la Isla," *Crónicas de Puerto Rico*, p. 210. He also mentions a number of Puerto Ricans who had been promoted in his day to canonries in Segovia, Tlaxcala/Puebla, Caracas, etc.

23. Other bishops of Puerto Rico born in America were don Francisco de Isasi (1654–1661) born in Jamaica before the English conquered it, don Marcos de Sobremonte (1677–1682) born in Caracas and dean of that city, fray Francisco de Padilla, O. de M. (1683–1685), a native of Lima, and fray Pedro de la Concepción Urtiaga, O.F.M. (1706–1713) born in Querétaro, Mexico. At least two other *criollos* were nominated in the seventeenth century but did not accept.

24. From a lecture by Fernando Picó, S.J., at the Northeast Pastoral Center for Hispanics, New York, July 16, 1981. The town of Utuado, whose social history Picó has exhaustively researched, had all native priests until well after 1850, but from that date they are replaced by Spaniards.

25. I heard this in high school as part of a talk by the diocesan director of vocations, an American priest. Traces of this belief appear in Ivan Illich, "Puerto Ricans in New York," *Commonweal* (June 22, 1956): 295, and in Raymond H. Schmandt, "The Origins of *Casa del Carmen*," *Records of the American Catholic Historical Society of Philadelphia* 97 (1986): 29. On the other hand Joseph Fitzpatrick, in "The Role of the Parish in the Spiritual Care of Puerto Ricans in the New York Archdiocese," *Studi Emigrazione* 3, no. 7 (October 1968): 14, is aware that the shortage of native priests in proportion to foreigners dates from after 1898.

26. O'Reilly, "Memoria Sobre la Isla de Puerto Rico," *Crónicas de Puerto Rico*, p. 257.

27. Ibid.

28. For the importance of context and style in popular Hispanic religiosity see Vidal, "Popular Religion in Newark," *Presencia Nueva*, pp. 258–261.

29. Fray Manuel de Mercado to Philip II and the Council of the Indies, San Juan, Sept. 8, 1573; Murga and Huerga, *Episcopologio*, II p. 279.

30. "Relación de la Reforma de Tierras que promueve Don Felipe Remíres de Estenós, Gobernador de Puerto Rico . . ." (1757) *Crónicas de Puerto Rico*, pp. 227–235.

31. O'Reilly, "Memoria," *Crónicas de Puerto Rico*, p. 242. For the same reason he reports that schooling in the country villages was non-existent.

32. "Constituciones Sinodales Hechas por el Ilustrísimo y Reverendísimo señor Don Fray Damián López de Haro, Obispo de la Ciudad de San Juan de Puerto Rico," Constitution XIV: "On the precept of hearing mass, and on how it is to be kept in the countryside," Murga and Huerga, *Episcopologio* III, pp. 359–360. Note that because of the priority given (quite rightly) to liturgical solemnities, those who lived farthest away would hear four masses in about five months, and then spend seven months without Mass. The same constitution, however, upholds the precept of abstaining from servile work for all persons, and reminds masters that this also applies to slaves.

33. Picó, "Institutional Catholicism," 189–190, based on an oral interview with an old peasant on conditions during his childhood.

34. Fray Iñigo Abbad y Lasierra, *Historia Geográfica, Civil y Natural de la Isla de San Juan Bautista de Puerto Rico* (1782) (Río Piedras, P.R.: University of Puerto Rico, 1979), pp. 192–193.

35. Blessed Carlo Spínola, S.J., "Letter to Father Fabio Spínola," reproduced as Appendix VIII in Antonio López de Santa Anna, S.J., *Los Jesuítas en Puerto Rico, 1858–1886* (Santander, 1958), pp. 184–90.

36. This was not a trained catechist or an authorized lay minister; they arose spontaneously and were recognized by the people as having a skill, like guitar playing, the improvising of song lyrics, or the carving of *santos*.

37. These are discussed at greater length in Vidal, "Popular Religion in the Lands of Origin of New York's Hispanic Population," *Hispanics in New York: Religions, Cultural and Social Experiences* (New York: Archdiocesan Office of Research and Planning, 1982), II: 1–48. This discussion reworks some of this material in a very condensed form.

38. Arizmendi voiced one of the first recorded statements of this consciousness in his farewell speech to the Puerto Rican delegate to the *Cortes* held at Cádiz in 1812. While not overtly—or maybe even consciously—disloyal to Spain, the speech clearly implied that the delegate should work in Spain for the interests of his *patria*, i.e., Puerto Rico. After this the governor of the island sought every opportunity

to undermine the bishop and the Crown never appointed a native of the island to the see again.

39. Puerto Ricans still commonly refer to an unbaptized child as being "still a Moor," i.e., not yet a Christian; the child is not yet "one of us" and thus gets assigned to the archetypal non-Christian group in Spanish experience. (Cf. the medieval Scandinavian custom of referring to unbaptized children as "still heathen.") In some parts of the Dominican Republic it is still customary for the godparents, upon returning the child to the parents after baptism, to say "You gave him to me a Moor, I return him to you a Christian."

40. Picó, "Institutional Catholicism," p. 192, n. 19.

41. Ibid.

42. See Dorothy Dohen, "Marriage, Family and Fertility Patterns among Puerto Ricans," *Hispanics in New York* II: 166, 170–171.

43. Picó, "Institutional Catholicism," pp. 190–192; some details are added from notes taken at a lecture by Picó, July 16, 1982.

44. Ibid.

45. Summarized from Dohen, "Marriage, Family," pp. 166–167, who obtains her information from H. Dubois, *Subcultural Variations in Courtship and Marriage in Puerto Rico* (1972).

2. The Attempt to Americanize Puerto Rico and the Problem of Identity

1. It was they who designed the present Puerto Rican flag, which is the Cuban flag with its colors reversed. Until 1950 this flag was associated with the idea of an independent Puerto Rico, and its use was banned on the island, but it was emotionally accepted by all Puerto Ricans as "their flag," and when Commonwealth status was granted it was the only possible choice for its official flag.

2. Picó, *Historia*, p. 230.

3. Ibid., pp. 232–233; 244–245.

4. Ibid., p. 243.

5. But note that this was a territorial, not a personal limitation; mainland Americans who moved to Puerto Rico could not vote either unless they maintained juridical residence in a state which accepted absentee ballots, while natives of Puerto Rico who moved to the mainland could vote in presidential elections as soon as they fulfilled the residency requirements of their new domicile. This is one of the cases where the provisions of the Jones Law are still in force.

6. Fernando Picó, *1898: La Guerra Después de la Guerra* (Río Piedras, P.R.: Ediciones Huracán, 1987), p. 198.

7. When I was a child my grandmother often told me how two American spinsters who ran her school would teach them Protestant hymns in English, and, when the class became sufficiently proficient, announced that the following Sunday they could sing them in their church. At that point the children's mothers caught on to what was afoot and had a very firm conversation with the teachers, which left the two ladies quite crestfallen. My grandmother's comment was that "the poor women had come here under the impression that they were going to educate savages."

8. My parents, for example, were voracious readers of English books, from history and literature to "whodunits," and as soon as I could read I was encouraged to read all of these. But they never spoke to me or to each other in English.

9. Salvador Tió, *Lengua Mayor* (Río Piedras, P.R.: Editorial Plaza Mayor, 1992), pp. 86–87.

10. Cf. Anthony Stevens-Arroyo, *Catholicism as Civilization: Contemporary Reflections on the Political Philosophy of Pedro Albizu Campos,* Caribbean Institute and Study Center for Latin America Working Paper, San Germán, P.R., Inter American University, 1992.

11. Picó, *Historia,* pp. 250–252.

12. Thus in 1936 the two Nationalists who had murdered the American Chief of Police Francis Riggs were shot without trial at the Police Station in San Francisco Street, San Juan; a year later, in an incident which shocked the whole island, twenty-one Nationalists who were participating in a parade (authorized at first, but forbidden by the mayor at the last minute) were massacred by the police in the streets of Ponce.

13. José Mercado (Momo) "La Lengua Castellana" in *Virutas* (San Juan, 1900), reprinted in C. Rosa Nieves, *Aguinaldo Lírico de la Poesía Puertorriqueña,* vol. I (San Juan: Edil, 1971), pp. 430–433.

14. "Yesterday this flag waved threateningly over the forts of my country, and I would have gladly given my life to see it go away, back across the ocean, with its red and gold colors. But today, when it has darkly folded in its headquarters, a fruitful idealism leaves us with her; a symbol of honor and chivalry. And, believe me, I don't know what I'd give now, alas, to see it rule over the whole wide world." Luis Muñoz Rivera, *Obras Completas, Poesía* (San Juan: Instituto de Cultura Puertorriqueña, 1960), p. 223.

15. *Los Símbolos Oficiales de Puerto Rico* (San Juan: Editorial Cordillera, n.d.), pp. 20–21. The short-lived seal referred to in Puerto Rican history as *"el escudo intruso"* is reproduced in A. C. Fox-Davies, *The Art of Heraldry* (London: Bloomsbury Books, 1986, 1st ed. 1909), p. 230.

16. Thus Puerto Ricans tended to get passionately involved in the problems of other Latin American countries which Americans used to ignore until recently. There was strong sympathy for the struggles against Somoza, Trujillo, and Batista in the 1950s, although this has been altered by the presence of Marxism in recent struggles for liberation.

17. This attitude was analyzed from a bitterly critical point of view by the independentist playwright René Marqués in his essay "El Puertorriqueño Dócil," *Ensayos* (Editorial Antillana, 1967), pp. 147–210; the essay caused a furor in Puerto Rico at the time of publication.

18. It is notable that while Mexican-Americans refer to members of the dominant culture as *Anglos*, Puerto Ricans refer to them as *Americanos*; the term "Puerto Rican–American" is practically unheard of in Puerto Rican circles. The implicit assumption is that while a Puerto Rican is an American *citizen*, he is not an *American*.

19. It is amusing—but also significant—that when the Statehood Party in 1968 won the Governor's Palace for the first time after almost thirty years out of power, its leader don Luis Ferré invited to his gubernatorial inauguration not the governors of nearby states, but the presidents of the nearby Latin American nations—and they accepted. Both in their eyes and in his, the Governor of Puerto Rico was the counterpart of the presidents of Venezuela, the Dominican Republic, etc., not of the governors of Florida or New York.

20. To this day the official title in English is "Commonwealth of Puerto Rico," and in Spanish "*Estado Libre Asociado de Puerto Rico.*"

21. For, 374,649; against, 82,923 (Picó, *Historia*, p. 270).

22. It might be instructive to compare these with the protestations of undying loyalty to Spain which proliferated between April and July 1898 in the Puerto Rican press, as reported in Picó's *1898: La Guerra Después de la Guerra*, pp. 43–47. The same politicians and journalists were often the first to welcome the "liberators" with open arms (ibid., pp. 73–74).

3. The Establishment of a North American Church Structure in Puerto Rico

1. The bishops of Puerto Rico were not members of the National Catholic Welfare Conference, nor of its post-Conciliar successor the NCCB, but eventually set up their own episcopal conference, which became part of CELAM, the Latin American Bishops' Conference. Feasts granted to the United States, such as St. Frances Cabrini, the

North American Martyrs, etc. were not celebrated in Puerto Rico, while those granted to Latin America, such as the proper masses of Our Lady of Guadalupe and St. Rose of Lima were celebrated in Puerto Rico, but not in the U.S.

2. For what follows I rely primarily on Elisa Julián de Nieves, *The Catholic Church in Colonial Puerto Rico: 1898–1964* (Río Piedras, P.R.: Editorial Edil, 1982). While the interpretation of the facts in this book is often clearly tendentious, the facts themselves are accurate, and no other ecclesiastical history of the island in this period exists.

3. This whole issue is treated in some detail in W. A. Jones, "Porto Rico," *The Catholic Encyclopedia* (New York: 1911), vol. 12, pp. 293–294, and exhaustively by Nieves, *The Catholic Church*, pp. 3–60. The ins and outs of the case are here drastically simplified.

4. A. J. Ennis, "Jones, William Ambrose," *The New Catholic Encyclopedia*. Julián de Nieves is very inaccurate on the early career of Bishop Jones, to whom she attributes the foundation of the Augustinian Universidad de Villanueva, which did not occur until decades later. Ennis, on the other hand, closes his entry on Jones with his appointment as bishop in 1906, as if that had been the end of his career, when in fact his achievements from 1906 to 1921, as bishop of Puerto Rico, are much more significant than anything he did before that.

5. *Codex Iuris Canonici* (1917), canons 391(1), 431(1), 435(1), 1532(3), 1541(2).

6. *Constituciones Sinodales* of 1645, const. 85; Murga and Huerga, *Episcopologio*, III: 416–417.

7. Nieves, *The Catholic Church*, pp. 90–93.

8. Ibid., p. 76.

9. Ibid., p. 75.

10. Joseph P. Fitzpatrick, *Puerto Rican Americans* (Englewood Cliffs, N.J.: Prentice-Hall, 1971), p. 2, see also pp. 124–125.

11. Nieves, *The Catholic Church*, p. 81.

12. Ibid., p. 83.

13. Ibid., p. 82. There were at the time 390 foreign religious priests serving in the island.

14. For the appeal of Spiritism to the nineteenth-century intellectuals see Vidal, "Popular Religion in Newark," *Presencia Nueva*, pp. 289–290.

15. Protestantism's appeal in Puerto Rico has been limited to the poor and the middle class, and Protestants have always been to a certain degree social outsiders; one simply does not hold a society wedding in a Protestant church.

16. Marqués, "El Puertorriqueño Dócil," pp. 175–176, relays this about lay Catholic organizations.

17. Both of these are men's organizations, and were designed to attract men to church. Although the women's counterpart of the Knights of Columbus was also introduced, on the whole the bishops were content to rely on the local women's confraternities, especially the *Hijas de María*.

18. Nieves, *The Catholic Church*, p. 81. This was offset by the fact that the population had increased at a comparable rate, from 953,243 in 1899 to 2,210,703 in 1950. (Vivas, *Historia de PR*, p. 318).

19. That the change of name was in imitation of the Catholic University of America can be seen by the new seal adopted at the time, which is a close adaptation of that university's arms; the only differences being that the central open book is replaced by the closed book and *Agnus Dei* of the arms of Puerto Rico, and the crescent moon symbolic of the Immaculate Conception in the dexter-chief canton is replaced by the three crescents of the arms of McManus. Once again the implied assumption that Puerto Rico is a country (and must therefore have its national Catholic University just as the U.S. does) is particularly ironic when one remembers that its founder and chancellor was an outspoken advocate of statehood.

20. The party won not only the governorship, but every municipal election except for the towns of San Lorenzo, which was won by the Statehood Party and Aguada, won by the Christian Action Party, but later nullified on charges of ballot stuffing. In the heated atmosphere of the time many suspected that this nullification of the PAC's only victory was purely vindictive.

21. Nieves, *The Catholic Church*, is especially useful on the remote antecedents of the controversies that led to the confrontations of 1960; unfortunately this information is scattered throughout her book, which lacks an index. The actual crisis is reported extensively in María Mercedes Díaz Alonso, *An Approach to Church-State Relations in Puerto Rico* (unpublished doctoral dissertation, Catholic University of America, 1972). For those who can read Spanish, Tarcisio Ocampo's *Puerto Rico: Partido Acción Cristiana, 1960–62: Documentos y Reacciones de Prensa* (Cuernavaca: CIDOC, 1967) is an indispensable collection of primary sources; unfortunately it is out of print.

22. Before leaving the island McManus disclosed that, although his resignation was ostensibly for reasons of health, it was actually in response to an explicit request from Rome. At Cardinal Spellman's invitation he became auxiliary bishop of New York, but had little to do with the New York ministry to Puerto Ricans. Considering that most

Puerto Ricans carried their party loyalties with them to New York, this was probably prudent (Nieves, *The Catholic Church*, p. 156).

4. The Great Migration

1. Picó, *Historia*, p. 161.

2. Joseph Fitzpatrick, S.J., "The Role of the Parish in the Spiritual Care of Puerto Ricans in the New York Archdiocese," p. 8.

3. Virginia Sánchez Korrol, "Survival of Puerto Rican Women in New York Before World War II," in Rodríguez et al., *The Puerto Rican Struggle* (Maplewood, N.J.: Waterfront Press, 1984), p. 47.

4. Ana María Díaz-Stevens, *American Catholicism's Encounter with the Religion of the Puerto Rican People* (Notre Dame, Ind.: Cushwa Center Working Paper, 1990), p. 55.

5. The word *Latino* was used at this time to characterize the Mediterranean culture of the nationalities which spoke Latin-derived languages; thus Spaniards, Portuguese, Frenchmen, and Italians were considered *Latinos*. Latin Americans were also *Latinos* precisely because they had been colonized by *Latino* countries and had absorbed their culture.

6. Not all Puerto Ricans shared this sympathy. The late doña Encarnación Padilla de Armas, a long-term leader of the Puerto Rican community and the first woman (of any ethnic group) to be vice-president of a party in New York State, was strongly opposed to him at the time and continued to have a much lower opinion of his role than is usual among Puerto Ricans who study the period. (Interview with Sra. de Armas, November 20, 1990.)

7. Díaz-Stevens, *American Catholicism's Encounter*, pp. 55–58.

8. Thus, for example, the Catholic Labor Schools which flourished at this time did not offer classes in Spanish, or target Puerto Rican workers; ibid., p. 57.

9. The population density of Puerto Rico in 1960 was of 670 persons per square mile according to J. L. Vivas, *Historia de Puerto Rico*, p. 248. To give us an idea of what this density implies, Vivas says that it would be the population density of the United States if all persons living in the world would move within its borders.

10. Picó, *Historia*, p. 266.

11. "Economic Survival in New York City," in Rodríguez et al., *The Puerto Rican Struggle*, p. 40.

12. In 1970 44 percent of the Puerto Rican families which qualified for welfare were *not* receiving it (ibid., p. 42).

13. This same period produced in Puerto Rico a major play on the theme of the migration, René Marqués's *La Carreta* (1963; Eng. translation *The Oxcart* [New York: Scribner's, 1969]). This traces the "descent into hell" of a Puerto Rican peasant family from an unviable mountain farm to a San Juan slum, and from there to the New York ghetto. In the last act the son, whose infatuation with American industrial opportunities had caused the move, dies in a factory accident, and the women of the family decide to return to their roots in the mountains of Puerto Rico. The problem is that in real life this is not so easy to do (the old farm, after all, *was* unviable) and that the younger generation cannot, by a "geographical cure," unlearn the contradictory values it acquired in the ghetto.

14. Rodríguez, "Economic Survival," p. 35. These and other factors are explained and demonstrated by the author in pages 36–39.

15. Ibid., p. 38.

16. For much of what follows I rely on Clara Rodríguez's dissertation, *The Ethnic Queue in the U.S.: The Case of the Puerto Ricans*, most of whose statements ring true by my own experience. Dr. Rodríguez published her dissertation in 1974 (R. and E. Research Associates, San Francisco) but this edition is no longer available; the original dissertation (Washington University, 1973) can still be obtained from University Microfilms. Since this is still available, I quote from the dissertation rather than the published version.

17. Rodríguez, *The Ethnic Queue*, p. 124. For a perceptive analysis of the issue of prejudice in Puerto Rico see Fitzpatrick, *Puerto Rican Americans*, pp. 101ff.; a long footnote on p. 101 offers an exhaustive bibliography on the issue.

18. Ibid., p. 125.

19. Even within the Catholic community the ethnic group which for historical reasons was in the best position to assimilate to the WASP image—the Irish, who arrived speaking English and with centuries of experience of the English system—became the leaders of American Catholicism, to whom later groups were expected to assimilate. And after Vatican II the efforts to break down the Catholic ghetto and "Americanize" the U.S. church have often come down to the shedding of whatever baroque Mediterranean trappings were still left, and final assimilation to the WASP traditions of stark simplicity.

20. This is shown, for example, in the way they answer questionnaires which include questions on race; they usually mark *both* "Puerto Rican" (or "Hispanic") *and* "white," even if the instructions clearly demand "mark only one." This is so widespread that many such questionnaires now read "Non-Hispanic White."

21. The *Report on the First Conference on the Spiritual Care of Puerto Rican Migrants, Held in San Juan, PR, April 11th to 16th 1955* speaks of "the relatively small number of those who remain on the Mainland in contrast to the very large number of those who travel back and forth to the Mainland" (MS. document in New York Archdiocesan Archives, p. 4). Eventually more and more migrants settled on the mainland, but the numbers of those who settle here only temporarily have always remained very high in comparison to other ethnic groups in U.S. history.

22. Illich, "Puerto Ricans in New York," p. 296.

23. Ibid., p. 294.

24. My translation.

25. Thus the burning of the American flag elicits reactions comparable to those of medieval Christians who heard of heretics spitting on the cross or desecrating the Eucharist. Similarly the strongly emotional negative reaction of many Americans when they hear Hispanics speak Spanish among themselves, ultimately embodied in the "English Only" movement, is more understandable when it is seen as a reaction to a symbolic rejection of America by refusing to give up the language of what ought to be by now "the old country."

26. It is significant that shortly after the presidency of John F. Kennedy—which was a symbol of the acceptance of Catholics by the generality of Americans—we begin to see the first instances of Catholics taking on a position as critics of America. Such criticism is a hallowed American tradition, but only persons or groups which feel secure of their place in American society feel they can afford to take it, since only insiders are allowed to criticize America, doing so from the point of view of American ideals.

27. An interesting contrast is presented by the Cuban exiles who, especially in the earlier days of their immigration, tended to be middle and upper class professionals. Although their forms of Catholicism were often quite alien to the American Catholic tradition, their values and mores were those of the middle class, and American clerics and parishioners tended to feel much more comfortable in dealing with them than they had with the Puerto Ricans.

28. Carmen Judith Nine-Curt, *Non Verbal Communication in Puerto Rico*, 2nd ed. (Cambridge, Mass.: Evaluation, Dissemination and Assessment Center, 1984), p. v.

29. Ibid., p. vi.

30. These issues have been developed by Edward Hall in his classic works *The Silent Language* (Garden City, N.Y.: Anchor Press, 1963), *The Hidden Dimension* (Garden City, N.Y.: Doubleday, 1966), and *Beyond*

Culture (Garden City, N.Y.: Anchor Press, 1976). A detailed comparison in these terms between Puerto Rican and American cultures has been made by Carmen Judith Nine-Curt in the work just cited, and these differences have been applied to the religious field in my essay "Popular Religion in Newark," pp. 258–261.

31. Jay P. Dolan, *The American Catholic Experience* (Garden City, N.Y.: Image Books, 1985), p. 221; these four traits are discussed extensively in the following pages.

32. George Kelly, "Catholic Survey of Puerto Rican Population in the Archdiocese of New York," unpublished document in the New York Archdiocesan Archives, p. 106.

33. The neighborhoods with the highest percentage of Mass attendance in New York City were Highbridge and Fordham in the Bronx, with 47.6 percent and 45.7 percent respectively; ibid., p. 97.

34. Cf. George Kelly, "The Puerto Ricans and the Church of New York," *Integrity* 8, no. 9 (1954): 15, 37, 39. Leo Mahon, *Report on the Inter-Diocesan Meeting of Priests concerning the Apostolate to the Spanish-Speaking of the East* (unpublished ms in the New York Archdiocesan Archives, 1957), pp. 4–5, speaks of "the indifference to Mass and Sacraments" found in the island, and denies that the island's Catholic culture has made Puerto Ricans "practicing Catholics." Fitzpatrick, *Puerto Rican Americans*, p. 127, says that "only a small percentage of Puerto Ricans in New York follow those religious practices which identify one as a practicing Catholic in the mainland."

35. Kelly, "Puerto Ricans and the Church of New York," p. 15.

36. Joseph Fitzpatrick, S.J., "Puerto Rican Story," *America* 103, p. 595.

37. Cf. Illich, "Puerto Ricans in New York," p. 297. (Illich is contradicting that position.)

38. These were principally by Illich or Fitzpatrick, but occasionally by others, e.g., John La Farge, S.J., "Conversation in Ponce," *America*, May 23, 1959, and Cynthia Hettinger, "Faith of the Puerto Rican," *America*, April 16, 1960.

39. "Dedication," *Report on the First Conference on the Spiritual Care of Puerto Rican Migrants, San Juan April 11th to 16th, 1955*, p. 2.

40. Kelly "Catholic Survey," p. 5.

5. The Rejection of the Ethnic Parish Model

1. Cf. C. Armanet, *Church of Our Lady of Esperanza* (New York: privately printed, 1921) and *Our Lady of Esperanza, New York: Fiftieth Anniversary* (New York: Custombook, 1963).

2. Robert Stern, "Evolution of Hispanic Ministry in the New York Archdiocese," in *Hispanics in New York: Religious, Cultural, and Social Experiences* (New York: Archdiocesan Office of Pastoral Research, 1982), vol. 2, pp. 294–295.

3. Ibid., p. 292.

4. *Report on the First Conference*, p. 9, and Paper 2, p. 3.

5. Ibid.

6. Cf. Stern, "Evolution of Hispanic Ministry," p. 306: "When Cardinal Spellman came to New York he declined to continue to establish national parishes."

7. Father Joseph Fitzpatrick, S.J., stressed the importance of O'Hara's advice in an interview with the author in the fall of 1989. While O'Hara was fluent in Spanish and very knowledgeable about Latin American affairs, he seems to have had little understanding of Hispanic attitudes beyond those of the statesmen and prelates whom he knew; cf. Schmandt, "The Origins of *Casa del Carmen*," 33–34.

8. Philip Gleason, "American Identity and Americanization," *Harvard Encyclopedia of American Ethnic Groups*, p. 47.

9. This mentality is clearly expressed in Spellman's introduction to the *Report of the First Conference on the Pastoral Care of Puerto Ricans*.

10. Ibid.

11. *Studi Emigrazioni* 3 (1966): 1–27.

12. Fitzpatrick, *Puerto Rican Americans*, pp. 124–125.

13. The report was edited by Fitzpatrick with William Ferree, S.M., rector of the Catholic University of Puerto Rico, and Ivan Illich.

14. Vol. II, pp. 306–307. Stern was archdiocesan director of the Spanish-Speaking Apostolate from 1969 to 1973, and had been involved in it since the 1950s.

15. The following paragraphs are taken, with significant expansions, from my article "The American Church and the Puerto Rican People," in the *U.S. Catholic Historian*, pp. 130–135, by kind permission of that review's editor.

16. Fitzpatrick, "The Role of the Parish," pp. 9–11.

17. Fitzpatrick, *Puerto Rican Americans*, p. 57.

18. New York City has only four parishes with more than 70 percent Hispanics, all in the South Bronx; four more in the South Bronx, and three in Manhattan, have more than 60 percent, and fourteen have more than 50 percent. Seventy-eight parishes in the city have between 10 and 49 percent, and another sixty-five have between 1 and 9 percent; no parish is without at least 1 percent Hispanic population, even in Staten Island (*Hispanics in New York*, I:8). The archdiocese of Newark, across the Hudson from New York City, has only one parish with

more than 70 percent Hispanic population; seven others have between 50 and 60 percent, and twelve have more than 30 percent; there are another 154 parishes where the Hispanic presence ranges between 1 and 30 percent. Even in Hudson County, where the Hispanic presence is strongest, twelve parishes have more than 30 percent Hispanics, twelve have between 11 and 30 percent, and ten have less than 10 percent. There is no parish in the archdiocese without at least a minimal Hispanic presence (*Presencia Nueva* [Newark: Archdiocesan Office of Research and Planning, 1988], p. 31; tables on p. 35 and complete list of parishes with population and percentages, pp. 101–103).

19. Fitzpatrick, "The Role of the Parish," p. 14.

20. Ibid.; *Puerto Rican Americans*, pp. 124–125. Spellman also emphasizes this in *Report of the First Conference*, "Dedication," p. 2.

21. I discuss some of the problems involved in having a community whose leadership is not of its own culture and identity in my article "Popular Religion in Newark," *Presencia Nueva*, pp. 262ff.

22. Frederick O'Brien, S.T.D., in a telephone interview with the author, Aug. 2, 1991. I checked this with Father Joseph Fitzpatrick, who informs me that ruling out the national parishes was without question a decision of Cardinal Spellman, later adopted by the American hierarchy, but that the Holy See was not in any way involved. (Telephone interview, same date.)

23. Fitzpatrick, "The Role of the Parish," pp. 6–7; *Puerto Rican Americans*, p. 125; Stern, "Evolution of Hispanic Ministry," pp. 306–307, with quote from the preceding. See also *Report of the First Conference*, p. 7 and Paper 2, p. 5, where the pastor of St. Cecilia's claims that the second and third generations feel there is a "stigma" attached to belonging to a national parish.

24. That this was still an issue at the time of the Puerto Rican migration is shown by a statement in the pastoral plan prepared by Msgr. Connolly, first coordinator of the Spanish-speaking apostolate in New York: "The suggested plan . . . will avoid the unhappy and undesirable evolution, in effect, of separate diocese within the Archdiocese" (*A Suggested Basic Plan for the Cooperation of Spanish Catholic Action in the Archdiocese of New York*, manuscript in the Archdiocesan Archives, p. 4).

25. *Report of the First Conference*, p. 2; similar sentiments are expressed on p. 4.

26. "It was remarked with some sadness that kindness towards Puerto Ricans is sometimes discouraged by the clergy lest it prompt more Puerto Ricans to come into the parish" (*Report of the First Conference*, p. 12).

27. Ibid., Document 2, p. 2.

28. Ibid., p. 3.

29. Ibid., p. 2. The situation of "English Masses in the main church, Spanish in the basement" later became symbolic of discrimination in the integrated parishes, and thus came to be resented by Hispanics. But as late as the 1980s I have come across parishes where the feeling that "it may be poor but it's ours" led the Hispanic community to decline the offer of a move to the upper church.

30. This feeling can be expressed by requests for a separate First Communion for their children at the Spanish Mass, for separate Holy Week services in Spanish and following the Hispanic style, for their own parish societies, etc.

31. The problems inherent in this shift of emotional commitment from the parish to the movements are discussed in Vidal, "Popular Religion in Newark," p. 333.

32. La Milagrosa's church building, in fact, was a converted synagogue (Stern "Evolution of Hispanic Ministry," p. 292).

33. See O'Dea and Poblete, "Anomie and the Quest for Community: The Formation of Sects among the Puerto Ricans of New York," in O'Dea, *Sociology and the Study of Religion* (New York: Basic Books, 1970), pp. 180–198.

34. E.g., in *Puerto Rican Americans*; "The Role of the Parish," and the *Report on the First Conference*, which he co-edited.

35. Fitzpatrick, *Puerto Rican Americans*, p. 124. A similar point is made briefly in "The Role of the Parish," p. 19, and in his presentation at the 1953 Conference on the Spiritual Care of Puerto Rican Migrants (*Report*, Document 9), where he went so far as to say that rapid integration would actually damage the Puerto Rican family by depriving it of the support of a stable Puerto Rican community and a strong Puerto Rican parish.

36. As early as 1951 we hear of a storefront congregation which built its own church after five years; "the new building cost $68,000 [pre-inflation] and every cent was contributed by Puerto Ricans. This seems to indicate that if the Puerto Ricans have the proper leadership, they will respond to it generously" (Encarnación Padilla de Armas et al., *Report of Some Catholic Women on the Religious Condition of Puerto Rican Immigrants in New York City* [manuscript in the personal archives of Joseph Fitzpatrick, S.J.], p. 7).

37. The delegate from Trenton—one of the few dioceses which held on to the national parish model—said in the 1957 Conference that "only sixteen Puerto Ricans would come to Mass [in Perth Amboy] before opening a church for them alone. Now we have a gratifying

assistance of 1,050 at Sunday Mass. . . . During the last twelve months eleven families who had joined Protestant sects returned to the Catholic Church" (Mahon, *Report on the Inter-Diocesan Meeting*, p. 41).

38. Thirty-two priests with Spanish surnames are listed as attending from Puerto Rico, plus three from the U.S. (none from La Milagrosa or Santa Agonía). Of these, eight (one from New York and seven from the island) were to my certain knowledge native Puerto Ricans, and eight were Spaniards; I do not know the origin of the rest.

39. The diocese of Camden, for example, set up a national parish for Puerto Ricans in 1953 (*Report of the First Conference*, "Report of Diocesan Activity," p. 1) while the delegate from Trenton categorically stated that "the Latin American parish is considered in central New Jersey as the best means to help the Puerto Ricans" (ibid., p. 20), which in the context of a conference sponsored and underwritten by Spellman has an almost defiant ring to it.

40. *Report on the First Conference*, p. 8, my emphasis.

41. *"Non possunt sine speciali apostolico indulto constitui paroeciae pro diversitate sermonis seu nationis fidelium in eadem civitate vel territorio degentium, nec paroeciae mere familiares aut personales; ad constitutas autem quod attinet, nihil innovandum, inconsulta Apostolica Sede."*

42. Thus at the time of the promulgation of the Tridentine Liturgy, orders and dioceses whose particular liturgical customs were more than 200 years old were given the option of holding on to them; however, all it took was one majority vote in chapter, then or at any time in the future, for the order or diocese to switch to the Tridentine-Roman rite. Once this decision was taken, however, no second thoughts were allowed. It is obvious that Rome favored conversion to the Roman usage.

43. *Acta Apostolicae Sedis*, vol. XIX, 13 (1952), pp. 649–704.

44. *"Quantum vero huiusmodi paroeciae, frequentissime a peregrinis expetitae, dioecesibus ac animabus profuerint, norunt omnes dignaque cohonestant existimatione. Ideoque ipsarum moderamini Codex Iuris Canonici, praescripto Canonis 216, ad par. 4, consulere non praeteriit ita ut, Apostolica Sede gradatim adprobante, plurimae paroeciae nationales potissimum in America usque numerentur et Sacrae Congregationis Consistorialis decreto, ne alia afferamus exempla, in Insulis Philippinis paroeciae pro Sinensibus nuperrime sint constitutae"* (*Exsul Familia*, p. 653; see also p. 660).

45. Ibid., pp. 700–701.

46. *Exsul Familia* was promulgated August 1, 1952; the first Mass at the Lorain chapel was held on the first Sunday of that September (September 7). Cf. Eugenio Rivera, "The Puerto Rican Colony of Lorain, Ohio," *Centro*, vol. 2, no. 1, p. 16.

47. "The Pastoral Care of Spanish-Speaking Catholics in the United States," in *The 1960 National Catholic Almanac*, ed. Felician Foy, O.F.M. (Paterson, N.J.: St. Anthony's Guild Press, 1960), p. 665.

48. Indeed, this position is central to the American Church's own desire to be allowed to develop its own style and its own identity within the greater Catholic unity, without being saddled with Mediterranean attitudes and practices which are alien to U.S. culture in the name of "unity."

6. Implementing the Vision

1. Msgr. Joseph F. Connolly, *Suggested Basic Plan*, p. 4.

2. Interview with Father Fitzpatrick, March 22, 1992.

3. His first talk on the issue outside of the classroom was to the Knights of Columbus in May 1952.

4. This story, together with much of my information on Illich, comes from Francine Du Plessix Gray, *Divine Disobedience: Profiles in Catholic Radicalism* (New York: Vintage Books, 1971). Illich verbally confirmed the general accuracy of this work's version of his story in a telephone interview in the fall of 1990.

5. Stern, "Evolution of Hispanic Ministry," p. 297.

6. Gray, *Divine Disobedience*, p. 248.

7. Ibid., p. 246.

8. Ibid., p. 244.

9. He would later be raised to auxiliary bishop, and eventually to coadjutor archbishop, although without the right of succession.

10. Kelly, *Catholic Survey*, p. 3.

11. A manuscript of 135 pages plus 49 pages of appendices; it was not intended for publication, but circulated within the chancery of the archdiocese.

12. Kelly, *Catholic Survey*, p. 11. Kelly tends to use the word "almost" in this and other passages as a diplomatic ploy to tone down the harshness of what he has to say; it is clear from the context (and must have been clear to his readers) that the word is inserted out of mere politeness, but that he meant not "almost" but "undoubtedly."

13. Ibid., p. 130.

14. Ibid. Numerical tables are given in pp. 131–132.

15. Ibid., p. 39. By "New York City" Kelly meant the boroughs which belong to the archdiocese; Brooklyn and Queens belong to the diocese of Brooklyn.

16. Ibid., p. 42.

17. Ibid., p. 12. "Spanish-speaking" did not mean here (as it tended to do when applied to the laity) "persons whose native language is Spanish," but "Americans fluent, or at least functional, in Spanish."

18. Ibid.

19. Ibid.

20. Stern, "Evolution of Hispanic Ministry," p. 299.

21. Ibid.

22. Press release, March 24, 1953.

23. Stern, "Evolution of Hispanic Ministry," p. 299. Gray, *Divine Disobedience*, pp. 243–244, quotes a number of Connolly's reminiscences of life with Illich, which evidence a warm, though not uncritical, admiration for the latter's creativity and dynamism.

24. Manuscript in the archives of the archdiocese of New York; there is a first draft and another revised on the basis of input from various departments.

25. Connolly, *Suggested Basic Plan*, 1st draft, p. 2.

26. Ibid., p. 3.

27. Ibid., p. 2.

28. Ibid., p. 4.

29. Stern, "Evolution of Hispanic Ministry," p. 300.

30. Two one-page documents in the New York archdiocesan archives.

31. Stern, "Evolution of Hispanic Ministry," p. 300. Details about celebrant, preacher, and the presence of the mayor are in the press releases.

32. Some members of the Puerto Rican community had previously organized a celebration of St. John's Day at the Polo Grounds, along the lines of the civic side of the traditional *fiestas patronales* of Puerto Rican towns (Díaz-Stevens, "From Puerto Rican to Hispanic: The Politics of the *Fiestas Patronales* in New York," *Latino Studies Journal* [Jan. 1990], p. 35). But being privately sponsored, this fiesta did not serve the psychological need for public presence and legitimation which was served by the pontifical Mass.

33. Stern, "Evolution of Hispanic Ministry," p. 309.

34. Thus the two press releases refer constantly to "Spanish-Americans" or "Spanish-speaking Catholics"; only at the end of the second press release do we find "and especially for Puerto Ricans." Msgr. Connolly speaks of the fiesta as "The Spanish-American equivalent of a St. Patrick's Day" (*Report on the First Conference*, Paper 5, p. 9).

35. For a very perceptive overview of the European-Mediterranean roots of this combination, and of its transfer to Spanish Americans, see Díaz-Stevens, "From Puerto Rican to Hispanic," pp. 28–35.

36. Gray, *Divine Disobedience*, pp. 246–247.

37. Ibid., p. 247; also Stern "Evolution of Hispanic Ministry," p. 300.

38. Stern ("Evolution of Hispanic Ministry," p. 309) attributes the suggestion to Illich.

39. Interview with Father Joseph Fitzpatrick, May 22, 1992.

40. Copies of the proceedings were sent by Connolly, at Spellman's direction, to all departments and agencies of the archdiocese which dealt with Hispanics in the course of their work, to all U.S. bishops who had Puerto Ricans in their dioceses, and to the bishops of the Southwest Conference, as well as to all participants in the Conference (*Report on the First Conference*, pp. 3–4).

41. Chicago sent five, Philadelphia three, and the other dioceses one or two each.

42. *Report on the First Conference*, pp. 1–2. This last point was especially relevant on the issue of the national parishes, where in spite of the questions raised in this regard by a number of participants, and of the misgivings which Fitzpatrick himself diplomatically but not cryptically expressed in his own presentation, nothing was done in the direction of reconsidering the matter or ascertaining the wishes of the New York Puerto Ricans (*Report on the First Conference*, p. 8). In this light it becomes clear that the purpose of the conference, in spite of all claims to free and open discussion, was not to find out what was the best policy, but to find out how best to implement the policy on which Spellman had made up his mind sixteen years before.

43. Stern, "Evolution of Hispanic Ministry," p. 317.

44. By the time Illich had developed a following among the younger priests his career had been deflected away from New York.

45. Interviews with Msgr. Wilson, now pastor at La Esperanza, and with Sister Aida Robles, who was his secretary during the time of his tenure as coordinator, November 1990.

46. Interview with Msgr. Wilson, November 1990.

47. Interview with Sister Aida Robles, November 1990. Neither she nor Msgr. Wilson, whom I consulted later, know whether any prints of this film are extant, or where they might be kept.

48. These features are described, and their cultural and psychological interdependencies analyzed, in Díaz-Stevens, "From Puerto Rican to Hispanic," pp. 36–39.

49. Ibid., p. 39.

50. Stern, "Evolution of Hispanic Ministry," p. 312.

51. Ibid.

52. He later described his Center for Intercultural Documentation at Cuernavaca as "a center of de-Yankeefication" (Gray, *Divine Disobedience*, p. 252).

53. Fitzpatrick, "Role of the Parish," p. 18.

54. *Report on the First Conference*, "Dedication," p. 2.

55. Fitzpatrick, "Role of the Parish," p. 18.

56. Gray, *Divine Disobedience*, p. 249.

57. Ibid., p. 245.

58. This brought up one of the problems of integration: the Americans who came for the next Mass were appalled to find that the Spanish Mass was still at the *Sanctus*, having started fifteen minutes late, and complained loudly about being forced to wait. This was solved in many places by making the Spanish Mass the last Mass of the day.

59. The whole quarrel between Muñoz and the bishops, and especially their founding of a Catholic Party and threatening to excommunicate anyone who voted for Muñoz, was a great embarrassment to Spellman at that time, since it provided an ideal weapon for opponents of Kennedy's presidential campaign. Thus Spellman had no qualms about embarrassing the Puerto Rican bishops in turn.

60. Gray, *Divine Disobedience*, pp. 250–251.

61. Fitzpatrick, *Puerto Rican Americans*, p. 126.

62. Cf. Ana María Díaz Ramírez, "The Life, Passion and Death of the Spanish-speaking Apostolate of the Archdiocese of New York," in Antonio Stevens Arroyo, *Prophets Denied Honor* (Maryknoll, N.Y.: Orbis, 1980), pp. 208–213. It was not until 1977 that a Spanish-speaking American and a Spaniard were appointed auxiliary bishops to Cardinal Cooke.

63. Stern, "Evolution of Hispanic Ministry," p. 310.

64. This attitude is clearly expressed in Spellman's "Dedication" of the *Report of the First Conference* and is central to the idea and ideology of the integrated parish.

65. Illich, "Puerto Ricans in New York," p. 294.

66. These developments fall mostly beyond the temporal parameters of this essay, but they must be brought up in order to evaluate the success and failure of Illich's program. Details may be found in Stern, "Evolution of Hispanic Ministry," pp. 317–323, in Mary Coles's *Summer in the City* (New York: Kenedy, 1968), and more critically in Ana María Díaz Ramírez, *The Roman Catholic Archdiocese of New York and the Puerto Rican Migration, 1950–1973*, unpublished doctoral dissertation, Fordham University, 1983, pp. 199–247. Illich himself has some implicit criticisms of his New York disciples in "The Seamy Side

of Charity," *Celebration of Awareness* (Garden City, N.Y.: Doubleday, 1970), pp. 67–68. The criticisms are of liberals who cannot implement their vision in the U.S. and volunteer for work in Latin America, but they are equally applicable to those who volunteered for work with Hispanics at home.

67. Díaz-Stevens, "From Puerto Rican to Hispanic," p. 42.

68. Ibid., pp. 41–43.

69. While the organizers of the new fiesta had perceived the Puerto Rican emphasis as "divisive" of the larger unity of the oppressed, the organizers of the parade saw the countercultural causes as "divisive," and the Puerto Rican emphasis as unitive; they wanted to emphasize what all Puerto Ricans shared, and deemphasize what some Puerto Ricans shared with some non-Puerto Ricans, but did not share with all Puerto Ricans. This meant an emphasis on *Puertorriqueñismo* and a deemphasis on denominational religion and on controversial causes.

70. The name means "Crash Course in Christianity." The next few paragraphs are taken with slight changes from my article "Popular Religion in Newark," and are reused by permission.

71. The letter authorizing women's Cursillos is dated September 29, 1960, and is reproduced in an appendix to the movement's *Manual de Dirigentes*, 6th ed., p. 357. The first women's Cursillo in New York took place in December 1962.

72. Cursillos were also offered in English with some success, but never came to be as important in the American Church as they became among Hispanics.

73. *Hispanics in New York*, vol. I, p. 91.

74. Stern, "Evolution of Hispanic Ministry," pp. 312–313.

75. Wilson, *Memo for the Use of His Eminence at the Priests' Retreats* (two-page typewritten document in the archdiocesan archives), p. 2.

76. Stern, "Evolution of Hispanic Ministry," p. 313.

77. Msgr. Fox was notoriously uninterested in the movement and out of sympathy with its clerical and lay leadership; see Stern, "Evolution of Hispanic Ministry," p. 323, and Díaz Ramírez, *The Roman Catholic Archdiocese*, pp. 237–241.

7. Beyond New York

1. They did not all live in the archdiocese of New York, since two of the city's five boroughs are in the diocese of Brooklyn. The two principal concentrations of Puerto Ricans at that time, Spanish Harlem (el Barrio) and the South Bronx, were both in the archdiocese

of New York. In spite of repeated efforts I have been able to obtain only negligible materials on the diocese of Brooklyn.

2. *Report on the First Conference*, p. 20.

3. The Mennonites were particularly zealous in this respect, and sometimes went so far as to present obstacles to their employees being bused to Mass, or to priests visiting them in their farms. Cf. Pistone et al., *Dedicación Solemne de la Iglesia Católica Hispana Cristo Salvador* (York, Penn.: 1980), p. 5 (this work is actually a short history of the Hispanic apostolate in the diocese of Harrisburg); also the Harrisburg diocesan report in *Report of the First Conference*, Section III, p. 5. For the less enthusiastic attitude of Catholic farmers, see *Report on the First Conference*, p. 20.

4. *Report on the First Conference*, Section III, p. 5.

5. Ibid., Section III, p. 1.

6. Ibid., Section III, p. 17; also Mahon, *Report on the Inter-Diocesan Meeting* (1957), p. 41.

7. Pistone, *Dedicación*, p. 5.

8. *Report on the First Conference*, Paper 11, pp. 1–3.

9. Ibid., Section III, p. 13.

10. It is not clear whether the reporter, Father Gerard Micera, is the same person as the priest who worked so successfully with this group in August.

11. *Report on the First Conference*, Section III, p. 1.

12. Ibid., Section III, p. 17.

13. Ibid.

14. Ibid., p. 18.

15. It is now a flourishing national parish in its own right, under the direction of the Servite Friars.

16. Mahon, *Report on the Inter-Diocesan Meeting*, p. 41.

17. Wister and Plunkett, "The Development of the Spanish Apostolate in the Archdiocese of Newark," *Presencia Nueva*, pp. 196–197.

18. Ibid., p. 215.

19. Ibid., p. 196.

20. Report of Sara Butler, M.S.B.T., General Concillor for New York/New Jersey to the Director of Research and Planning, Archdiocese of Newark, March 13, 1985.

21. Wister and Plunkett, "The Development of the Spanish Apostolate," p. 197, attribute this work to Father Faulkner and do not mention Carmody, but Faulkner himself (*Report on the First Conference*, Section III, p. 6) attributes it to Carmody and does not mention his own contribution.

22. *Report on the First Conference*, Section III, p. 6.

23. Ibid., p. 7. The problem was not limited to Jersey City; it is also mentioned in Illich, "Puerto Ricans in New York," p. 295.

24. *Report on the First Conference*, Section III, p. 7.

25. Ibid., Section III, p. 1.

26. Verrill, "Some Points of Interest in the Apostolate History," in *Hispanic Pastoral Plan* (Archdiocese of Boston, 1990), p. 15.

27. Telephone interview with Father O'Brien, August 2, 1991.

28. Verrill, "Some Points of Interest," p. 16.

29. Mahon, *Report on the Inter-Diocesan Meeting*, p. 39.

30. The 1950 Census reported 1,910 Puerto Ricans in Philadelphia; by 1952 they were estimated at 3,100 and by 1954 at 7,300. Schmandt, "The Origins of *Casa del Carmen*," p. 28.

31. Ibid., p. 29.

32. Ibid., p. 30.

33. This had been founded in 1912 for Spaniards and Latin Americans, and was served by Spanish Vincentians of the Barcelona Province—not connected, therefore, with the Madrid Vincentians who served in Puerto Rico and at La Milagrosa and Santa Agonía in New York.

34. Schmandt, "The Origins of *Casa del Carmen*," p. 32.

35. Ibid.

36. Ibid., p. 37. Schmandt goes further and says that the name *Casa del Carmen* was selected because it "had no religious connotations at all" and thus was "more in keeping with the center's temporal mission" (ibid.). But at least for Puerto Ricans the name would be a clear and unmistakable allusion to Our Lady of Mt. Carmel (*La Virgen del Carmen*), patroness of ten towns in Puerto Rico. (The article *del* is never used in Spanish with Carmen as a given name; it is used only in the Marian title.)

37. In 1957 there were fifteen Spanish-speaking priests (seven with experience in Puerto Rico) distributed among nine parishes; the program was then a year old (Mahon, *Report on the Inter-Diocesan Meeting*, p. 39).

38. Schmandt, "The Origins of *Casa del Carmen*," p. 34.

39. Memo of Mrs. McGarry, quoted in ibid., p. 40, n. 30. This notion of Catholic education as a panacea for the "Puerto Rican problem" is also stated in the Philadelphia section of the 1957 *Report on the Inter-Diocesan Meeting*, p. 39. It should be remembered in this context that fifty years of schooling in English had not succeeded in Americanizing the Puerto Ricans at home.

40. Ibid., p. 40.

41. Data from a questionnaire returned to the author by Msgr. John Campbell, director of Hispanic ministry for the diocese of Allentown.

42. All information in this section is from Joseph E. Koch, "The Puerto Ricans Come to Youngstown," *Commonweal* 59, no. 1 (Oct. 1953): 9–11. There is also a brief notice in *America* (Aug. 9, 1952): 452.

43. Koch, "The Puerto Ricans," p. 11.

44. "Underscorings," *America* (Aug. 9, 1952): 452.

45. Koch, "The Puerto Ricans."

46. Telephone interviews with Father John Daly, pastor of St. Rose of Lima, and Ms. Isa Garayúa, director of the *Organización Cívica Cultural Hispano Americana* of Youngstown.

47. Eugenio Rivera, "The Puerto Rican Colony of Lorain, Ohio," *Centro* 2, no. 1; p. 11.

48. "Rigid Examination for Puerto Ricans," Gary, Ind., *Post Tribune*, June 8, 1948, quoted in ibid., p. 12.

49. Rivera, "The Puerto Rican Colony," p. 13.

50. As seen above, the coast was dominated by the sugar economy, which had depended on slave labor, while the mountain coffee plantations employed free white peasants of primarily Castilian descent.

51. Ibid., p. 14.

52. Ibid., p. 16.

53. William Arroyo, "Lorain, Ohio: The Puerto Rican Experiment: A History Unexplored," *Extended Roots* (New York: Centro de Estudios Puertorriqueños, Hunter College), p. 33. Without naming the parishes, Rivera (p. 16) corroborates that "members of the colony had attempted to attend Mass in those churches only to find that they were not welcomed."

54. "City, Church Effort Proposed to Improve Puerto Rican Status," *Lorain Journal*, August 10, 1951, quoted in Rivera, "The Puerto Rican Colony," p. 16.

55. Rivera, "The Puerto Rican Colony," p. 16.

56. Data on the chapel's work as of 1955 is from the *Report on the First Conference*, Section III, p. 4.

57. Arroyo, "Lorain, Ohio," p. 33, refers to the role of the Pentecostal Churches in the community as part of the "unexplored history" of Lorain, since the contribution of the Catholic Capilla has absorbed the attention of observers so far.

58. Interview with Sra. Carmen Meléndez, Lorain, Ohio, and Rivera, "The Puerto Rican Colony," p. 16. The *Trinitarios* turned the parish over to the diocese in the same year it received parochial status, after three decades of service.

59. Zentos, "Hispanic Community," *The Encyclopedia of Cleveland History* (Bloomington and Indianapolis: Indiana University Press, 1987), p. 508.

60. Ibid., p. 509.

61. Ibid.

62. In 1950 New York had some 246,000 Puerto Ricans; in 1955 Chicago had 20,000. By 1960 New York had some 612,000 and Chicago 32,371. The New York figures are calculated on the basis of information given in Picó, *Historia*, p. 266; the 1955 Chicago figure is from the *Report of the First Conference*, Section III, p. 2, and the one for 1960 from Félix Padilla, *Puerto Rican Chicago* (Notre Dame, Ind.: University of Notre Dame Press, 1987), p. 78.

63. Padilla, *Puerto Rican Chicago*, p. 57.

64. Manuel Martínez, *Chicago: Historia de Nuestra Comunidad Puertorriqueña* (Chicago: privately printed, 1989), pp. 93–94.

65. Ibid., p. 94. The CYO involvement is described in Roger L. Treat, *Bishop Sheil and the CYO* (New York: Julian Messner, 1951), pp. 146–148. This work describes the situation of the contracted servant girls as "virtual slavery" (p. 146). A report on abusive conditions of both the domestics and the foundry workers, dated November 25, 1946, is reproduced in Martínez, *Chicago*, pp. 103–105.

66. Martínez, *Chicago*, p. 97. This pioneer work with Chicago's Puerto Ricans is not mentioned in Padilla's *Puerto Rican Chicago* or in the archdiocese's reports at either the 1955 or the 1957 conferences on Puerto Rican apostolate; all three of these practically equate the archdiocese's ministry to Puerto Ricans with the Cardinal's Committee and the Caballeros de San Juan.

67. Ibid.

68. Treat, *Bishop Sheil*, p. 148.

69. Padilla, *Puerto Rican Chicago*, pp. 82–83.

70. Ibid., p. 128; Martínez, *Chicago*, p. 129.

71. Padilla, *Puerto Rican Chicago*, p. 128.

72. Carroll and Mahon, *Memorandum to His Eminence Albert Cardinal Meyer*, 1961. Typewritten manuscript in the archives of the archdiocese of Chicago, p. 1. Emphasis in the original.

73. Gilbert Carroll, "The Latin American Catholic Immigrant," in Thomas T. McAvoy, C.S.C., ed., *Roman Catholicism and the American Way of Life* (Notre Dame, Ind.: University of Notre Dame Press, 1960), p. 166.

74. Ibid.

75. Father Mahon to Manuel González, July 14, 1961, reproduced in Padilla, *Puerto Rican Chicago*, p. 248.

76. Mahon, *Report on the Inter-Diocesan Conference*, p. 28; Carroll and Headley, *Report of the Cardinal's Committee for the Spanish Speaking*, January 14, 1964 (typewritten document in the Archives of the archdiocese of Chicago), p. 1; Martínez, *Chicago*, p. 129.

77. Padilla, *Puerto Rican Chicago*, p. 126.

78. Ibid., p. 131.

79. The clergy associated with the Cardinal's Committee had a rather low opinion of the ministry these parishes were offering the Mexican community (cf. Carroll and Mahon, *Memorandum to Archbishop Meyer*, p. 2, and Carroll, "The Latin American Catholic Immigrant," p. 169) and hired a lay organizer to work with the Mexicans, hoping his work would "direct the Mexicans here into a more American and more Catholic mold" (Carroll and Mahon, *Memorandum to Archbishop Meyer*, p. 2).

80. Ibid., p. 1.

81. The names of the two full-time organizers are in Donaldo Headley, *Chicago History of the Catholic Church in the Hispanic Community* (typewritten manuscript in Father Headley's personal files), p. 1. Carroll ("The Latin American Catholic Immigrant," p. 169) mentions that the organizer for the Mexicans was a layman of that nationality, but does not give his name.

82. Both in Carroll, "The Latin American Catholic Immigrant," p. 165.

83. Carroll, ibid.; Mahon, *Report on the Inter-Diocesan Meeting*, p. 27.

84. "Current Comment," *America*, June 30, 1956, p. 314.

85. Mahon, *Report on the Inter-Diocesan Meeting*, p. 27; in the 1955 conference at San Juan, where he had presented the report for his archdiocese, he had already said: "It is hoped by stressing this assimilation that this purely Puerto Rican organization can eventually disappear" (*Report on the First Conference*, Section II, p. 3).

86. Padilla, *Puerto Rican Chicago*, p. 137. The "assimilationist" agenda implicit in the organization of the Caballeros de San Juan is analyzed in detail by Padilla in pp. 128–130 of the same work.

87. Carroll and Headley, *Report of the Cardinal's Committee*, p. 2.

88. Ibid., p. 1. The influence of the Office of the Commonwealth of Puerto Rico rankled all the more since in 1957 the first St. John's Day Parade, under the auspices of the Caballeros, was perceived by its organizers as "serv[ing] notice on civic, religious and welfare agencies that the Church considered the Spanish-speaking its own particular domain" (Mahon, *Report on the Inter-Diocesan Meeting*, p. 26).

89. Mahon to Cardinal Meyer, December 17, 1962. Letter in the archives of the archdiocese of Chicago.

90. See Vidal, "Popular Religion in the Lands of Origin," pp. 24–25.

91. Headley, *Chicago History*, p. 6. Of course, once they were ordained to the diaconate they were, in fact, clerics—and usually the only Puerto Rican clerics anyone got to see.

92. Padilla, *Puerto Rican Chicago*, p. 136.

93. Ibid.

Conclusion

1. *Report of the First Conference*, Appendix 2, p. 1.

2. Joseph Fitzpatrick's book *Puerto Rican Americans* is a notable exception, but the title was not his choice; it was imposed on him by his editors so that the book's title would be consistent with those of other books in the same series (interview with Father Fitzpatrick, April 17, 1993).

3. *Hispanics in New York*, vol. I, p. 91.

4. The term "inculturation" is of later date, but the idea it expresses is encouraged in the Constitution.

5. According to the survey in *Hispanics in New York* (Vol. I, p. 91), 28.8 percent of the respondents declared that the Charismatic Renewal was important in their lives. Since the survey sampled the total Hispanic population of the archdiocese, and not the Hispanic Catholics exclusively, one could estimate that between one quarter and one third of the Hispanics in New York have been affected by the Renewal, even if not all of these may be active in it.

6. For a detailed evaluation of the positive and negative aspects of the Charismatic Renewal in the Northeast U.S. Hispanic community see Vidal, "Popular Religion in Newark," pp. 308–328.

PART II: CUBAN CATHOLICS IN THE UNITED STATES

1. The Catholic Church in Cuba: A Weak Institution

1. Ramón Fernández Piérola y López de Luzuriaga, Bishop of Havana, in a letter to Cayetano Sánchez Bustillo, August 4, 1880. Reproduced in Manuel Maza Miquel, S.J., *El alma del negocio y el negocio del alma, testimonios sobre la iglesia y la sociedad en Cuba, 1878–1894* (Santo Domingo: Pontificia Universidad Católica Madre y Maestra, 1990), p. 12.

2. Richard Henry Dana, Jr., *To Cuba and Back* (1859; rev. ed., Carbondale: Southern Illinois University Press, 1966), p. 118.

3. Robert P. Porter, *Industrial Cuba* (New York: G. P. Putnam's Sons, 1899), p. 389.

4. Juan Bosch, *Cuba, la isla fascinante* (1955; reprint ed., Santo Domingo: Editorial Alfa y Omega, 1987), p. 203.

5. Calixto C. Masó, *Historia de Cuba*, 2nd ed. rev. (Miami: Ediciones Universal, 1976), p. 467.

6. Dana, *To Cuba and Back*, p. 117.

7. Manuel Santander y Frutos, bishop of Havana, in a letter to Angelo di Pietro, papal nuncio in Madrid, June 5, 1888. Reproduced in Maza Miquel, *El alma del negocio*, p. 76.

8. Manuel Santander y Frutos, bishop of La Habana, in a letter to Victor Balaguer, Minister of Colonies, June 5, 1888. Reproduced in Maza Miquel, *El alma del negocio*, p. 77.

9. Leví Marrero, *Cuba: economía y sociedad*, 14 vols. to date (Madrid: Editorial Playor, 1972–), 13:114–116.

10. Samuel Farber, *Revolution and Reaction in Cuba, 1933–1960: A Political Sociology from Machado to Castro* (Middletown, Conn.: Wesleyan University Press, 1976), p. 173.

11. Marrero, *Economía y sociedad*, 1:132–160 and Masó, *Historia de Cuba*, p. 48.

12. Fernando Portuondo, *Historia de Cuba, 1492–1898*, reprt. of 6th ed. (La Habana: Instituto Cubano del Libro, 1965), pp. 144–146.

13. Ibid., p. 136.

14. Louis A. Pérez, Jr., *Cuba: Between Reform and Revolution* (New York: Oxford University Press, 1988), p. 37.

15. Maza Miquel, *El alma del negocio*, pp. 2–3.

16. Hugh Thomas, *Cuba: The Pursuit of Freedom* (New York: Harper & Row, 1971), p. 12.

17. Marrero, *Economía y sociedad*, 3:53.

18. Ibid., 8:120.

19. Ibid., 8:111.

20. Maza Miquel, *El alma del negocio*, p. 18.

21. Santander y Frutos in a letter to di Pietro, June 5, 1888. Reproduced in Maza Miquel, *El alma del negocio*, p. 80.

22. Commission on Cuban Affairs, *Problems of the New Cuba* (N.Y.: Foreign Policy Association, 1935), p. 288.

23. Lowry Nelson, *Rural Cuba* (1950; reprinted ed., New York: Octagon Books, 1970), pp. 174–175.

24. The sugar revolution is extensively discussed in virtually every source on Cuban colonial history. The major work on the revolution itself and its consequences, and one that is primarily used here, is

Manuel Moreno Fraginals, *El ingenio, complejo económico social cubano del azúcar*, 3 vols. (1964; rev. ed., La Habana: Editorial de Ciencias Sociales, 1978).

25. Jorge Castellanos and Isabel Castellanos, *Cultura afrocubana I: El negro en Cuba, 1492–1844* (Miami: Ediciones Universal, 1988), pp. 126–128.

26. Moreno Fraginals, *El ingenio*, 1:128.

27. Manuel Moreno Fraginals, *The Sugarmill: The Socioeconomic Complex of Sugar in Cuba, 1760–1860*, trans. Cedric Belfrage (New York: Monthly Review Press, 1976), p. 18.

28. Franklin W. Knight, *Slave Society in Cuba During the Nineteenth Century* (Madison: University of Wisconsin Press, 1970), p. 22.

29. Moreno Fraginals, *The Sugarmill*, pp. 52–53.

30. Ibid., p. 53.

31. Ibid., p. 59.

32. Castellanos and Castellanos, *Cultura afrocubana I*, p. 112.

33. Juan Bautista Casas, quoted in Maza Miquel, *El alma del negocio*, p. 50.

34. Maza Miquel, *El alma del negocio*, p. 12.

35. Marcos Antonio Ramos, *Panorama del Protestantismo en Cuba* (San José, Costa Rica: Editorial Caribe, 1986).

36. Rafael Cepeda, "Un análisis de los juicios de los misioneros americanos sobre Cuba, los cubanos y la iglesia en Cuba, 1899–1925," in *La Herencia Misionera en Cuba*, ed. Rafael Cepeda (San José, Costa Rica: Departamento Ecuménico de Investigaciones, 1986), pp. 37–40.

37. Margaret E. Crahan, "Protestantism in Cuba," *Proceedings of the Pacific Coast Council on Latin American Studies* 9(1982): 59–60.

38. Ramos, *Panorama*, pp. 634–635.

39. Ibid., pp. 637–638.

40. Ibid., p. 635.

41. Manuel Moreno Fraginals, "Extent and Significance of Chinese Immigration to Cuba (19th Century)," in *Asiatic Migrations in Latin America*, ed. Luz M. Martínez Montiel (Mexico, D.F.: El Colegio de Mexico, 1981), pp. 53–58; Max J. Kohler, "Los judíos en Cuba," *Revista Bimestre Cubana* 15 (January–June 1920): 125–129; Robert M. Levine, *Tropical Diaspora: The Jewish Experience in Cuba* (Gainesville: University Presses of Florida, 1993).

42. Centro de Estudios Demográficos, *La población de Cuba* (La Habana: Editorial de Ciencias Sociales, 1976), p. 75; and Oficina Nacional de los Censos Demográfico y Electoral, *Censos de Población, Viviendas y Electoral, 28 de enero de 1953, informe general* (La Habana: P. Fernández y Cía, 1955), p. 82.

43. Maza Miquel, *El alma del negocio*, p. 58.

44. Ibid., pp. 59–60.

45. Ibid., p. 60.

46. Jan Knippers Black et al., eds., *Cuba: A Country Study*, reprt. of 2nd ed. (1976), Area Handbook Series of American University (Washington, D.C.: U.S. Government Printing Office, 1985), p. 124.

47. Ibid.

48. Leonel-Antonio de la Cuesta, ed., *Constituciones cubanas desde 1812 hasta nuestros días* (New York: Ediciones Exilio, 1974), p. 139.

49. Ibid., p. 254.

50. Black, *Cuba: A Country Study*, p. 124.

51. *Gaceta Oficial de la República de Cuba* 28 (1939): 2189–2193.

52. Mateo Jover Marimón, "The Church," in *Revolutionary Change in Cuba*, ed. Carmelo Mesa-Lago (Pittsburgh: University of Pittsburgh Press, 1971), p. 401.

2. The Nineteenth-Century Cuban Experience in the U.S.

1. Lisandro Pérez, "The Cuban Population of the United States: The Results of the 1980 U.S. Census of Population," *Cuban Studies/ Estudios Cubanos* 15, no. 2. (summer 1985): 17.

2. The volume of the academic and popular literature, especially the latter, on migration from socialist Cuba and the dynamics of the exile communities is evident in the most comprehensive, although now somewhat dated, bibliography on the topic: Lyn MacCorkle, *Cubans in the United States: A Bibliography for Research in the Social and Behavioral Sciences, 1960–1983* (Westport, Conn.: Greenwood Press, 1984).

3. José Rivero Muñíz, "Los cubanos en Tampa," *Revista Bimestre Cubana* 74 (January–June 1958): 5–140. Other early works, somewhat less comprehensive than Rivero's are: Nestor Carbonell, *Tampa, cuna del Partido Revolucionario Cubano* (La Habana: Imprenta Siglo XX, 1957); Orlando Castañeda, *Martí, los tabaqueros y la revolución de 1895* (La Habana: Editorial Lex, 1946); Gerardo Castellanos García, *Motivos de Cayo Hueso* (La Habana: Ucar, García, y Cía, 1935). During the 1960s and 1970s there were four theses or dissertations on this topic written at U.S. universities: Marshall M. True, "Revolutionaries in Exile: The Cuban Revolutionary Party" (doctoral dissertation, University of Virginia, 1965); Joan Marie Steffy, "The Cuban Immigration of Tampa, Florida, 1886–1898" (master's thesis, University of South Florida, 1975); Carol A. Preece, "Insurgent Guests: The Cuban Revolutionary Party and its Activities in the United States, 1892–1898" (doctoral dissertation, Georgetown University, 1976); and L. Glenn Westfall, "Don

Vicente Martínez Ybor, the Man and His Empire: Development of the Clear Havana Industry in Cuba and Florida in the Nineteenth Century" (doctoral dissertation, University of Florida, 1977).

4. The works of Gerald E. Poyo are central to the new body of historical literature on the Cuban communities in the U.S.: Gerald E. Poyo, "The Evolution of Cuban Separatist Thought in the Emigré Communities of the United States," *Hispanic American Historical Review* 66, no. 3 (1986): 485–507; Gerald E. Poyo, "The Impact of Cuban and Spanish Workers on Labor Organizing in Florida, 1870–1900," *Journal of American Ethnic History* 5, no. 2 (spring 1986): 45–63; Gerald E. Poyo, "The Anarchist Challenge to the Cuban Independence Movement, 1885–1890," *Cuban Studies/Estudios Cubanos* 15, no. 1 (winter 1985): 29–42; Gerald E. Poyo, "Cuban Communities in the United States: Toward an Overview of the 19th Century Experience," in *Cubans in the United States*, ed. Miren Uriarte-Gastón and Jorge Cañas Martínez (Boston: Center for the Study of the Cuban Community, 1984); Gerald E. Poyo, *With All, and for the Good of All: The Emergence of Popular Nationalism in the Cuban Communities of the United States, 1848–1898* (Durham: Duke University Press, 1989). Other important works: Gary R. Mormino and George E. Pozzetta, *The Immigrant World of Ybor City: Italians and their Latin Neighbors in Tampa, 1885–1985* (Urbana: University of Illinois Press, 1987); Susan D. Greenbaum, *Afro-Cubans in Ybor City* (Tampa: University of South Florida, 1986); Susan D. Greenbaum, "Afro-Cubans in Exile: Tampa, Florida, 1886–1984," *Cuban Studies/Estudios Cubanos* 15, no. 1 (winter 1985): 59–72; Louis A. Pérez, Jr., "Cubans in Tampa: From Exiles to Immigrants, 1892–1901," *Florida Historical Quarterly* 57, no. 2. (October 1978): 129–140.

5. U.S. Bureau of Statistics, *Immigration into the United States, Showing Number, Nationality, Sex, Age, Occupation, Destination, etc., from 1820 to 1903* (Washington, D.C.: Treasury Department, n.d.).

6. For a lengthy discussion of this concept, see U.S. Congress, Senate, *Reports of the Immigration Commission. Dictionary of Races or Peoples* 61st Congress, 3rd session, Document no. 662 (Washington, D.C.: U.S. Government Printing Office, 1911). The consequence of this definitional deficiency is that long-time foreign-born residents of Cuba (including naturalized Cuban citizens) who migrated to the United States were supposedly not counted as Cubans or Cuban immigrants. On the other hand, Cuban-born persons (or of Cuban "race or people") who migrated to the United States but were previously long-time residents of third countries were presumably counted as Cubans. It is likely, however, that the latter are far less numerous than the former, thus leading to an undercount of immigration from Cuba, especially

during the late nineteenth century. Migration from Cuba to the United States during those years included a noticeable number of persons born in Spain but who were long-time residents of Cuba. Many of them were employed in Cuba's cigar industry and were partly responsible for the establishment of the Havana tobacco industry in the United States during those years. While this shortcoming of the data does not seriously handicap the analysis, it is important to keep it in mind. It means that in reality the data do not refer to migration from Cuba to the United States, but rather to the migration of Cubans to the United States.

7. Portuondo, *Historia de Cuba*, p. 490.

8. Ibid., p. 256, and José Martí, "Heredia," speech delivered at Hardman Hall, New York, 30 November 1889, in *José Martí: obras completas*, vol. 5 (La Habana: Editorial de Ciencias Sociales, 1975), pp. 163–176.

9. Portuondo, *Historia de Cuba*, p. 360.

10. U.S., Customs Service, "List of Passengers Arrived from Foreign Ports into the Port of New Orleans, 1820–1875," microfilm, Genealogy Room, Centroplex Library, Baton Rouge, Louisiana.

11. Robert E. May, *The Southern Dream of a Caribbean Empire, 1854–1861* (Baton Rouge: Louisiana State University Press, 1973) and C. Stanley Urban, "A Local Study in 'Manifest Destiny': New Orleans and the Cuban Question During the Lopez Expeditions" (master's thesis, Louisiana State University, 1938).

12. Portuondo, *Historia de Cuba*, p. 361.

13. Cirilo Villaverde, *Cecilia Valdés ó la loma del angel* (1882; reprint ed., La Habana: Consejo Nacional de Cultura, 1964).

14. The extensive bibliography on Varela can be divided into three areas, reflecting the different facets of Varela's life and work. His contributions as a philosopher are the subject of the following: Gustavo Serpa, *Apuntes sobre la filosofía de Félix Varela* (La Habana: Editorial de Ciencias Sociales, 1983) and Humberto Piñera Llera, *Panorama de la filosofía cubana* (Washington, D.C.: Secretaría General de la Organización de los Estados Americanos, 1960), pp. 38–49. His political activities and ideas in relation to Cuban independence are the principal focus of these works: Juan P. Esteve, *Félix Varela y Morales: análisis de sus ideas políticas* (Miami: Ediciones Universal, 1992) and Joaquín G. Santana, *Félix Varela* (La Habana: Ediciones Unión, 1982). There are two works that emphasize his pastoral work in New York: Joseph McCadden and Helen M. McCadden, *Félix Varela: Torch Bearer from Cuba*, 2d ed. (San Juan: Félix Varela Foundation, 1984) and Felipe J. Estévez, *El perfil pastoral de Félix Varela* (Miami: Ediciones Universal, 1989). Since the latter facet of Varela's work is emphasized here, those

two works are heavily relied upon for the account of Varela's life in New York. Extensive use is also made of two comprehensive biographies of Varela: Antonio Hernández Travieso, *El Padre Varela: biografía del forjador de la conciencia cubana*, 2nd ed. rev. (Miami: Ediciones Universal, 1984) and Eusebio Reyes Fernández, *Félix Varela, 1788–1853* (La Habana: Editora Política, 1989).

15. McCadden and McCadden, *Felix Varela*, pp. 51–52.

16. Jay P. Dolan, *The Immigrant Church: New York's Irish and German Catholics, 1815–1865* (Baltimore: The Johns Hopkins University Press, 1975), p. 64.

17. Gaspar Betancourt Cisneros, letter to Jose Antonio Saco, June 3, 1849, quoted in McCadden and McCadden, *Felix Varela*, p. 121.

18. Antonio Lluberes, S.J., "Cuba, iglesia y revolución: la causa de la canonización del Padre Varela," *Estudios Sociales* 67 (1987): 69–72.

19. Westfall, "Don Vicente Martínez Ybor," p. 22.

20. U.S. Bureau of Statistics, *Immigration into the United States*, p. 4366.

21. The description given here of the events leading up to the establishment of Ybor City was compiled from the accounts in the following sources: Rivero Muñíz, "Los cubanos en Tampa," pp. 9–20; Westfall, "Don Vicente Martínez Ybor," pp. 23–47; Durward Long, "The Making of Modern Tampa: A City of the New South, 1885–1911," *Florida Historical Quarterly* 49 (1971): 333–345; Durward Long, "The Historical Beginnings of Ybor City and Modern Tampa," *Florida Historical Quarterly* 45 (1966): 31–44; Pérez, "Cubans in Tampa," pp. 129–140; and Steffy, "The Cuban Immigrants."

22. U.S., Census Office, *Twelfth Census of the United States, Taken in the Year 1900, Census Reports, Volume 1, Population, Part I* (Washington, D.C., Government Printing Office, 1901), p. 742.

23. U.S., Department of the Interior, Census Office, *Statistics of the Population of the United States at the Tenth Census, June 1, 1880* (Washington, D.C.: Government Printing Office, 1883), p. 501.

24. U.S., Congress, Senate, Committee on Immigration, *Report to Accompany Senate Resolutions of July 16 and December 14, 1892*, 52nd Cong., 2d sess., 4 February 1893, S. Rept. 1263, p. I.

25. Ibid., p. 3.

26. Ibid., pp. 3–5.

27. Portuondo, *Historia de Cuba*, p. 413.

28. Ibid., p. 395, and "Francisco Vicente Aguilera," *Bohemia* (July 25, 1983): 81.

29. True, "Revolutionaries in Exile"; Preece, "Insurgent Guests"; Poyo, *With All and for the Good of All*; and Jorge Mañach, *Martí, el apóstol* (6th ed.; Madrid: Espasa-Calpe, 1975), pp. 198–205.

30. True, "Revolutionaries in Exile," p. 35.

31. Ibid., p. 74.

32. Ibid., pp. 75–76; Hugh Thomas, *Cuba: The Pursuit of Freedom* (New York: Harper and Row, 1971), p. 314; and José Martí, "La reunion en New York," *Patria*, 22 April 1893, reprinted in Martí, *Obras completas*, vol. 2, pp. 307–310.

3. The Cuban Communities in the U.S., 1900–1958

1. U.S., Department of Justice, Immigration and Naturalization Service, *Annual Report 1948*.

2. U.S., Department of Justice, Immigration and Naturalization Service, *Annual Report 1958*.

3. Federal Writers' Projects, Tampa Staff, "Ybor City," (unpublished manuscript, Jacksonville, 1935–36), p. 298. The pages in the manuscript were not numbered sequentially by the typist. This copy, however, has sequential page numbers written in pencil. It is those penciled page numbers that are used in the references.

4. José Yglesias, "The Radical Latino Island in the Deep South," reprint of a letter appearing in *Nuestro*, August 1977, pp. 6–7.

5. In the most comprehensive work on the political activities of the émigré communities (Poyo, *With All and for the Good of All*) there is no mention at all of religion, in fact, the words "religion," "Church," and "Catholic" do not even appear in the book's subject index. In another work that is fairly detailed and comprehensive (Rivero Muñíz, "Los cubanos en Tampa") there is also not a single mention of religion, religious organizations, priests, or churches, despite the depth of his article in mentioning organizations, publications, and leaders. Note in the previously cited bibliography on Ybor City that virtually all works focus on the political activities of the émigrés in relation to the homeland.

6. Louis A Pérez, Jr., "Reminiscences of a *Lector*: Cuban Cigar Workers in Tampa," *Florida Historical Quarterly* 53(1975): 443.

7. Poyo, "The Impact of Cuban and Spanish Workers," p. 59.

8. Pérez, "Reminiscences of a *Lector*," p. 443.

9. Ibid., pp. 445–446.

10. Yglesias, "The Radical Latino Island," p. 6.

11. Ibid.

12. Federal Writers' Projects, *Ybor City*, p. 264.

13. Ibid., pp. 436–437.

14. Antonio del Rio and Emilio del Rio, *Yo fuí uno de los fundadores de Ybor City* (Tampa: Emilio del Rio, 1950), pp. 47–50.

15. Federal Writers' Projects, "Ybor City."

16. Ibid., pp. 277–278.

17. Ibid., pp. 261–264.

18. Ibid., pp. 240–245.

19. For an excellent analysis of black Cubans in Ybor City, see Susan D. Greenbaum, *Afro-Cubans in Ybor City* (Tampa: University of South Florida, 1986). Consistent with the rest of the literature on Ybor City, this fairly comprehensive work on Afro-Cubans contains no mention of religious practices.

20. Westfall, "Don Vicente Martínez Ybor," p. 95.

21. Commissioner General of Immigration, *Annual Report for the Fiscal Year Ended June 30, 1909* (Washington, D.C.: U.S. Government Printing Office, 1909), p. 9.

22. Much of the material on music in this section is derived from John Storm Roberts, *The Latin Tinge: The Impact of Latin American Music on the United States* (New York: Oxford University Press, 1979).

23. Much of the material on boxing is derived from Julio Ferreiro Mora, *Historia del boxeo cubano* (Miami: Selecta Enterprises, n.d.).

24. Much of the material on baseball is derived from Angel Torres, *La historia del beisból cubano, 1878–1976* (Los Angeles: Angel Torres, 1976).

4. The Exodus from Revolutionary Cuba and the Catholic Church in South Florida, 1959–1965

1. Manuel Fernández, *Religión y revolución en Cuba* (Miami: Saeta Ediciones, 1984), pp. 35–43.

2. John M. Kirk, *Between God and the Party: Religion and Politics in Revolutionary Cuba* (Tampa: University of South Florida Press, 1989), pp. 81–82.

3. Raúl Gómez Treto, *La iglesia católica durante la construcción del socialismo en Cuba* (Matanzas: Centro de Información y Estudio Augusto Cotto, 1988), p. 44.

4. Fernández, *Religión y revolución*, p. 115.

5. For analyses of the political context of the U.S. immigration policy towards Cuba during this period, its origins and consequences, see: Félix Roberto Masud-Piloto, *With Open Arms: Cuban Migration to the United States* (Totowa, N.J.: Rowman and Littlefield, 1988) and Silvia Pedraza-Bailey, *Political and Economic Migrants in America: Cubans and Mexicans* (Austin: University of Texas Press, 1985), pp. 18–52.

6. Sergio Díaz-Briquets and Lisandro Pérez, "Cuba: The Demography of Revolution," *Population Bulletin of the Population Reference Bureau* 36 (April 1981): 25.

7. Lisandro Pérez, "Cubans in the United States," *The Annals of the American Academy of Political and Social Science* 487 (1986): 129–130.

8. Michael J. McNally, *Catholicism in South Florida, 1868–1968* (Gainesville: University of Florida Press, 1982), pp. 127–166.

9. Ibid., p. 144.

10. Ibid.

11. Ibid., p. 149.

12. Ibid., p. 145.

13. Ibid., p. 147.

14. Ibid., p. 145.

15. Bishop Coleman F. Carroll, quoted in McNally, *Catholicism in South Florida*, p. 151.

16. McNally, *Catholicism in South Florida*, p. 151.

17. Ibid., pp. 152–154.

18. Ibid., p. 147.

19. Ibid., p. 148. See also Everett M. Ressler, Neil Boothby, and Daniel J. Steinbock, *Unaccompanied Children: Care and Protection in Wars, Natural Disasters, and Refugee Movements* (New York: Oxford University Press, 1988), pp. 51–57.

20. Two of Castro's biographers have placed considerable emphasis on the formative impact of Belén on the young Fidel. See: Tad Szulc, *Fidel: A Critical Portrait* (New York: William Morrow and Company, 1986), pp. 118–134, and Georgie Anne Geyer, *Guerrilla Prince: The Untold Story of Fidel Castro* (Boston: Little, Brown, and Company, 1991), pp. 37–44.

21. Richard C. Chisholm, S.J., to Bishop Coleman F. Carroll, 4 November 1960, copy provided to the author by José M. Izquierdo.

22. Ibid.

23. Ibid.

24. Interview with José M. Izquierdo, S.J., 7 January 1993.

25. Ibid.

26. Chisholm to Carroll.

27. Bishop Coleman F. Carroll to Ramón Calvo, S.J., 29 August 1961, copy provided to the author by José M. Izquierdo.

28. Ibid.

29. Ibid.

30. Ibid.

31. Ibid.

32. Interview with Izquierdo.

33. The legend associated with the building is that years prior to housing the dance academy, it was used by Al Capone as a whiskey warehouse.

34. José M. Hernández, *Agrupación Católica Universitaria: los primeros cincuenta años* (Miami: Agrupación Católica Universitaria, 1981), p. 7.

35. Ibid., p. 8.

36. Interview with Antonio Abella, 7 January 1993.

37. Hernández, *Agrupación Católica Universitaria*, p. 15.

38. Ibid.

39. The ACU's lay co-founder, Juan Antonio Rubio Padilla, for example, was a principal figure of the anti-Machado struggle.

40. Interview with Abella.

41. Ibid.

42. Interview with Amando Llorente, S.J., 8 January 1993.

43. Interview with Abella.

44. Pablo J. Carreño and Enrique Hernández Miyares, "Entrevista con el Padre Llorente," *Esto-Vir* 41 (August 1992): 8.

45. Ibid.

46. Ibid.

47. Interview with Abella.

48. Interview with Llorente.

49. Ibid.

50. McNally, *Catholicism in South Florida*, p. 163.

51. There is an extensive bibliography on the Afro-Cuban religions. For the classical work on the subject see Lydia Cabrera, *El Monte* (Miami: Rema Press, 1968).

Contributors

Jay P. Dolan is Professor of History at the University of Notre Dame and former Director of the Cushwa Center for the Study of American Catholicism.

Lisandro Perez is Associate Professor and Director of the Cuban Research Institute at Florida International University.

Jaime R. Vidal was the Assistant Director of the Cushwa Center for the Study of American Catholicism from 1990 to 1994.

Index

Abbad y Lasierra, Iñigo, 20
Africa, Africans, 2, 13, 14, 23, 153
Afro-Cuban cults, 21, 153, 181, 206–7
agriculture: colonial Cuba, 151;
    Puerto Rico 54, 55; seasonal farm
    workers, 112–14. *See also* sugar
    industry
Agrupación Católica Universitaria,
    201–6
Aguada, PR, 18
Aguas Buenas, PR, 141
Aguilera, Francisco Vicente, 170
Albizu Campos, Pedro, 30, 31, 48
Alfonso XIII, king of Spain, 70
Alinsky, Saul, 130
Alvarez, Placido, 117
American Church, 3, 22, 37, 64, 65–69
Americanization: and the Church, 43,
    44, 45, 94; of immigrants, 29, 74,
    78, 85; of Puerto Ricans, 4, 5, 59,
    112, 135–38; and Puerto Rico, 31,
    37, 39, 48, 49. *See also* assimilation
Amoros, Sandy, 188
annexation, U.S.: of Cuba, 160, 161;
    of Puerto Rico, 27, 54
anti-Americanism, 34, 62, 63, 143
anti-Castro underground, 203
anti-Catholicism, 46, 78, 140, 163
anticlericalism, 6, 17, 48
Aponte Martinez, Luis, 53, 104
Arecibo, PR, 18, 20
Arecibo diocese, PR, 50
Arizmendo y de la Torre, Juan Alejo,
    16, 22, 48, 104, 213
Arnaz, Desi, 186
Arroyo, Felipe, 201

assimilation: and Cubans, 7, 196, 200;
    and Puerto Ricans, 5, 60, 86, 102,
    103, 105, 121–22, 125, 133, 142
asylum, political, 193, 203
Augustinian Recollects, 110
Augustinians, 42
Augustinians of the Assumption, 70
authority: attitudes toward, 21,
    160; ecclesiastical, 107; and
    institutional loyalty, 67
Azpiazu, Don, 186

Badillo, Herman, 108
Balbuena, Bernardo, 16
Balmes, Jaime, 30
Baltimore, MD, 45, 79
Barbeito, Francisco, 203
Bardeck, Phillip, 79
barrio, 54, 128–29
Batista, Fulgencio, 34, 148, 174, 185,
    189, 202
Bauzá, Mario, 186
Bay of Pigs Invasion (1961), 190, 203
Bayonne, NJ, 88
Belén Jesuit Preparatory School (El
    Colegio de Nuestra Señora de
    Belén), 198–201, 202, 205, 206
Benedictines, 117
Betancourt, Alonso, 161
Betancourt Cisneros, Gaspar, 161,
    164
birth control, 49, 51
Blenk, James Humbert, 40, 42, 43, 44,
    48, 50, 52
blue collar jobs, 58
Bosch, Juan, 147
Boston, 54, 119

249

Bronx (New York), 71, 72, 91, 92
Brooklyn (New York), 54, 171
Bucaná, PR, 20
Buffalo diocese, 114

Caballeros de San Juan, 129–33
Caguas, PR, 124
Caguas diocese, 50
Callaghan, Robert, 120, 121
Calvo, Ramón, 200
Camarioca, Cuba, 192
Camden (NJ) diocese, 83, 85, 114
Campaneris, Bert, 188
Canary Islands, 13–14
Cardenal, José, 188
Cárdenas, Leo, 188
Cardinal Cushing Center for the
    Spanish-Speaking, 119
Cardinal's Committee for the Spanish
    Speaking in Chicago, 130
Carmelites of Charity, 47
Carmody, James, 118, 232
Carroll, Coleman F., 195, 198, 199–200
Carroll, Gilbert, 131, 132
Carroll, John, 15
Casa del Carmen (Philadelphia), 121
Casa María (Centro María), 72
Casas, Juan Bautista, 155–56
Casita María (New York), 72, 121
Cassville, NJ, 117
Castro, Fidel, 34, 185, 189, 193, 198,
    203, 246
Catalonia, 17
Catholic Action, 4, 7, 93
Catholic Church: colonial Cuba,
    147–49, 150–51, 153–54, 155–56;
    Iberian, 12; Puerto Rico, 38–53;
    revolutionary Cuba, 190–91
Catholic Student Youth, 208
Catholic Welfare Bureau (Miami),
    201
Catholic Youth Organization (CYO),
    127–28
celebration, 66, 101. See also holidays
center for social services, 114, 118,
    122

Centro Católico de Información
    (Jersey City, NJ), 118
Centro del Cardenal (Boston), 119
Centro Hispano Católico (Miami),
    195
Channel, Joseph, 124
Chapelle, Placid, 40, 42
chapels, 84, 112, 114, 116, 117, 121,
    125
Charismatic movement, 81, 140, 141
Chávez, César, 140
Chelsea (New York), 54
Chicago, IL, 6, 11, 60, 62, 113, 119,
    127
Chicago archdiocese, 130
Children of Mary, 80
Chisolm, Richard C., 198
Church and State: colonial Puerto
    Rico, 38, 41; Cuba, 148, 155–56,
    190–91, 197; Muñoz Marín, 55
churches (buildings), 65, 76, 84, 85,
    126, 162–63; Puerto Rico, 15, 18,
    41, 80; renting and building, 81,
    85. See also chapels
church finance, 16, 23, 40, 43, 82, 148,
    150
churchwardens, 43
Cigar Makers International Union,
    166–67
cigar manufacturing, 6, 158, 164–65,
    166–69, 170, 172, 173, 174, 177–78,
    181, 183
citizenship: hearings, 58; immigrants
    and, 85; Puerto Rico, 5, 27, 37,
    135–37
civil rights movement, 120, 142
Claretians, 114, 116, 130
class: Afro-Cuban religion, 207;
    American middle class, 4;
    church lay societies, 49; colonial
    Cuba, 152; differences, 64; Great
    Migration, 24; Hispanics in U.S.,
    110; parish model, 77; Puerto
    Rican education, 46, 48; Puerto
    Ricans, 33, 50–51; revolutionary

Cuba, 191; white American
communities, 56, 59
clericalism, 133
Cleveland, OH, 126
Clot, Juan, 120, 121
clubs: CYO, 128; hometown clubs,
92; in national parishes, 82;
revolutionary activities, 171, 178
Coamo, PR, 18, 20
color (race), 4, 13, 33, 55, 58, 59, 137
commerce, 54, 149, 174
Committee for the Independence of
Cuba, 26
Commonwealth of Puerto Rico, 5,
36, 132
community organizing, 131; la
comunidad hispana, 81; Cursillo,
11, 139; ecclesially centered Puerto
Ricans, 112; geographical focus
for, 82; local church, 80, 86; local
neighborhood, 66; nuns and
religious, 47; Puerto Rican and
American views, 69; Puerto Rican
communities, 12, 96, 138; Ybor
City, FL, 168
conduct of life: Afro-Cuban religion,
207; Cubans in Ybor City, FL,
180; Institute of Intercultural
Communication, 103–4
Conference on Spiritual Care of
Puerto Rican Migrants, 83, 98, 99
119
Connolly, Joseph F., 93–94, 96, 97,
99, 110, 224, 228, 229
contraception. See birth control
contract labor, 127, 166
credit unions, 133
crime, 71, 118, 149, 193
Cuba Church, 198
Cuban constitution, 156, 189
Cuban Council of New York, 161
Cuban Insurrection (1868–1878),
164–66, 171
Cuéllar, Mike, 188
culture: American, 29, 56, 58, 64,

73–74; Catholic, 16, 25, 78, 121;
counterculture, 107, 142; Cuban,
160, 184–87; cultural imperialism,
80; Irish and Hispanic, 105;
language and culture, 58; Latin
culture, 104; otherness, 103, 143;
Puerto Rican, 5, 13, 30, 32–35, 87,
129, 132, 133, 137, 139
Curley, Michael, 180
Cursillos de Cristiandad, 6, 81,
109–11, 139, 140, 141, 206
customs, 65
CYO. See Catholic Youth
Organization

Dana, Richard Henry, 147, 148
Davis, James P., 53, 98
Daytona Beach, FL, 185
del Rio, Antonio, 178
democratization of Puerto Rico,
26–27
Dente, Vincent M., 180
Depression (1929+), 55, 174, 182
devotions: seasonal farmwrokers,
115; vernacular, 73. See also rosary
diaconate, 133, 141, 142
Díaz Alonso, María Mercedes, 218
diBuono, Pasquale, 114
dictatorships: Batista, 185, 202;
Castro, 185; Machado, 185, 202;
Trujillo and Batista, 34
Díez, Genadio, 117
Dingley Tariff Act (1897), 181
diocesan priests. See priests
diocese: government of, 42; Puerto
Rico, 14, 39; unity of, 78, 94, 98,
103
discrimination in housing, 76, 100
disestablishment of Church, 39, 41
dispensation fees, 24
divorce, 24, 156
Dolan, Jay P., 67
Dominicas de Fátima, 47
Dubois, Jean, 163

East Harlem (New York), 71

economic conditions: cigar industry, 168–69, 180, 181; Cuba, 174, 192, 193; Puerto Rico, 27, 34, 35
Ecumenism, 140–41
education: bishops, 15–16; Cuba, 4, 156; Europe and U.S., 54; Puerto Rico, 29, 45–46; transplanted institutions, 197–208
Eisenhower, Dwight D., 192
elections: Puerto Rico, 5; U.S., 52, 127, 136
elites, 5, 110, 202, 203
Elizabeth, NJ, 117
emigration: emigrant aliens, 183–84; exiles from Cuba, 192; Puerto Rico, 61
employment: abandonment, 60; Agrupación Católica Universitaria, 204–5; Cuban immigrants, 173, 174; Great Migration, 56–58, 60; Lorain, OH, 124; sugar industry, 113; Youngstown, OH, 122–24
English language, 29, 33, 36; Belén school, 200; Catholics, 72–73; decision-makers, 81; priests, 196; Puerto Rico, 50, 135; teaching in, 49; vernacular Mass, 80
Estado Libre Asociado, 36
Estrada, Noel, 62–63
Estrada Palma, Tomás, 171
ethnic parishes, 78, 81
ethnic revival, 142–43
ethos, American, 64, 103
Europe, European, 3, 12, 14, 20, 22, 25, 37, 42, 54, 56, 62, 85, 129, 151, 154, 204. See also Mediterranean Catholicism
Eustace, Bartholomew, 116
Evangelical Foreign Missions Association, 154
excludables (Marielitos), 193
exiles: Cuban, 6–7, 160, 170, 182, 191, 195, 199, 204; Puerto Ricans, 2, 26, 54

exports, 169, 181
Exsul Familia, 83–84, 85, 112, 116, 125

family life: of migrant workers, 114; Great Migration, 60–61; Puerto Ricans, 113; slavery, 23
farm workers, 112–16. See also agricuture; migration
Fatima Social Center (NJ), 116
Faulkner, Joseph, 118, 232
Ferdinand V, king of Spain, 15
Ferdinand VII, king of Spain, 162
Fernández Piérola y López, Ramón, 147
Ferré, Luis, 48–49, 216
Ferree, William, 101
Fiesta de Cruz, 21
Fiesta de San Juan, 94, 95, 101, 107
fiestas patronales, 97
Fitzpatrick, Joseph, 6, 75, 81, 88–89, 96, 97, 98, 138, 212, 222, 223, 224, 229
Florida, 6, 170, 171, 172, 174, 177, 181, 192
folk Catholicism, 22
Foraker Law, 27
Fox, Robert, 105, 106, 108, 231
Fredericks, Paul, 125
Freemasonry, 3, 22, 47, 154, 156, 181
fundamentalism, 141

Galveston, TX, 167
Gargol, Bernardino, 167
Gaudium et Spes, 140
Gauthier, Felisa Rincón de, 97
ghetto, 46, 120
González, Gerardo (Kid Gavilán), 187
González, Tony, 188
Great Migration, 24, 37, 45, 54–69, 75, 91, 136, 137, 138
Greenbaum, Susan D., 245
Gregory XVI, pope, 22
Griffiths, James, 94
Grillo, Frank, 186
Guánica Bay, PR, 26

Guayama, PR, 13
Guerra, Benjamin, 171
Gutiérrez, Gavino, 167, 168

El Habanero (serial), 162
Harlem (New York), 55
Harrisburg diocese, 114
Havana, 42, 149–50, 151, 156, 170,
    174, 182, 197, 198–200, 201–2
Haya, Ignacio, 167, 168
Headley, Donaldo, 132, 134, 236
Heredia, José María, 160
Hermanas del Buen Pastor, 47
Los Hermanos de la Familia de Dios,
    133
Herrera de la Iglesia, José Martín,
    150
Hervás, Juan, 110
Hickey, James A., 127
Hillsborough County, FL, 169
Hispanic Society of America, 70
holidays, 19, 21, 87, 94, 95, 97, 101,
    107. See also celebration
Holy Cross Cathedral, Boston, 119
Holy Name Society, 49, 51, 52, 80,
    125
Home Rule, Puerto Rico, 2, 26, 31, 32
housing, 76, 122, 125, 128, 168, 196
Hughes, John, 163
Hunt, Lester, 131,
Huntington, Archer, 70

Iasi, Francisco de, 212
identity: Chicago Puerto Ricans,
    132; Great Migration, 59, 136;
    immigration, 11, independence,
    36; oppressed people, 143; Puerto
    Ricans, 30, 31, 34, 95–96, 101;
    Puertorriqueñismo, 37, 63, 133,
    135, 137; and U.S., 37, 62
Illich, Ivan, 60, 62, 89, 93, 95, 96, 97,
    98, 100, 101–6, 138, 139, 212, 227,
    228, 230–31
immigration: Agrupación Católica
    Universitaria, 203–4; colonial
    Cuba, 154, 172; Cuban, 158–73,
    165, 169–70, 174–88, 189–207;
    Puerto Ricans, 37, 59. See also
    migration
Immigration Law (1924), 64, 122
imports, 169, 182
income, Chicago, 127
independence, Puerto Rico, 28, 30,
    48, 135–36
industrial workers, 122
Institute of Intercultural Communca-
    tion, 102
Institute of Misssionary Formation,
    102
institutional church in Puerto Rico,
    21, 25, 38–53, 77, 136
integrated parishes, 6, 85, 86, 90, 92;
    beyond New York, 112; Chicago,
    131; and ethnic revival, 143; NJ,
    117; New York, 73, 78, 82, 79, 88,
    100, 111; Philadelphia, 120; and
    vernacular liturgy, 140
intelligentsia, Puerto Rico, 22, 48
Interdiocesan Meeting of Priests
    Concerning the Apostolate to the
    Spanish-speaking of the East, 120,
    121
intermarriage, 12, 13, 58, 122
Ireland, Irish, 95, 96, 105, 108, 163,
    164
Italy, Italian, 54, 55, 82, 87, 180, 204
Iznaga, Alberto, 186
Iznega, José Antonio, 161

Jacksonville, FL, 178
Jayuya, PR, 124
Jersey City, NJ, 118
Jesuits, 7, 48, 179, 198–201, 202, 203,
    204, 206
job recruitment in Puerto Rico,
    124–25, 127
Jones, William Ambrose, 42, 44, 48,
    50, 52
Jones law, 27, 28

Kansas, 205
Kelly, George, 69, 90–92, 97, 138, 227

Kennedy, John F., 46, 142, 221, 230
Kerhonkson Valley, NY, 115
Key West, FL, 158, 164–66, 167, 168
King, Martin Luther, Jr., 142
Kingston, NY, 115
Kirk, John M., 190
Knights of Columbus, 51, 52, 129
Korean War, 28

labor management relations, 182
labor movement, 55, 58, 166–67,
    176–77
Ladies Altar Guild, 126
La Guardia, Fiorello, 55
laity, 42, 43, 49, 82, 93, 110, 133, 139,
    140, 142
Lakehurst, NJ, 117
language: and culture, 58; and
    parishes, 70, 73, 81, 140; Puerto
    Ricans, 29, 59, 137; training in, 94,
    97, 102
Laredo, TX, 110
Lares, PR, 124
leadership: Chicago archdiocese,
    130, 132; clergy and politicians,
    52; Cursillo, 110, 139; in ethnic
    parishes, 82; Great Migration, 136;
    and hierarchy, 77; laity, 140, 142;
    Puerto Rican bishops, 16
Lecuona, Ernesto, 185
Lee, Muna Muñoz, 127
Lesley, John T., 168
Liberation Theology, 140
Lindsay, John, 108
Llorente, Amaando, 203–6
Loíza Aldea, PR, 13
Lope de Vegas. See Vega y Carpio,
    Lope de
López, Narciso, 161
López, de Haro, Damián, 19, 42, 213
Lorain, OH, 6, 85, 124–25
Louisana, 40
Luque, Adolfo, 187

MacCorkle, Lyn, 240
McGarry, Anna, 120, 121

Machado, Gerardo, 185, 202
Machito. See Grillo, Frank
McKinley, William, 147, 181
McKinley Tariff, 181
McManus, James E., 53, 94, 98, 104,
    218
McNally, Michael J., 194, 206
Madres del Sagrado Corazón, 47, 48
Mahon, Leo, 129, 131, 132, 133, 134,
    222, 226, 236
Manhattan (New York), 91, 92
Manrara, Eduardo, 167–68
Manso, Alonso, 15, 16
manufacturing jobs, 57. See also
    cigar manufacturing; steel
    manufacturing
Marcantonio, Vito, 55
marginalization of the Church, 3
Marianists, 48
Maricao, PR, 12
Mariel boatlift, 193, 207
Marists, 40
Marqués, René, 216, 220
marriage: Cuba, 148; intermarriage,
    122; interracial, 58; of permanent
    deacons 141; Puerto Ricans, 23–24,
    46, 68; of slaves 23; in Ybor City,
    FL, 180
Martí, José, 156, 171
Martínez, Manuel, 128
Martínez Ybor, Vicente, 165, 166–68,
    177, 179, 182
Marxism, 34
Masó, Calixto, 148
Mass: attendance, 66, 67, 68, 91, 157;
    Camden, 114; Cuban exiles, 197;
    language of, 79, 87; Latin Mass,
    140; Lorain, OH, 126; outdoor,
    96, 101; Philadelphia, 122; Puerto
    Rico, 19, 46; schedules, 104;
    weekly obligation, 51
Matheson, Hardy, 200
mayordomo de fábrica, 42
Meagan, Peter, 127
Medeiros, Humberto, 77

Mediterranean Catholicism, 13, 25, 39, 48
Mediterranean culture, 18
Melgarejo, Juan, 12
melting pot, 59
Mercado, José, 18, 32
metal industries, 122
Metuchen, NJ, 116
Mexican Americans, 125, 130
Mexico, 14, 160–61, 192
Miami, FL, 185, 192, 194–97, 204, 205
Miami diocese, 194–97, 199–200
Micera, Gerard, 232
midwives, 22–23
migration: Cuba, 3; farm workers, 112–14; Great Migration, 54–69, 91; Puerto Rico, 11, 28, 60
military vicariate, 94
Minguella de la Merced, Toribio, 40
Miñoso, Orestes (Minnie), 188
Miquel, Maza, 155
Missile Crisis (October 1962), 192, 194
Missionary Servants of the Blessed Trinity, 118, 125
missioner, ethnic, 84
Mobile, AL, 167
monarchy, 27, 38
Monroe County, FL, 169
Montalbán, Ricardo, 100
Moore, John, 179
Morales Lemus, José, 170
moralism, Irish-Catholic, 68
Moreno Fraginals, Manuel, 239
Morrison Act of 1883, 169
Muñoz Marín, Luis, 35–36, 52, 53, 55, 56, 104, 135, 230
Muñoz Rivera, Luis, 32, 215
music, 101, 175, 185–86
mutual aid societies, 178

National Catholic Community Services, 123
nationalism: colonial Cuba, 156; Puerto Rico, 36

Nationalist Party (Puerto Rico), 30, 55
nationality, Puerto Ricans, 59, 62
national parishes, 3, 70, 74, 77–78, 91, 112; Chicago, 131; Youngstown, OH, 123–24
neighborhoods, 45, 77–78, 81, 128, 131. See also barrio
Nelson, Lowry, 151
New Jersey, 110, 113
New Orleans, LA, 40, 42, 161, 179
New York, NY, 11, 54, 56, 57, 60, 61, 62, 67, 68, 69, 137, 158, 160 , 161, 166–67, 170–71, 172, 174, 185, 186, 187, 188
New York archdiocese, 6, 75, 84, 87, 88–111, 119, 138, 162, 163
Newark (NJ) archdiocese, 117
non-denominational centers, 123
Northern European Catholicism, 25
Nuevo, Jesús, 201
nuns. See sisters

O'Brien, Frederick, 77, 119, 224
Ocampo, Tarcisio, 218
Office of Migration (Puerto Rico), 124–25
Office of Spanish Catholic Action (New York), 93–94, 110
Office of Spanish Community Action (New York), 105
O'Hara, John F., 74, 120, 121, 122
Ohio, 122–24
Oliva, Tony, 188
oppression: colonial Cuba, 148, 155–56; colonial Puerto Rico, 12; Irish Catholics, 66; minorities, 143
O'Reilly, Alejandro, 17, 20, 213
Ortiz, Roberto, 188
Our Lady of Charity shrine, 71, 196–97

Padilla, Elena, 127
Padilla, Felix, 128, 132
Padilla, Francisco de, 212

parades, processions, 18; Fiesta de San Juan, 94–95, 101, 108; in Hispanic culture, 66; Peace Procession, New York, 108; in Puerto Rico, 21; Puerto Rico Day, 96; St. Patrick's Day, 95

parish: bilingual personnel in, 72; colonial Puerto Rico, 18; Cuban, 180, 196; ethnic model, 70–87; New York, 163–64; structure of, 45, 51, 100. *See also* integrated parishes, national parishes, territorial parishes

parish societies, 49–50, 51, 90–91

Partido Republicano (Puerto Rico), 27

Partido Revolucionario Cubano, 171

Pascual, Camil, 188

Paso de Palma, PR, 19

passive resistance, 34, 63, 74, 108, 142–43

pastoral ministry: 20, 112–34, 102, 108, 152

pastors, 84, 99, 100

patriotism, 22, 64, 74

Pedro Pan Operation, 197

Peña, Orlando, 188

Pennsylvania, 113, 114

Pensacola, FL, 167

Pentecostals, 76, 81, 125, 126, 141

Pérez, Tany, 188

Pérez Prado, Dámaso, 186

permanent diaconate, 133, 141, 142

Perth Amboy, NJ, 114, 116, 117

Philadelphia, PA, 54, 74, 162, 187

Philadelphia archdiocese, 120

Philip II, king of Spain, 12

Pius XII, pope, 83–84

Platt Amendment, 182

political activism, Cuban, 161, 171, 177, 185, 202–4

Polk, James K., 161

Ponce, PR, 18, 26

Ponce de Léon, Juan, 11, 212

Ponce diocese, PR, 50, 53, 94, 101

popular Catholicism, 12–13, 14, 25, 136, 180

Popular Democratic Party (Puerto Rico), 35, 36, 49, 51, 56, 136

popular religion, 68–69

population: Cuban, 152, 154, 158, 165, 169; Puerto Rican, 12, 17–19, 56, 116, 122

Porter, Robert, 147

poverty. *See* wealth and poverty

Power, John, 163

Poyo, Gerald E., 177, 241

Pozo, Luciano "Chano," 186

prejudice, 65, 128, 137. *See also* discrimination

priests: Chicago, 131; Cuban, 5, 7, 150, 191, 196; diocesan, 91; for farm workers, 116; and Great Migration, 136; immigrant, 84; and language, 88, 98, 113, 120–21, 126, 194–95; New York, 77, 108, 138; Puerto Rican, 17, 44, 47, 50, 65; training of, 101–2, 105. *See also* pastors

Prío Socarrás, Carlos, 185

Proctor, Redfield, 170

Protestants: anti-Catholic, 140; in Cuba, 148, 153–54, 163, 171; proselytizing, 113, 121, 138; in Puerto Rico, 21 29, 47; societal influence, 45, 48, 78, 82, 96. *See also* Pentecostals

public opinion: birth control, 51–52; Caballeros de San Juan, 130; clubs and New York archdiocese, 92; Great Migration, 56–58, 138; Puerto Rico, 30–31

public schools, 29, 45, 50

Public School Society, 163

Quesada, Gonzolo, 171

Quinlan, John, 179

race: Cuban, 159, 175, 183, 184; and culture, 32–33; integrated parishes, 79; integration, 58;

Puerto Rican, 120, 124, 137. *See also* segregation
railroads, 167, 168
Ramos, Marcos Antonio, 154
Redemptorists, 45, 72, 114, 115, 179
religion: Afro-Cuban cults, 206; American Protestantism, 29; Catholicity of Puerto Ricans, 13, 96; Great Migration, 66; plurality in, 63
religiosity: American institutional church, 25; colonial Puerto Rico, 20; Cuban, 147–48, 156–57, 180, 188; Mediterranean Catholicism, 39, 48; popular, 90; Puerto Rican, 19, 136. *See also* religious life; spirituality
religious education, 50, 52, 115, 119, 198, 202
religious life: Cuban, 147–49; Cuban exiles, 161–62
religious orders, 14, 16, 44–45, 108, 191, 195
religious practice, 20, 130, 133, 176–81
retreats: Agrupación Católica Universitaria, 205; Caballeros de San Juan, 130; Cursillo, 109; Puerto Rico, 49
revolving door immigration, 5, 6, 117, 170, 174, 175
Rey de Castro, Felipe, 201–2, 203
Richter, Joseph, 123, 124
Riggs, Francis, 215
riots, 108, 193
Ripoll, Luis, 201
ritual, 67, 107
Rivero Muñiz, José, 158, 244
Robles, Aida, 229
Rodríguez, Arsenio, 186
Rodríguez, Clara, 56, 103, 220
Rodríguez, Domingo, 127
Rodríguez de Olmedo, Mariano, 16
Rojas, Octavio "Cookie," 188
Román, Agustín, 196–97
rosary, 114

Rubio Padilla, Juan Antonio, 247
Ruiz, Ceferino, 198
rural areas: Cuba, 150, 151; Puerto Rico, 18, 19–20, 114, 124; U.S., 116–17

Saco, José Antonio, 161, 162, 164
sacraments: baptism, 22–23, 141; confession, 73, 80; confirmation, 105. *See also* marriage, Mass
St. Augustine, FL, 162
St. Augustine diocese, 179, 180
St. Joseph's Cursillo Center (New York), 110
Salamanca, Diego de, 18
Salamanca, Spain, 15, 119
Salesian Fathers, 179
Sánchez, Serafín, 168
San Germán, PR, 20
San Juan, PR, 101
San Juan diocese, 50, 53, 75
Santamaría, Ramón "Mongo," 186
Santander y Frutos, Manuel, 148, 150
Santería, 2, 21, 207. *See also* Afro-Cuban cults
Santiago de Cuba, 150, 201
Sardiñas, Eligio (Kid Chocolate), 187
Schmandt, Raymond H., 221
schools: Catholic schools, 121; in Cuba, 190–91, 197–208; parochial and public, 65–66
secularism, 6, 17, 49, 55, 188; Cuba, 147, 150, 151, 153, 156
segregation, 13, 74, 75, 123, 128
seminaries, 17, 22, 43, 102, 110, 136, 198
settlement houses, 72, 121
Seville, Spain, 15
Shaw, Artis, 186
Sheil, Bernard, 127, 128
Sigüenza, Spain, 40
sisters, 45, 47, 91, 118, 126, 180
slavery, 12–13, 23, 126, 151–53, 161
Sobremonte, Marcos, 212
Socarrás, Alberto, 185

social action, 106, 119, 127–28, 129, 131

socialism, 55, 156, 177, 181, 189–90, 207, 208

Sociedad Católica Puertorriqueña, 128

Sorolla y Bastida, Joaquín, 71

Spain, Spanish, 1, 2, 12, 20, 22, 26, 29, 31, 38, 40, 44, 49, 55, 109, 149–50, 151, 154, 155–57, 160, 167, 168, 169, 181, 191, 192, 199, 203, 204

Spanish American War, 154

Spanish Harlem, 54, 121

Spanish language: and acculturation, 59, 102; parity with English, 36; and priests, 88, 99, 103, 194–95, 196; Puerto Ricans, 6, 30, 31, 49, 50, 58, 76–77, 135; second language, 70; Spanglish, 35

Spellman, Francis J., 69, 72, 74, 75, 78, 81, 84, 87, 95, 96, 97–98, 99, 102, 106, 107, 134, 218, 224, 226, 229, 230

Spinola, Carlo, 20

Spiritism, 3, 47, 22

Spiritualism, 21, 153

sports, 175; Caballeros de San Juan, 130; Cuban professionals, 186–88

statehood, Puerto Rico, 27, 35, 39, 75

steel manufacturing, 123

Stern, Monsignor, 105, 111, 223

storefront churches, 76, 77, 81, 138

Straits of Florida, 193

street gangs, 57

strikes, 167, 166, 168, 182

Stritch, Samuel, 130

students: Cuban elite, 175; Cuban exiles, 197; Miami Belén, 201, Puerto Ricans, 50–51, 121. See also seminaries

sugar industry, 23, 29, 30, 54, 151–53

Sullivan, Charles, 114

supernatural world, 67, 107

symbol system, 2–3, 25, 31, 47

syncretism, 153, 207

Tampa, FL, 158, 166, 168, 169, 176, 178

Tampa Bay, FL, 167

Taylor, Tony, 188

teachers, 29–30, 45, 47, 117

Ten Year War. See Cuban Insurrection

territorial parishes, 72, 83, 84–85, 90, 92, 121, 125, 196

Thomas, Hugh, 149–50

Tiant, Luis, 188

Tió, Lola Rodríguez de, 2

Torres Vargas, Diego de, 16, 211

tradition, 106, 139, 155

travel: by air, 56, 61, 192; and Cuba, 170, 176; Great Migration, 60, 61; internal migration, 61; and Puerto Rico, 98; restrictions on, 187–88

Treat, Roger L., 235

Treaty of Paris (1898), 26, 41

Trent, Council of, 79

Trenton (NJ) diocese, 83, 85, 114, 116

Trinitarian Sisters, 126

Trujillo, Rafael Leonidas, 34

Truman, Harry S., 31

Unaccompanied Children's Program, 197

Unionista Partido (Puerto Rico), 27

United Community Defense Services, 123

United States of America: "American way," 64, 142: Bureau of Statistics, 159: Commissioner General of Immigration, 183; Congress, 11; and Cuban exiles, 192; Department of State, 98; Department of Justice, 194; Federal assistance, 194–95; Federal Writers, 176, 178, 180, 181; foreign relations, 27, 28; Great Migration, 54; interest in Cuba, 154, 160; Senate Committee on Immigration, 170

United Steel Workers of America, 122

Urtiaga, Pedro de la Concepción, 212

Utuado, PR, 19, 124

Valdés, Patato, 186
Valdés y Noriega, Francisco, 40
Valencia, Spain, 165
Varadero, Cuba, 192
Varela y Morales, Félix, 161–64, 242
Vatican, 7, 77, 83, 89
Vatican Council II, 11, 46, 106, 110, 139–43
Vázquez de Arce, Martín, 16
Vega y Carpio, Lope de, 16
Versalles, Zoilo, 188
Vietnam, 28, 142
Villaverde, Cirilo, 161
Vincentians, 71
Vivas, J. L., 211
vocations, 17, 43–44, 47, 141, 151, 155
von Hoffman, Nicholas, 131

voodooism, 181

Walsh, Emmet M., 123
War on Poverty, 107
Washington Heights (New York), 70, 89
wealth and poverty, 17, 24, 33, 56–57, 64, 151, 107
West Side Story, 57
Williams, Ramon O., 170
Wilson, James J., 99, 101, 110, 229
World War I, 28
World War II, 28, 74, 106

Ybor City, FL, 158–59, 166–69, 171, 172, 174, 176–81, 182, 183
Yglesias, José, 176
Young Lords, 143
Youngstown, OH, 122–24, 125